Trading
Cultures
in the
Classroom

A

Kolowalu

Book

University

of Hawaii

Press

Honolulu

Lois
Muehl
&
Siegmar
Muehl

Trading

Cultures

in the

Two
American
Teachers in
China

Classroom

University

of Hawaii

Press books

are printed

on acid-free

paper and

meet the

guidelines for

permanence

and

durability

of the

Council on

Library

Resources

Printed in the United States of America

98 97 96 95 94 93 5 4 3 2 1

Library of Congress Cataloging-in-Publication Data

Muehl, Lois Baker.

    Trading cultures in the classroom : two American teachers

in China / Lois Muehl & Siegmar Muehl.

    p.   cm.

    "A Kolowalu book."

    ISBN 0–8248–1442–8

    1. English philology—Study and teaching—China. 2. English

language—Study and teaching—Chinese speakers. 3. Americans—

China—History—20th century. 4. English teachers—China—

Biography. 5. China—Civilization—1949– 6. Muehl, Lois Baker.

7. Muehl, Siegmar. I. Muehl, Siegmar. II. Title.

PE1068.C5M84   1993

428'.0092'251—dc20

[B]   92–42272
                                               CIP

Designed by Richard Hendel

Contents

Background, Up Front

This is a book about growth and exploration, about teaching and learning on both sides of a classroom desk. The place was Nanjing (formerly Nanking), People's Republic of China. The period covered two semesters, from September 1987 to July 1988. The participants were nineteen mainland Chinese postgraduates in English, one auditing college instructor, and two United States teachers, freshly retired from decades in University of Iowa classrooms (Lois in the Rhetoric Program, Sieg in the College of Education).

The classes that kept us all hopping began at 7:30 every morning, Monday through Friday, and involved twenty hours a week. We divided them among reading, writing, speaking/conversation, and vocabulary. Sometimes our lessons were serious, formal—as when our students, ranging in age from twenty-two to thirty-four, practiced English by writing essays about a range of topics like their grandparents, their or their families' experiences during the Cultural Revolution, and their own attitudes toward property.

At other times, exchanges of ideas popped up informally, spontaneously. For instance, one day during a conversation class we were discussing games we all played as children. Lois mentioned that in her neighborhood she used to be convinced if she just dug a hole deep enough in her back yard down through the center of the earth, she would emerge somehow in China.

"For us the same!" exclaimed one woman student. "Only we believed we would come up in the middle of America."

We became involved in the postgraduate English program at Hehai by a mixture of China's educational needs, our own previous experiences teaching in Asia, and our wish for further exposure to people and cultures in this part of the world that, in so many ways, is different from America.

Encouraged by China's policy of increasing openness to the West for economic development, Hehai Hydraulic Engineering College in Nanjing planned a short-term program to train new teachers to strengthen its own English classes. Since Hehai wanted native speakers of English as models, the college circulated flyers in the United States announcing faculty needs.

An Iowa colleague knew of our previous teaching stints in Asia, twice in Thai refugee camps for Hmong and Khmer refugees, once for a semester teaching English as a Second Language to undergraduates at Kyungnam University in Korea. Our colleague waved Hehai's announcement under our ever-curious noses.

"How would you like to go teach in China?"

We read the flyer, debated (briefly), said yes, applied, and—after months of suspenseful negotiations, after half a year trying to amplify our extremely skimpy knowledge of that vast country—received word the opportunity was indeed ours. Instant elation. Instant anxiety. Still feeling massively ignorant, we stepped up our reading about China's history and customs. We invested in text and tapes for studying Mandarin, kept an atlas open since we had never previously traveled that specific part of the world, and did what we could, long-distance, to prepare for the coming ten months' experiences within the People's Republic of China.

One thing troubled us especially. We couldn't find enough information about what it would be like to communicate daily in a Chinese classroom. We had endless questions. We wondered, for instance, which Chinese attitudes and past or present government policies would require sensitivity on our part as we worked with our students and the university's administration.

We said a few words back that China's leaders at the time we applied to teach there encouraged more openness to Western ideas. They also showed somewhat more tolerance for individual opinions than in earlier decades. Former chairman Mao Zedong's 1956 call for people's ideas to be expressed without fear ("Let a hundred flowers blossom. Let a hundred schools of thought contend.") and his subsequent 1957 crackdown on critics was thirty years past. The infamous Cultural Revolution, that physically and intellectually lethal decade from 1966 to 1976, had died along with Mao. Deng Xiaoping, himself a victim of the revolution, now led his people in a pragmatic attempt to modernize the country and raise its standard of living.

In January 1985, members attending the Chinese Writers' Association Congress felt the political climate right to urge more artistic freedom. The Communist Party, in response, promised new creative freedoms in a charter that, according to the official New China News Agency, advised Chinese writers "to emancipate their minds and to be bold to break new ground." A Party directive further encouraged universities and colleges to develop economic exchanges with foreign countries. The directive praised "educational changes . . . intended to train millions of independent thinkers and bold trailblazers to push the modernization program."

True, in the well-known climate of political shifts, there had been a new surge of restraint on freedom of speech and ideas a few months before we arrived. During the turbulent winter of 1986–1987, Beijing student demonstrations for a more democratic society met strong government opposition and police confrontation. That same January prominent dissident intellectuals were publicly blamed for touching off waves of student unrest, for falling prey to "bourgeois liberalization." Some were expelled from the Communist Party. Many lost key positions. Among them, Fang Lizhi, an astrophysicist with moderate views much admired by students, was dismissed as vice-president of the University of Science and Technology of China in Hefei. Intellectuals received repeated warnings: all debate must proceed under "Marxist guidance."

And yet, outside exchanges continued to occur. Tourism prospered. China sought foreign investors who could bring in needed hard currency, foreign experts who could help the country modernize. In September, the month we began classes, officials allowed two reporters from Taiwan's *Independent Evening Post* to travel through mainland China and file critical observations. By October, Deng Pufang, Deng Xiaoping's son who had been disabled by a fall or push from a second-story window during the Cultural Revolution was traveling in the United States as head of a delegation representing China's handicapped.

So, during this period of mixed orthodoxy and openness, we arrived on Hehai campus to take up residence in an apartment building that housed five other Western teachers. Mr. Guo Kun, chairman of the Foreign Languages Department at Hehai, radiated welcome. In line with his country's announced modernizing hopes, he instructed us to provide our students with "a Western-style classroom."

We did, exploring as we went, interacting almost daily with our students, and reacting as teachers must to changing needs and circumstances. In the amalgam of narrative, journal, and formal/informal student responses that makes up this book, you will hear the voices of young contemporary Chinese adults as they wrote and talked freely, with increasing fluency, during two semesters. We used a range of interrelated assignments—essays, stories, poems, skits, letters, speeches, and frequent discussions—encouraging our students always to value and to express their personal views in English.

The class, wholly educated in traditional Chinese schools, found our student-centered approach novel and, at first, upsetting. Because of their intensive prior training in English and because they had qualified for this postgraduate program through stiff, nationwide competitive exams, this group proved far more in command of English, especially written English, than we had expected.

Their undergraduate years, however, had given them very little practice writing papers and none in class discussion. They described their college classes in China as large, typically based on a lecture format. Each student's task, they said, was to take notes, absorb every text or lecture meticulously, then give it all back on one or two major exams during a semester. Most did prepare a required, closely supervised research paper in their senior years, but no writing assignment had ever asked them, as we did, to reflect freely on or to express their own thoughts and experiences. These, they had always assumed, were insignificant compared to profound statements from "experts" and "authorities."

The various responses sampled chronologically in the coming pages show that this particular group of students, as they practiced and relaxed through daily, individual involvement in reading, speaking, talking, and writing, noticeably strengthened their use of English and the courage and sureness to use their own voices. The selections within these pages, although sometimes shortened, are in their own words.

If their turn of phrase occasionally sounds a bit odd, blame us. We helped them change major departures from standard usage but tended to enjoy the fresh way they made us view our own language and, yes, culture. If our use of the present tense in recounting a past adventure seems strange, it is because the richness of those Nanjing days, even the exasperations, stay vivid in our minds.

Readers may wonder why, given two authors' names on the front cover, the narrative voice throughout the book is in the first-person singular. With Sieg's corrections and additions, Lois wrote the first draft—an unwieldy ninety-one chapter account—for personal and family purposes. To focus more on Chinese classroom interactions and student contributions—the kind of book we couldn't find before going to China ourselves—Sieg cut, recut, and helped smooth the manuscript for publication. (Our marriage did indeed survive. We're used to working as each other's preliminary editors.)

Not surprisingly, our Nanjing students taught us as much or more than we taught them. These writers and speakers, whose willingness to share grew in proportion to their trust, led us gradually, with seriousness and humor, to see their country, its culture, customs, problems and delights, from a diverse but always Chinese point of view. We hope they received in return a glimpse of some of the same from a Western viewpoint.

For their gifts to us of knowledge, of friendship, we will always remain grateful.

Acknowledgments

We owe a special note of appreciation to Professor Liang Ruiju, president of Hehai University, and to Mr. Guo Kun, head of the Foreign Languages Department, who had the vision and willingness to implement the advanced English program in which we taught.

We also want to thank Iris M. Wiley and Cheri Dunn, of the University of Hawaii Press, and the skillful copy editor Susan Stone and designer Rich Hendel for their constructive suggestions and expert shepherding of this manuscript into print.

Although all nineteen students and one auditing instructor gave us permission to include their work, several requested we use not their real names, but a pseudonym that each provided.

It was our practice in the classroom always to address the students by Miss, Mr., or Mrs., according them the respect they deserved as young adults. We've continued to use their titles throughout the narrative to help readers identify names easily confused.

This book is dedicated to the generous individuals who made it possible:

Miss An Ran	Mr. Li Jian
Miss Bin Qilin	Miss Li Yanping
Miss Chen Hong	Miss Liu Jie
Mr. Chen Pingnan	Miss Lü Shu
Mrs. Ching Chao	Mr. Lüe Shi
Miss Chun Xu	Mr. Mao Yanyang
Mr. Fan Rui	Miss Xi Yang
Miss Feng Yunxia	Mr. Xue Hai
Mr. Ku Qiu	Miss Zhuang Zi
Mr. Lao Sheng	Mr. Zhuo (Zuo) Niannian

1 : Setting and Settling

Our host institution in Nanjing, Hehai Hydraulic Engineering College, is a walled, iron-gated complex tucked into wooded hills and flats on the southwest side of a city that teems with more than three million inhabitants.

A rusting red star decorates Hehai's main gate. Day and night, alert men guard this gate. They forbid entry except by persons on official business—visiting lecturers, food suppliers, construction workers, regular students and teachers who can show their yellow or red badges of unit identification.

The few foreigners who live within this secluded compound are Third World engineering students, mostly from Africa, and a handful of Western teachers. We all room and eat in modern buildings segregated from Chinese dorms atop what once was called "Marxist-Leninist Hill" but has now metamorphosed into "Friendship Hill."

Its present name commemorates a formal occasion when Japanese and Chinese representatives, meeting here in friendship, sought to dim memories of horrible events in 1937 when Japanese soldiers, in a bloodbath known to history as the "Rape of Nanking," systematically killed three hundred thousand Chinese in six bitter winter weeks. Hehai campus was one of the many local killing grounds.

Although a moving memorial to this citywide tragedy exists on campus, all seems peaceful, even jolly, in the small park surrounding the monument now. Students park bikes nearby. Cheerfully, they carry out surveying assignments around the park's central obelisk. Other students, laughing, talking, bookbags in hand, stroll along wide avenues shaded from the September sun by massive carefully trimmed plane trees.

In nearby fields, peasants bend, lift, and haul, exactly as they must have done on the same land for two thousand years. They grow lush green vegetable gardens that they fertilize by ladling from large storage vats a malodorous slurry of well-aged night soil. Beyond their hand-cultivated fields rise formidable remains of an ancient wall that ringed the city as early as A.D. 212.

The wall invites climbing. From its top, we can see distant industrial suburbs and the vast plain of the Yangzi River where it flows eastward toward Shanghai and the sea. Leaving the wall, by taking a roundabout way back to campus, we pass through one of the jammed, bustling street markets where the same families who work the fields sell their produce from "free-enterprise" carts and stalls.

Wherever we look, on campus, across fields, in markets and streets, it's a scene thronged with people.

Our second day at Hehai, Mr. Guo Kun, a slender, lively man in his forties who heads the Foreign Languages Department, arrives by appointment at our apartment door.

We discuss class schedules and content—reading, writing, conversation, and vocabulary—with classes beginning at 7:30 in the morning, running with a mid-morning break until 11:30. This will happen five days a week—"unless there are holidays," Mr. Guo adds.

We ask him to tell us something about the specific students.

"They come from several provinces, north and south," he says. "They range in age from twenty-one to thirty-four. Some have had teaching experience already."

"More men than women?" Sieg asks.

Mr. Guo considers. "I believe there are eleven women and eight men."

"What would you say about their abilities in English?" I ask.

"I think you'll find them quite good. Of course, there are differences.

Some are not so good in pronunciation especially. There is one young man from the South—" Mr. Guo pauses. He almost shudders. "Even his Chinese is hard for us to understand."

Clearly, he thinks we have our work cut out for us with that one.

"Do you have any warnings for us on sensitive areas in the classroom? Things we shouldn't bring up?"

Mr. Guo ponders Sieg's question with eyebrows raised. "Just don't bring up politics—Chinese politics." He laughs. "In fact, I want you to give our students, as much as possible, American-style teaching. I have studied in your country. I know how different things are." He rises. "Any more questions?"

"Not at the moment."

Mr. Guo whisks us on a tour of the campus so we'll know where to find his office and our classrooms. Almost every building seems under some stage of construction or repair. Jumbled piles of red bricks and sand lie dumped by the road. Dust coats every brick, every board, every tangle of steel rods. Inside the buildings, cement floors and plaster walls, darkened by both foot- and handprints, echo our footsteps. Within classrooms, heavily chalk-dusted blackboards are palimpsests of past teachers' lecture outlines. Each classroom has a lectern set on a desk raised, in its turn, on a wooden platform.

Cracked or missing window panes make us wonder what winter will be like in these rooms that have no heat of any sort. To save fuel reserves, we understand, China permits central heating only north of the Yangzi. Nanjing lies just south.

During the tour, we find we don't need any Chinese characters to locate restrooms. Eye-watering, nose-pinching fumes that waft from open doors are signal enough.

Every classroom, small or large, has fixed seats.

"Is it possible," Sieg asks, "to find classrooms with movable chairs?"

"Not possible," Mr. Guo responds firmly.

Back at the Management Building, where our tour started, Guo Kun instructs us to meet him here at 7:20 the next morning so he can introduce us to the students.

He bids us farewell, mounts his bike, and rides off.

We return to our apartment to brace for the first day of unfamiliar classes in a new land.

2 . Face to Face

The next morning, at 7:25, Mr. Guo leads us upstairs in the Management Building to the classroom where our students wait. When we enter, they stand and burst into applause. Briefly, Mr. Guo introduces us. He admonishes the students: "Study hard! Learn from experts!" Then he disappears. We are on our own.

Fortunately, this first class calls for conversation. We need to get acquainted, to start learning names. We give the students folded cards and ask them to print their names large enough so we can read the name propped on the front of each desk. They open their pen cases and print their names slowly. Some consult across rows, not sure how to spell the sound of their own name in English.

Today we want to hear their spoken English and let them hear ours. Before the first two hours are over, *everybody* is going to talk.

"When you meet a stranger," Sieg begins, "what do you like to find out about that person?"

4

The students look nervous to be asked anything at all. A few of the braver ones speak up: name, where they live, what family they have, what training, experiences, and hobbies.

As the list grows, I write it on the board. Then, using their suggestions, standing not on the wooden platform above them, but at floor level, Sieg and I model in turn the kind of brief self-introduction we'd like each student to give.

One by one, they venture their first solo English words to us. They hesitate. They glance often at the list on the board. What comes out sounds too structured. Even with follow-up questions, it's too formal for conversation. It dismays us that students feel they must leap to their feet to "recite." A more relaxed atmosphere will have to come later.

Miss Lü Shu, front row, for instance, is single. She graduated from Nanjing University. "My hobbies are travel, photography, and talking with friends." She starts to sit, stands again, waiting to be asked to sit down. We release her from public glare.

Mr. Ku Qiu comes from Hunan Province. "My brother and father are peasants." He likes to play basketball, volleyball, badminton, and chess, but mostly basketball. At 5′4″, he's an enthusiast.

Miss Li Yanping is petite, pale, and brief. In excellent, if halting, English, she tells us she has two sisters and she graduated "from Nanking Normal in 1987."

We check in surprise, hearing this more familiar version of the city's name. "You say 'Nan*king* Normal'?"

Miss Li blushes. "That's the old way. I mean Nan*jing*."

Mr. Zhuo Niannian is thirty-two, married, the father of a year-old son. His wife is a shop assistant. She works "fifty percent of time." He comes from Hubei Province, has been a teacher of English in a factory. He likes to travel and read.

Three other students are married—Mrs. Ching Chao, Mr. Lao Sheng, and Mr. Xue Hai. When Mr. Xue states this, a murmur runs through the class.

"Recently married," Miss Chun Xu teases him.

Mr. Xue blushes. He has left his wife, a dentist, he says, to study far from her in this year-and-a-half-long program.

Several students come from large families. Mr. Li Jian has "eight brothers and sisters," a family cluster soon to be rare in this country whose leaders, facing urgent and escalating problems of overcrowding, food shortages, pollution, and unemployment, are trying to enforce (with some mostly rural exceptions) a strict one-child-per-couple limit.

The class members continue to introduce themselves. Four say they like to sing. No one mentions playing a musical instrument. When we ask about that, they look at each other.

Mr. Zhuo says simply, "No money."

We've made it through all nineteen students. Which is the one whose English is supposed to be so dreadfully accented? They all have predictable patterns of trouble with *l, r, s,* and some vowel sounds, yet they're fluent enough that we aren't going to have to hobble our own choice of words.

The real challenge lies in getting them to relax, to be less frightened of speaking English, to accustom them to a more democratic classroom ambience. Many need to know each other better. During the twenty-minute break between the first and second two-hour classes, they don't yet mingle and chatter as a cohesive group. But then neither do American students on their first day of class.

3 . First Assignments

Yesterday, following our get-acquainted session, we handed out individual copies of a slender paperback reader and text I put together five years ago. Its purpose in Iowa was to meet complex needs involving reading, writing, speaking, and listening for our Rhetoric Program. There, they wanted an inexpensive guide, with simple-to-hard selections designed especially for teachers new to our program's intensive fusion of varied communication skills. Who would have guessed we'd be using it here, now for Chinese postgraduates? But Mr. Guo Kun had forewarned us to bring books if possible. Not only was this English program brand new on campus, with its first students hungry for "new materials"; Hehai's library was also limited, he had written, since it serves mostly engineering students and therefore concentrates its holdings on technical materials.

Yesterday, students took the new books in their hands almost with reverence. Overnight, I notice, nearly all have made a neatly fitted paper jacket to protect their precious new book's cover. Most students have their heads bent. They're softly reading aloud the day's assigned preface for practice!

I hate to interrupt this preoccupied buzzing, but it's time to plunge in. The text begins with some brief reading advice from Professor John T. Frederick, one of my most respected teachers: "Bring yourself to the book."

"What does that say to you?" I ask.

There follows that long silence which makes young teachers squirm inwardly and break out in a sweat before rushing to answer their own questions. I wait. Even among these modest and reticent students, someone, perhaps a former teacher who understands the spot I am in, will answer.

Sure enough, Mr. Lao Sheng who has taught in a middle school for eight years, starts to rise, then remembers to sit. In the back row, Sieg cups his ear to hear Mr. Lao's soft, tentative answer.

"Perhaps that we should bring our best selves to each reading?" he ventures.

"What do you mean by 'best selves'?"

"We should be quiet. And thoughtful," Mr. Lao explains.

Once again, a student has given an answer I didn't expect but is right. From some long-forgotten passage, I recall a description of a Chinese scholar approaching his desk in the morning. Nothing lies on the desk but a single book. Nothing fills the room but simplicity, order, quiet, sunlight.

Mr. Lao Sheng clearly belongs to this tradition.

"Quiet. Thoughtfulness." I repeat. "Right! What else?"

"Bring what you already know," Mrs. Ching Chao says, and we're off and running.

We discuss their encounters with reading generally for fifty minutes, then take a ten-minute break. We spend the next hour exploring vocabulary and ideas in this particular preface. It's not the most exciting literary piece, but Sieg and I want the students to become used to talking, to questioning, even —radical step—to criticizing a text while, at the same time, we get a clearer notion of what blocks their understanding.

They question simple words like "backpack" and harder ones like "pejorative." After clearing up that two-dollar meaning, we get into practicing American versus British pronunciations: peJORative, PEjorative. After all, they need to be bi-English, depending on where they travel or what speakers they encounter. I want them fully armed with instant recognition.

Besides, our students have reminded us twice in these two days of classes, they are *post*graduates. They seem to share an elitist's distrust of any teaching that looks informal or "easy" to them. Their remarks suggest they feel demeaned by anything that smacks of a "simple" assignment.

If equipping them with useful jawbreakers and variable pronunciations will reassure them they're really learning, I'll grab every multisyllabic chance that comes along. But, concurrently, how are we going to get them to recognize and use the power of simple English words?

No one morning is long enough to meet that last challenge. After the break, it's time to get them up on their feet, up on the teacher's dais individually, reading aloud the short family pieces they wrote as their writing assignment last night.

Sieg calls for volunteers. No one, not even experienced pros like Mr. Lao Sheng or Mrs. Ching Chao, offers to be first. Apparently, in China it's thought wiser to wait for authority to speak. So Sieg calls on them in turn.

One after another, casting agonized side-glances at their peers, they stumble onto the platform and slouch behind the lectern. They bury their heads in their papers. The papers tremble in universally shaking hands. Often their voices catch, or rip along too fast, or can't be heard.

The process proves tense for us also, realizing from our back row listening posts how terrified each one feels. We try to reassure them. We put a few questions gently, easy ones they can answer because who better knows their own families, the subject of their essays?

Each student strains to hear and understand our questions, just as we strain to hear their deliveries. Most of them reply readily enough, then relax on finishing their public ordeal. All scuttle for their seats at twice the speed they left them.

We end the morning knowing that platform poise, gained through repeated chances to practice, is a goal we need to work toward steadily for these postgraduates.

Back at the apartment, just before lunch, I look at the paper Mr. Ku Qiu, the basketball player, turned in. Now that I can read the words he wrote, I can understand more of what we heard:

> My mother is a country housewife. She is now 45 years old. Since she was born in old China, and her family was too poor to afford her to go to school. So she is illiterate and can't read and write. That's a terribly unfortunate thing. But I love her from the bottom of my heart because she loves me with heart and soul. I can't say in words how much she loves me. Here I'll tell you a story about my mother. Last Spring Festival

when I was already 24 years old coming back home for the winter vacation, I found a packet of cards and a packet of chess on my desk which my mother had brought for me to have a wonderful time during the vacation. What engraves on my mind is that at the end of the vacation when I left home my mother accompanied me to the bus stop. She didn't turn back until I disappeared in the distance.

I can't help saying that mothers' love to their children is the truest love in the world.

Wordlessly, I pass the paper across to Sieg. He reads it, looks up. His eyes shine with the same excitement I feel. Yes, the paper has problems. But in today's China, Mr. Ku Qiu has come so far.

And I was worrying about teaching these students the power of simple words.

4 . Adages

It's still the first week, Wednesday. We make another short writing assignment based on the new text that they bring to class every day. An early chapter contains several maxims dating back to Ovid, Aesop, Cicero, and other classical writers. Quintilian's "A liar should have a good memory" is one example.

We ask the students to consider these brief adages, think about their meanings, and supply a modern example for one of them.

"You'll read your work aloud in class again tomorrow," I say.

Some students peer at once into their texts to see how hard the assignment will be.

Thursday, they keep their papers hidden inside their folders. No one volunteers to go first.

"You call on someone," Mrs. Ching insists.

Miss Xi Yang, whose cheekbones Hollywood studios would vie for, has written on Ovid's "Nothing is stronger than custom." She smooths the paper down on the lectern, as if she were getting more used to standing behind it. She reads in a clear, strong voice.

Custom sometimes can't be changed by anything, since it is an established socially accepted practice. For example, in some poor areas of China, especially in the countrysides, when young people are engaged, a young lady always extorts many expensive gifts or a huge amount of money from her lover for showing off themselves. Some poor men are not rich enough. They sometimes borrow money from others so as to meet her needs. In fact, they are married in debt themselves. Of course, some women are good. They wouldn't like to demand much money, because they know very clearly that sooner or later they have to return those money which their husbands borrowed before engagement. But unfortunately some women's relatives and friends are good at making irresponsible remarks so that these women can't bear it. In this way, vanity makes them do what they wouldn't like to do. Obviously it's a kind of ostentation and extravagance. But nobody in those places is brave enough to get rid of it. If there is, she (or he) must be in a sorry condition.

Miss Xi starts toward her seat.

Sieg stops her. "Wait a minute. What kind of gifts does the young woman expect?"

Miss Xi ticks off on her fingers, "A television, a refrigerator, a washing machine, all kinds of furniture, and quilts."

"A sewing machine," Miss Lü Shu says.

"A tape player," Mr. Li adds.

"That's what *you* want," Miss Liu Jie guesses, and the class laughs.

"Do people really go that much into debt?" Sieg asks.

"Sometimes," Miss Zhuang Zi confirms from under her thick black bangs, "they can't pay it off for years."

"Or you can not spend all that." Mr. Lao Sheng waves both hands in a flat, palms-down gesture. "Just take a travel vacation, and then live simply. That's what my wife and I did. We didn't go in debt."

"May I see your paper?" I ask Miss Xi.

She hands it to me. I skim quickly, seeing places we need to make individual responses later, such as explaining the visual benefits of paragraphing, but finding what I wanted to mention.

"I like your use of the words 'ostentation' and 'extravagance.' They fit exactly and sum up well."

Miss Xi Yang sits down, glowing.

Sieg surveys the class. "Anyone else write on custom?"

Mr. Li Jian, bless him, raises his hand.

"Let's hear it."

Mr. Li takes his time at the podium. He's beginning to like it up there. Just so we won't forget the adage, he reads, "Nothing is stronger than custom."

> Current example: In our village, there is a widow who is very young now. When her husband died of a sudden attack of serious flu, she was even younger. But she remains single by the custom that if a woman marries for the second time, she will be said frivolous and fickle. After her death, she would be splitted into two by her two husbands.

"Is that really true?" Sieg asks.

Mr. Li shrugs. "Who knows what happens after?"

"I mean," Sieg amends, "is it true that Chinese people look down on a woman who remarries?"

"True," says Mr. Li. The class agrees.

"What about in the larger cities?"

"Perhaps it's a little better there," says Miss Liu, who comes from Nanjing.

"What if she marries a second time, and her second husband dies too?" I ask.

The class groans. "Then she will be thought a witch," someone says.

We have to hurry on, or we'll never get around to every class member in two hours.

"Any others on custom?" Sieg checks.

Thoroughly schooled in tradition, these postgraduates apparently found the subject attractive. Miss Chun Xu, whose precise spoken English reflects her previously expressed interest in languages, gives us another example:

> There is a custom in my home town that before Lunar New Year, every family should make a lot of cakes. Since in Chinese, "cake" has the same pronunciation as "going up," people believe that the more cakes you make, the better life they will live in the next year. So people make as many cakes as they can before every Lunar New Year, even though the cakes will go bad in several days.

"When is Lunar New Year?" I want to know.

The students hold a quick conference.

"We don't know the exact date. Some time next spring," Miss Chun says.

Mr. Fan Rui, the one I keep confusing with Mr. Li Jian, offers his thoughts on the same adage:

> Whenever I'm thinking about some problems, I can't help scratching my hair without my knowing. The heavier I catch my hair, the more difficult the problem means. Each time after I've got the key to the problem, I always find my hair in the mirror spreading disorderly like a mad man. So I'm determined to give up this unpleasant habit. But the result, you see, is not always as expected.

I check Mr. Fan's hair. Sure enough, he seems to have been agitating it hard. Of course, he may have tousled it to support his last sentence. Or, perhaps he's considerately given me the means to identify him without fail. We're all amused by his self-critical revelation.

"There were ten adages to choose from. Didn't anyone pick a different one?" I ask.

Mr. Zhuo Niannian raises his hand. He always stands in a stiffly upright, dignified manner. During class breaks, he walks by himself. He has chosen Cicero's "He plants trees to benefit another generation."

Mr. Zhuo blinks as he reads:

> The walls of our dormitory were terrible. They were really colorful: Red for soy sauce, yellow for cooking oil, green for vegetable leaves, blue for writing ink, and black for foot marks. It was our achievement of four years.
>
> But when we left it on graduation, the walls became as white as snow again. Why? We whitewashed them. We did it for new students.

The class approves Mr. Zhuo's example and his consideration. I like his color details. They fit what we've seen every mealtime here on campus. Most students do not eat in dining halls.

Instead, they stand in long lines at rows of small windows inside dark, bare, cavernous halls. Students collect their portions of rice, vegetables, and sometimes a little meat or fish, in tin or plastic containers, then carry them back toward their dorm rooms.

Always, there's a sense of hurry. They bring their containers to class, so they can rush straight from class to the canteens.

"Otherwise," Miss Lü Shu says, "they run out of delicious dishes."

Often they start eating as they walk back to their dorms. Whenever it's warm, like today, many students stop and eat standing around outdoor concrete ping-pong tables that have bricks across the middle for nets. Or they sit on stone walls with friends.

Except for the elements, there's little to lure them back to their rooms. Although our students have only two roommates, they have described how undergraduates are housed: seven to a small, rectangular room, which contains eight bunks and one window. No dressers. The eighth bunk stores their seven suitcases. A narrow aisle runs between the bunks. Such cramped conditions explain why we see them studying alone on the lawns at dawn or until 10:00 P.M. in lighted classrooms that at least provide a seat, a desk, and quiet, no matter how many other students have joined the impromptu study hall.

We go on listening and responding as more students read their current Chinese applications of ancient Western adages. But Mr. Zhuo's vivid food images have disquieted Miss Chun Xu. She shuffles her feet under the desk and chants, not loudly enough to interrupt but strongly enough to hint, "Lunch-ee. Lunch-ee."

I glance at my watch. It's only 11:20. Class is supposed to end at 11:30. Several students have already set food containers on top of their closed books. I suddenly realize why Chinese teachers in nearby classrooms always dismiss the last morning class five minutes earlier than this. First in line at the canteens get the best food.

Quickly, I collect their papers. With a happy clatter of feet, the class escapes.

5 . What "Fish" Means to You

During this week, the class has read and discussed an essay from the text, Samuel Scudder's nineteenth-century description of how Professor Louis Agassiz, Harvard's eminent zoologist, led a beginning student to look closely at a series of laboratory fish.

For follow-up, I announce at discussion's end, "Over the weekend, write in two or three hundred words what the word 'fish' means to you."

"Write anything?" Mr. Xue Hai asks doubtfully, as if I hadn't spelled out enough rules.

"*Anything.* You know what fish meant to Scudder so long ago. But each one of you today brings different associations to that word. Maybe you like fish. Maybe you hate it. Write your own reactions, your own experiences."

Mr. Fan Rui scowls. "Do we hand this in?"

"Yes. Both of us will read your work and give you feedback on your writing. But you'll be sharing them aloud in class too."

This longer writing assignment should please Mr. Chen Pingnan, the college English instructor who has officially qualified for auditor status in the class. He has already let us know he finds our assignments much too short. We've heard no such complaints from students.

Mr. Xue Hai is our first reader on Tuesday. His title is "The Enlightenment of Going Fishing." He reads fast, this time from an untrembling paper:

> I remember my first time of going fishing as it happened yesterday. It had been a cheerful time in the small lake located in the south, not very far from our house. Usually, at sunset of summer afternoon, my cousin took me to go fishing in that small lake.
>
> My cousin had much experience in going fishing, and chose a favorable point quickly. I threw out my fish hook with the fishing rod in my right hand, sitting on a big stone as I had so often seen others do. I kept waiting anxiously for a bite, moving my fishing-rod up and down in imitation of the leap of a frog. Nothing came of it. Then I stopped moving my fishing-rod, just waiting patiently and patiently.
>
> Suddenly, something tugged at my fish hook and swept off with it into deep water. Jerking it up, I saw a fine carp wriggling in the sun.
>
> "Cousin!" I cried, looking back in great excitement, "I have got a fish!"
>
> "Not yet," said my cousin. As he spoke, there was a plash in the water, I caught the gleam of a scared fish jumping into deep water and running away like an arrow. I was so disappointed that I threw my fishing rod away.
>
> "Boy, do remember," said my cousin, with a shrewd smile on his face, "never boast of catching a fish until it is on dry ground. It is no use to boast of anything until it is done, right?"
>
> I nodded my head gently. Since then, I have been reminded of the fish that I didn't catch! When I hear people boasting of a work undone I call to mind at once the good advice of my cousin on that summer afternoon. It seems to take the form of a wise saw.

There is a murmur of approval.

Mr. Li Jian asks to see Mr. Xue's essay.

Some students have not been listening with full attention either to the paper or to its following discussion. They lean over their own pieces, mouthing them at a subdued mutter in fervent practice before their own turn.

Mr. Zhuo Niannian, sitting next to Mr. Xue, is up next. He stalks to the lectern with his usual stiff assurance and begins,

The full colour of Chinese idioms and proverbs say a lot about fish. Let me fish out some for your enjoyment.

It's a good habit to continue studying. Never stop. Fish or cut bait. But never work yourself to death, like draining the pond to get all the fish. Let the work suit you. Otherwise you may become a fish in a small stream, at the mercy of shrimps.

He continues to produce examples. Each time he also gives the proverb in Chinese. With delight, the class joins in, completing the familiar saying. He goes on:

In shoal water you get fish and shrimps, while in deep ocean you catch flood dragon.

I have advice for you. Don't conflict with your colleagues or school-mates. It's not good for both of you. When a crane and a clam fight, it's the fishman who gets the profit. . . .

Perhaps I'm offering to teach fish to swim. Now I'll stop, because you have other fish to fry.

There's a spattering of applause. Mr. Zhuo moves erect, smiling back to his seat.

Mrs. Ching Chao tells us about eating "delicious fish." The way she rolls the phrase around in her mouth makes us almost taste the carefully prepared treat she describes. But in her speech, Miss Zhuang Zi recalls a fish she encountered that "had a bad smell!"

Mr. Ku Qiu draws us back into memories of his days as a schoolboy:

One day in my childhood Father bought a big fish from the market. Mother cooked it with vinegar, soy sauce and gourmet powder. It smelt sweet and tasted delicious. From then on I took a great love of eating fish.

I wanted to go fishing myself. I thought the fish caught by me would be even more delicious.

A few days later I saw many people groping for fish in a nearby up-dried pond on my way to school. Thinking of the delicious fish I threw down my schoolbag near the pond, and dashed into it. I began to grope for fish like the other people.

To my disappointment, after half an hour I got nothing but dirty mud around my legs and hands. I decided to give up when a fish jumped up in front of me. I immediately jumped on it and caught it. The fish weighed almost two pounds! I cried out with joy. Quickly I put it at the bottom of my schoolbag. All the way to school I was madly content.

But things turned wrong. I was late for school and felt nervous when I entered the classroom. The teacher saw through my secret and scolded me seriously. What was more, I was kept in the school in lunch time because of being late.

I really felt hungry. The more hungry I was, the more delicious the fish in the schoolbag seemed to be, but I couldn't eat a bit of it. I felt awful.

Now the word "fish" means "thorns" as well as "roses" to me.

We're up against the end of class. Too late for more than a word about his lively account. But I notice some interesting dynamics taking place around Mr. Ku Qiu.

Last week, although he sat in rows alongside other males, no one seemed to address him. He stayed quiet unless called on. Often he looked withdrawn. Perhaps because he came from a distant province and was the last student to arrive on campus, he seemed "foreign," too unapproachable.

Today, with this story, he has lowered those invisible barriers. Mr. Fan smiles as he makes way for Mr. Ku to sit down again. Someone—is it Miss Feng?—taps him on the shoulder, wanting to read his paper.

Bit by bit, the class is beginning to cohere. This reading aloud, which they found so frightening at first, is helping us all learn more about each other.

I know one further fact about Mr. Ku Qiu. His composition ends with a reference to a proverb, "Truth and roses have thorns about them." The proverb doesn't appear in our text until page 88. In lessons so far, we have worked as a class just to page 12. Perhaps Mr. Ku knew that proverb before, but I doubt it.

He is one of the few who look ahead, who want to know what's coming next.

With this class, so do we.

6 : Coming into Focus

Yesterday, students read "Ways to Get Around a Block," a covering title for two excerpts from Robert Pirsig's *Zen and the Art of Motorcycle Maintenance*. In one, Pirsig persuades a Montana student not to write about the grand idea she first considered ("a five-hundred-word essay about the United States") but to focus instead "on the front of the Opera House on the main street of Bozeman."

"I like this essay!" Mrs. Ching Chao bursts out.

"Why?" I'm curious to see what intrigued her.

"It tells us how to write."

"It's easy to read," Miss Li Yanping says.

"How is it easy?"

"There aren't so many hard words. And there is a lot of talking."

"Good point, Miss Li. You might try tucking dialogue into your own work."

"I like the motorcycle," Mr. Fan confesses, "where the man and his son go riding."

"What are hot cakes?" Miss Liu wants to know.

"And maple syrup?" Miss Bin Qilin asks.

We spend some time discussing these strange foods, what they are, where they come from, how they look. Ready knowledge like this helps make us instant "experts" in a foreign country. But as I try to draw a maple tree and syrup bucket on the board, I wish I'd spent more time taking art courses.

We clear up other unfamiliar words, like "stumped" and "in a heavy grip," where "grip" doesn't mean "suitcase." We look at ways Pirsig chose to build his narrative. The students practice reading aloud several paragraphs for pronunciation. They have persistent troubles with short *i*. The word "it" comes out "eat." "This" sounds like "theees." We practice saying "lips" and "leaps," with their different spellings on the board.

Finally, just before class ends, we zero in on the extension of today's reading into their own use.

"Just like Scudder," I recap, "Pirsig got his student to focus closely on one object. He also showed his son Chris how to make a list of points he wanted to cover in his letter. In your next writing assignment try combining both approaches.

"Choose a simple object. Make a list of everything you can think of to say about that object, in any order. Your list doesn't have to be logical. Just use it as a resource to help you develop a lively, focused piece about whatever you choose."

"How long?" Mr. Fan, ever practical, asks.

"No more than four hundred words. Keep it short. Revise it until it says exactly what you want."

I wish I could understand their comments in Chinese as they leave. At least Mr. Fan isn't scowling today. Or mussing up his hair.

It is Mr. Fan Rui's object description that most amuses the class the next day when they read them aloud.

"A mirror," he announces from the lectern.

It is a common sense that young girls like seeing their appearance or appreciating their beauty in the mirror. You can find every girl has a mirror with herself no matter where she goes and they use mirror frequently.

Here I want to inform you that, however, now things are changing toward the opposite direction. Today young boys uses mirror more often even than girls. Also, I'm no exception.

Now let me tell you the history of my owning the mirror. I've bought my mirror just on my entering Anhui University. It is a middle-size rectangular mirror. Its length is about 10 centimetres, width about 5 centimetres, and the glass is inlaid in the green plastic bottom with a white plastic frame in it. At the back of the glass is an attractive girl smiling at you. Unfortunately, I forgot to bring its stand when I left Anhui University. Otherwise I can set it upright on the desk of my bedroom and use it more conveniently.

Once I've read a piece of news in the newspaper. It was counted that now most of young boys watch mirror more often than girls a day. At first, I couldn't believe this strange phenomenon. I thought it was totally in error. But after this I began to watch my roommates. It turned out that they all had a small or a big mirror. Everyday, I found they saw their pictures in the mirror for at least 3–4 times. Some guys even got the highest point of 7–8 times.

Generally speaking, under such circumstances, they uses mirror more commonly, such as before calling on a friend, a teacher, or before making a speech, taking part in a dancing party, especially before making date with their girlfriend in order to give a graceful impression to the public.

So far as I'm concerned, to tell you the truth, I watch mirror about 3 times a day. One purpose for me to see myself in the mirror is that I don't want to show a bad impression to others. The other one is that by watching mirror, I feel more confident. Perhaps it is a psychological process.

So, ladies and gentlemen, if you don't believe what I've just said, would you please watch your friends around you?

Mr. Fan starts to nip from the platform.

"Wait a minute," Sieg says. "Any questions for Mr. Fan?"

No questions. Class members still don't like to speak up. They refuse to put a classmate on the spot with any negative remark.

"What he says is true." Mr. Lao Sheng breaks the silence. "I have seen it happen."

"Is it true that every woman keeps a mirror with her?" Sieg asks.

The women in the class, who still call themselves "girls," as the men call each other "boys," look sidewise at their seatmates. Giggling, they cover their mouths with their hands.

"Yes, it's true," admits Miss Li Yanping. Miss Zhuang Zi shoves her friend's arm to punish her for this revelation.

Mr. Chen Pingnan has time to be in class today. As a teacher/auditor, in a different position than these students, he has asked not to have his work read aloud, but he has responded in his own way to the title of the Pirsig excerpts, "Ways to Get Around a Block."

Back at the apartment, over a glass of hawthorn wine, we both read Mr. Chen Pingnan's essay:

> As a teacher of English, I experienced many blocks in my teaching, such as no response from the students, no communication between the teacher and the students, students' troubles in memorizing and so on. My way to get round the blocks was not positive but passive, and it's proved successful for the time being.
>
> Psychologically, the Chinese students are quite different from the foreign students. Foreign students like to do something freely with less limitation and fewer instructions. On the contrary, the Chinese students like to walk the way the teacher has paved for them. If the teacher gives them much time to have free activities, the students would feel quite at a loss and criticize the teacher's "bad" method and attitude. So we Chinese teachers usually make full preparation and bring enough materials and facts to class with which we stuff our students.
>
> Here is an example. One day, after I finished the text I asked the students to read the text and corrected their pronunciations. I asked them to raise questions, but there was only silence. I thought reading the text was the better way to overcome the silence.
>
> Several days later, I was told that the students were not content with my teaching. Then I changed the way of teaching. After finishing the text, I asked them questions, and gave them further explanations and more exercises. The students liked it very much.
>
> So for Chinese students, the more you feed them, the more welcome you will receive.

I put down his essay. "I think he's trying to tell us something. We aren't stuffing our students enough."

"Guo Kun wants them to learn Western ways," Sieg reminds me.

"Mr. Chen gave me another warning after class today. He told me he liked my teaching, but Chinese students don't like to listen to students' work. They want the teacher to explain. He said, 'It is better to pick out just the best students' work and make explanations and comments, rather than hear from everybody.' "

"What did you tell him?"

"That we had a difference in philosophy of teaching, and that I'd like to discuss it when we had more time."

Sieg laughs. Somebody knocks on the closed door. Sieg gets up to open it.

"Ah, Mr. Guo. We've been expecting you."

"I have been busy." Mr. Guo comes in . He sits down with assurance. "I hope everything is all right?"

"We *think* it is." One of our fellow American teachers, Dan Younkin, who lives just down the hall, has warned us it's time for Mr. Guo's critical supervisory visit. So I leave room for disagreement, and wait for him to launch into a list of problems.

Mr. Guo isn't to be rushed to the point. He discusses a few administrative matters. Then he says, "You and Dr. Muehl are always together."

"We like each other," I say.

"It is very unusual to have two teachers in the classroom."

"Do the students object?" Sieg never minds being blunt.

"Not at all. They find it—strange."

"It's called team-teaching." Sieg explains why we like it. He adds, "It's also a big help to me. I have some trouble hearing. Lois can fill me in if I haven't caught something in a student's question."

"Ah." Mr. Guo accepts this reason and our odd preferences. He pauses.

His fingertips touch in their most judicial manner. "The students like your teaching—so far. You are having them write a great deal."

"They're writing often," I agree, "but so far the assignments are short."

"They appreciate your many comments on their papers."

Mr. Guo does keep close tabs on what's going on, probably through the monitor system. In all Chinese classrooms, the monitor functions as part-spy, part-assistant, part-ombudsman for administrators, students, and teachers. Mr. Lüe Shi, as far as we know the only Communist Party member in the class, is our monitor this semester. He has no doubt reported regularly to Mr. Guo.

"Is there anything the students don't like?" Sieg asks.

Mr. Guo smiles. "They think Mrs. Muehl is very strict. They say you are not so strict."

"Good!" I tell him. "Then they will keep doing their assignments."

Privately, I'm glad they haven't realized quite so soon how much I'd prefer just to appreciate their wit and knowledge than to correct their sometimes awkward but often fresh use of English.

7 · Journals and Poems

Classes have barely started rolling when, suddenly, we face a four-day vacation. China's National Day, October 1, celebrates the founding of the People's Republic of China in 1949. Given two official days off plus a weekend, we set rejoicing students free with no more assignment than to keep a brief-entry journal and to bring one sample in to read aloud to the class.

At 7:30 Monday morning, several students look tired, but they have no trouble talking. Everyone chooses a single journal entry to read aloud in front of the class and then answers questions based on the selection.

Mr. Xue Hai smiles widely as he begins his:

> It was a splendid morning, and I wanted to go out. So I got up very early, having my breakfast and getting everything ready. To my surprise, as soon as I went out of my dormitory, I saw my wife. Being travel-worn

and weary, with a big heavy bag in her right hand, she stood there, looking at me with a kind smile on her face.

I eyed her narrowly from her head to foot. No doubt! It is my wife. So I ran to meet her, taking the heavy bag over from her hand, showing her into my dormitory, asking her to sit down, offering a cup of tea for her quickly.

Then I looked up my head and talked to her. I inquired her some daily affairs at home, but she stared at me instead of speaking.

After awhile, she said unhappily, "You've just been here days, you even can't recognize me!"

I answered humorously, "Oh! You can still recognize me, that's better than I do."

I knew that what she said was just for fun, but her coming broke down my plan for going out.

"And did you go out some time?" Mr. Li Jian slyly asks Mr. Xue.

He brushes his hand across his mouth, laughing. "Oh, yes. We had a very nice walk in the park."

"Mr. Xue," Sieg says, "how long since you had seen your wife?"

"Perhaps three weeks."

"And you'd already forgotten what she looked like?"

"I wasn't expecting her," Mr. Xue defends himself. "And you see, we haven't been married very long."

The class roars. Mr. Xue, ducking his head, returns to the obscurity of his seat next to the wall.

Like me, Sieg pictures to himself the other two roommates popping in and out of Mr. Xue's dorm room. Where *do* a married couple go for privacy under these circumstances? They can't afford to rent a hotel room. We've seen young couples in the parks. With so many people around, with so many customary Chinese inhibitions, they seem to touch rarely. It's not a question to ask this recent bridegroom here. All Sieg says is "Good account, Mr. Xue!"

Miss Zhuang Zi, fortunate enough to go home for the holidays, reads next. She chooses to share the second of three entries. Later, at our apartment, we scan all of her handwritten journal. We're eager to see her full account of this Chinese celebration, to hear how she translates her recent experience into English.

> Oct. 1. We stand up and propose a toast to my grandparents. We wish them good health and a long life. Tears in their eyes, my grandparents

seem very excited and they drink beer mouthfully. At last, my grand-father gets a little bit drunk!

Oct. 2. This is the second day of the holidays. The entire city of my hometown is still permeated with a holiday atmosphere. I go out to see the sights with my friends by bike. Both of the streets are decorated with many coloured lights. A lot of people, with the best clothes, are walking along the streets. The children follow the adults with coloured balloons in their hands. Suddenly a little boy is careless and sets the balloons free. They rise up and up. At last, they disappear. How interesting!

Oct. 3. I never care about the businesses in the countryside, such as when the peasants plant crops and when they get them in, since I've grown up in the city. Before I went to the countryside with my friends this morning, I didn't even realize what season it was and what the peas-ants were doing. When we got there, I saw many peasants were busy get-ting in rice and cotton. This busy scene suddenly reminded me that it was autumn, a harvest time which I learned from the textbooks.

Sieg rereads her conclusion. "She obviously didn't get sent to the country-side during the Cultural Revolution."

"Too young, probably." I do a quick count in my head. The Cultural Rev-olution lasted from 1966 to 1976. Miss Zhuang would have been about three when it started. Or perhaps her family wasn't sufficiently rich or educated to be punished during that stringent, anti-intellectual decade. Aloud, I wonder, "Do we dare ask the students about their or their families' experiences in the Cultural Revolution?"

"I don't see why not. The government officially criticizes that period now." Sieg jots a reminder in his indispensable shirt-pocket notebook. "I'll check it out with Monitor Lüe."

For a change of pace this week, we shift from prose to poetry. The latest major Western poet our students seem to recognize is Wordsworth. Since market carts glow with heaps of gold-to-orange persimmons now, we bring in Gary Snyder's "The Persimmons." He wrote this close observation of people and scenes from firsthand knowledge of Beijing and its surroundings in some past October.

As usual with short items, I read the poem aloud. Although I've never asked them to do it, most students mutter along a split second later. This practice gives a lagging, disjointed antiphony, but if it improves their pronun-ciation, fine.

We discuss words they question, like "riffle." Then the class reads the poem aloud for a second hearing. They like the mention of things they know: the yard-wide baskets, tricycle trucks, sellers spreading their wares on gravel; the Ming tombs, the Great Wall, Genghis Khan. We talk about wider implications in Snyder's final line, "the people and trees that prevail."

Some students think every line should begin with a capital letter. Miss Feng feels poetry ought to rhyme. This does neither. We bring up freedoms that twentieth-century Western poets have wrested for themselves, how structure often hides in their work beneath seeming informality, how sensitive choices blend serendipity with control.

Miss Feng looks skeptical but willing enough to listen to suggestions for their next writing assignment. They are to take some scene, some experience thoroughly familiar to them, and write a short, unrhymed poem in natural word order. We ask them to fill it with details and, if possible, to relate it to a larger human experience than just the immediate scene they're describing. Like Gary Snyder's last line.

After class, Mrs. Ching Chao says, "I can't write a poem."

"This is your chance to experiment," I tell her.

"What if I don't do well?"

Mrs. Ching is forever anxious about performance. Everything we've seen of hers has been good, thoughtful, thorough, if not sparked by whimsy. She is one of those people always tied up in knots of high self-expectation. Maybe that contributes to her current physical distress. She is miserable with shingles, so acutely uncomfortable that sometimes in class she picks up her dress and fans her legs, trying to cool the burning.

In these first weeks of getting acquainted, we haven't graded a single paper. We've settled instead for written responses from both of us on every piece handed in. Grades or no grades, Mrs. Ching habitually frets her class standing.

I'd love to release her from this school-bound tension, to move her more toward enjoying the process of creation than craving the final stamp. "Take some experience, sad or happy, that moves you," I repeat. "Just let your ideas, your words flow. If it helps, write it in prose form first, then break it up into shorter lines. See what happens. Remember, it doesn't have to be a great poem."

"I'll do my best," Mrs. Ching promises doggedly.

The day our next writing class meets, Mrs. Ching Chao comes in with a poem called "The Celebration of Mid-autumn Festival."

Nanjing has barely gotten beyond its festivities for National Day when

October's moon, in this month they call "the golden time," waxes full, when moon cakes—hamburger-sized disks of pielike crust stuffed with various sweet fillings—arrive at our door as gifts from the university to the teaching staff. It's also the time when students string colored lanterns along rooftops and hold parties up there, the better to view the moon.

Mrs. Ching Chao delivers her poem to the class with a kind of modest, disbelieving pride in her work:

> On the Mid-autumn Festival night
> we went to Xuan Wu Park.
> Decorated with multicoloured flags
> and lanterns, the Park looked
> exciting to us.
>
> We sat in a circle as round as the moon,
> near the Xuan Wu lake,
> waveless and wide.
>
> We felt intoxicated,
> watching the moon,
> full and bright in the sky.
>
> While eating sweet and delicious moon cakes,
> we talked and laughed,
> sang and danced
> to our hearts' content.
>
> Sitting in a corner,
> speechless and happy,
> I stared at the moon.
>
> All of a sudden,
> I seemed to see Zhang E—
> the female celestial,
> more beautiful than ever,
> flying gracefully onto the moon.
>
> At lightning speed
> Wu Gang appeared,
> the mythological old man,
> holding a cup of wine
> fermented with osmanthus flowers.

To Zhang E he offered the wine.
Cheerfully they both smiled.

Oh, how charming the night was!
How wonderful to be here
in the Xuan Wu Park!

"Mrs. Ching, you make me feel as though I were there with you! May I see your poem?"

Beaming, she hands it to me. I debate taking time to talk about phrases like "to our hearts' content." Clichés, which by their easy familiarity sound like very smooth English to these nonnative speakers, aren't simple to identify and avoid. I'd like to know more about Wu Gang, Zhang E, and the special power of osmanthus flowers. But if each poem proves as long as Mrs. Ching's, we'll have trouble hearing everyone's today. Maybe I can follow up with questions in a later conversation class.

Mr. Ku Qiu has gone back to his rural childhood to write "An Aspect of Spring Morning." He looks quiet, slight, unassuming on the platform, but as he reads, his classmates follow intently.

In the early morning of spring
The stars are still twinkling
But the birds begin whistling.
A little cowboy
Bouncing, jumping and singing,
Leads a large cow
That is strong, golden, and milky
Followed by her young darling
That is mooing, lowing and springing
Along a murmuring stream
That runs into a river
Alive with fish swimming.
On the back of the cow
The boy sitting crosses the river
And comes to a grassland
Dotted with sweet-smelling flowers
That stretches to the distant horizon.
Then, the East is red
And the sun is rising. . . .

The cowboy turns back
To take hold of the cow's tail
To beat her hips
To add to her appetite
And looks at the rosy sky sometimes.
Content with the cheerful sight
He takes out his bamboo flute
To which a silk ribbon is tied.
In a graceful manner
He puts the flute to his mouth
And out the tune flies.
The gentle breeze carries the tune so far
That it attracts the attention of a group of children
Who are on their way to school
And gives their imagination wings
That takes them to paradise.
Then comes along an old peasant with a pipe.
"Who is this boy
That is playing the flute so fine?"
"Brother John," the children cry.

Mr. Ku Qiu looks up in time to catch appreciative smiles and murmurs from his listeners.

"I like that detail of beating the cow's hips to—to do what?" Sieg asks.

"To make her eat more," says Mr. Ku.

"Does it work?"

Mr. Ku smiles enigmatically. "Perhaps."

We talk about the differences between what "cowboy" means in China and in the western United States. Although there are picky points to note in Mr. Ku's lines, I'm still transported back by his work into that spring meadow and fresh morning, and at the same time, forward. I'm even more excited now about further possibilities for poetic reading and writing by these students. It's not we who have taught them this much, this soon. They are obviously drawing on a culture that has prepared them, given the chance, to develop their own insights.

I glance at my watch. The hour's almost gone. "Anyone have a short one?"

Miss Chun Xu volunteers. Looking regal and poised, she strolls to the lectern.

"Break Time in Middle School," she announces.

> Not willing to waste the twenty minutes
> between the second and third period,
> the girl-students are dancing gaily
> in a circle in front of the classroom.
> Some are laughing, some singing.
> No study in their thoughts, just enjoying.
> Sitting far back in the room,
> the boy students are deliberately looking
> out of the window, pretending
> that they pay no attention
> to the girls' playing,
> but under the desks, their feet
> are beating time very very softly,
> following the rhythms
> of what the girls are singing.

I find it difficult to speak.

It isn't often that a teacher's heart pounds with pleasure during a class. This has been the kind of morning that makes me glad to be here in China, in this bare room, working daily with young women and men like these in front of us—young people who, however, as much as they too have enjoyed the poems, crave to escape the classroom confines for lunch.

8 : Closer Acquaintance

We finally overcome the fixed seat handicap for conversation classes, which meet twice a week. By splitting the group into two smaller units, we arrange for one to meet upstairs with Sieg in the common room of the teachers' Guest House. It will just barely seat a crowded nine or ten.

The second group gathers downstairs with me in our apartment. Cramming in folding chairs, we can fit nine students flank to flank. Despite their initial protests ("The teacher should take the place of honor facing the door!"), I perch on the desk, my feet dangling, which leaves a bit more foot room for them.

As they come in, the earliest students sink with sighs of luxury into the four overstuffed chairs. They look around curiously at our relatively large private quarters, so different from their spartan dorms. We have curtains, four rooms, even a TV! Mr. Mao Yanyang looks at the blank screen with longing but doesn't touch the switch.

Miss Liu Jie spots the portable typewriter. She asks before class, "Can I use it?"

"Of course," I say.

She borrows paper, rolls it in, and touches the keys tentatively, while others crowd around, standing, to watch. Reluctantly, they leave this novel machine to begin class.

From the first day of these smaller classes, the students talk more. In Sieg's group today, the subject of marriage rules pops up. Undergraduates cannot get married, they say. Someone adds, "unless the woman is twenty-five and the male twenty-seven, and then they must have permission."

"What if a woman gets pregnant?" Sieg asks.

"That's impossible in China!" someone objects.

"Or if she does," says Mr. Fan, "both she and the boy must leave school."

"What about people who are not in school? Do they have to wait so long for marriage?"

"If the woman is over twenty-one and the man twenty-three, then they can marry. But it is very hard. They may not have a place to live. So they must wait longer or move in with their parents."

In my group, talk turns to superstitions. We trade folk beliefs. It intrigues them, always hungry for foreign details, that Westerners say black cats, Friday the thirteenth, breaking mirrors, and walking under ladders might bring bad luck.

In China, for the same reason, they try not to see a crow, a fox, a snake, a mouse, or a comet. They avoid the number seven. No one gives a clock to a couple about to marry, because the word for clock has the same sound as the word for death.

What's more, they never send a white flower to a friend. That also suggests death.

"And if a parent dies before a son or daughter's marriage," Miss Bin Qilin says, "then the wedding must be postponed for three years."

"Do some couples go ahead anyhow?" I ask.

The group looks serious. "No, it would be bad luck," Miss Zhuang confirms.

"Also, you must not marry when you're twenty-two," says Miss Chen Hong.

"Why not?"

She shrugs. "I don't know. Except it's bad luck."

So is cutting a pear with friends. And putting on a shirt backwards.

"Isn't there anything that's good luck?" I tell them about our wishing on a load of hay, wishing on a wishbone, rubbing a rabbit's foot.

"Someone born in the Year of the Ox has long life," Miss Lü Shu says.

"But if someone is born in the Year of the Dragon and their boyfriend in the Year of the Tiger, they will fight. So they shouldn't marry," says Miss Feng.

The hour has been all too short. Our smaller numbers and informal setting have helped break the students' usual classroom habit of passivity.

Miss Liu lingers to try out the typewriter one last time. Later, I see her lay on her classroom desk a keyboard she has inked onto cardboard. She practices fingering the cardboard against some future day when she too may have regular access to a machine.

As Sieg and I are comparing postclass impressions and agreeing to alternate groups so that we get to know each student better and students have repeated chances to relate to different speakers of English, someone knocks on the apartment door.

Mr. Chen Pingnan, our sometimes auditor who has not been in writing class recently ("I have many other teaching duties," he apologizes), hands us a previously assigned essay on the subject of teaching and hurries off. Our regular students commented in their papers largely from a student point of view. We look forward to reading Mr. Chen's older, more experienced ideas:

I was working in my hometown as a peasant after my graduation from the middle school in 1968. I was labouring from morning till night together with other peasants in the production team. I thought I was born in the countryside and had to work in the rice fields, but I should have any chance to change my destiny as a peasant for I got a little pay and was looked down upon by the citizens.

From then on I worked harder and wrote some articles and also did some extra work for the brigade. I was praised by the peasants and the leaders of my brigade. Fortunately I was chosen to be sent to the teacher training course for a year's study and I would be a middle school teacher after the course. That was the first time I had real happiness. I failed to fall asleep in the night after I got the news. I thought I would be no longer looked down upon by others. I would no longer work in the boiling water in the rice fields with bare foot in summer and labor in the cutting wind in winter. I would stand before the students wearing neat clothes and leather shoes.

I went round to tell my friends and relatives the good news. From that time on, the leaders in the brigade and the people's commune offered greetings to me and encouraged me to work harder.

That is the first real happiness I've ever had.

My eyes shift from Mr. Chen Pingnan's paper downward, to our shoes. Straight from class, we are both wearing Kmart joggers that have traveled many a dusty mile.

9 . Prejudices

This week's reading and writing lessons center on a chapter from Maya Angelou's *I Know Why the Caged Bird Sings*.

Over the past weeks, our students have shown much curiosity about racial attitudes in the United States. We're not sure what lies behind their questions —whether, with their own possible futures in mind, they've learned that some Asians encounter resentment in America because of their success in school and business, or whether, closer to home, as native students enrolled in Hehai, they resent the noticeable presence and greater perks of African and Nepalese foreign students on campus. Perhaps they want to find out from us if American and Chinese attitudes jibe.

In some ways, Chinese students have a right to ruffled feelings. Undergrads must share narrow unheated dorm rooms with seven other roommates; graduate students live three to a room. Foreign students from Third World countries occupy heated quarters with only one or two persons to a room. They have hot showers in their building; Chinese students must walk to a central bath house. The foreign students also get a generous stipend from the Chinese government that is considerably larger than the pay of younger college teachers on campus.

Students voice other complaints. Food in foreign students' segregated dining halls is far better and more varied, they know, than in their own canteens. Foreign students can take food to tables in pleasant surroundings, much like a restaurant. And although every official effort is made to discourage social mixing, Chinese men see a few Chinese women going to visit foreign students in the dorms. What's more, between semesters, the Waiban (Foreign Student Office) provides paid vacation travel in China for foreign students, a luxury not available to native Chinese.

We never see any of our own students socializing with dark-skinned foreign students from Africa, Nepal, or Pakistan as they pass in the halls, on classroom stairs, or along the streets. It is against this background of nearly total separation that we turn to Maya Angelou and her sensitive revelations of differences between white and black elementary schools, between black and white views of her childhood world in Stamps, Georgia, U.S.A.

After thorough discussion of the text, we ask the students to turn insights gained from Angelou's recollections toward their own awareness of attitudes in China.

"Your writing assignment for next time," I explain, "is to give an example from your own experience or knowledge where prejudice against a minority or against someone different made trouble for that group or individual. You can choose any kind of example. As usual, we'll share results."

When we next gather for writing class, they're loaded.

Miss Liu Jie leads off. Normally, she burbles with songs or jokes in teasing her classmates. Today she stands formal, serious, behind the lectern as she reads.

> We have a saying, "Like father, like son." If the father is a hero, the son will be a brave man; if the father is a criminal, the son will be looked down upon as if he is a criminal.
>
> Ling Yi, my middle school classmate, suffered a lot from this saying. When Ling Yi was 14 years old, his father was sentenced to four years imprisonment for cheating. From then on, Ling's carefree life perished. It seemed that it was he himself who was found guilty of cheating. People looked at him with curious and contemptuous eyes, read his face

carefully so as to find the signs of guilt. Old friends became strangers to him. No one would trouble himself to speak to him.

When someone lost something, he was always the suspected character. What's more, if he got high marks in exams, others would think he practiced fraud.

At last, he could no longer bear the insults, and left school. Prejudice won the battle by changing Ling's life.

Today, prejudice still exists in China, but the situation is getting better. More and more people begin to see how sinful prejudice is, and try to judge a person more objectively.

The class agrees Miss Liu has given an accurate picture for both past and present.

Miss An Ran provides an example from typical academic conditions in every province.

It is impossible for every student to pass the examination. Only a small percent can enter universities or colleges. The failures bear a heavy pressure on their shoulders, particularly those who do a very good job in their ordinary study and anticipate succeeding.

Circumstances turn unpleasant for them. Their family, their relatives, and even the colleagues of their parents—all members of their small "world"—talk about their failure, are discontented with them, and say some unpleasant words, such as: "You're a fool," or "You're useless." Most parents express their disappointment by their looks. The failures can "read" the same words written on their parents' faces.

The prejudice against these students is so strong that they can't hold their heads up and are forbidden to go out, just do the housework at home. Perhaps later their failure will gradually move to other things and the psychological attack on them is so heavy that some leave their homes or take suicide.

Sieg looks back at his notes. "You said, 'Only a small percent can enter universities or colleges.' Do you have any idea what that percent is?"

"Perhaps 4 percent?" Miss An guesses. "It is not very many."

Other students concur. They cite friends who did not make it through the dreaded exams or were so afraid they would fail they didn't even try.

"When we go back home and talk with our friends, they are often very sad. They envy us," Mr. Li says. "Some of them work now in factories and feel hopeless."

"What about studying while they work?" Sieg asks.

"They can do it on their own, but it is not easy."

Miss Lü Shu's paper on prejudice takes us to a different problem.

China's long preference for male children still has a strong influence upon people today. Especially in the countryside, families need boys more urgently than girls because the male can do heavier labor than the female. And they think that male can pass on their offsprings. If having no boy in one family, their neighbours will look down upon them. So most people prefer to give birth to male child, even running counter to the policy of family planning, "One family, one child."

For instance, one couple of my acquaintance has already had a daughter. But under the pressure of special custom, they try every effort to produce their second baby.

Having known the case, the leader of this countryside often found troubles with them, and fined them three thousands Yuan for the birth of the second. Otherwise, their house would be pulled down under the order of the leader.

That's the situation happened in some places, and the feudal ideas of regarding men as superior to women still exist.

"That is also true in the city," says Miss Liu. "Every family wants a boy."

"I like my daughter!" Mr. Lao Sheng protests.

"You are different," sayd Mrs. Ching Chao. "Your daughter is lucky."

"Plenty of women today would argue that males are not necessarily stronger," Sieg says. "Are there other reasons for wanting a boy beside his muscles?"

"When the parents get old, they go to live with the oldest son," Miss Feng says.

"What if there is no son?"

"Then perhaps the oldest daughter."

"Or, in the old days, sometimes they adopted a nephew. Then he was their son."

"There is another reason families do not want girls," Miss Zhuang Zi offers. "Girls leave father and mother when they marry. From then on, they live in their husband's family, and help the mother-in-law. So they are of no use to their own parents."

This sparks a heated argument. Miss Feng feels that boys are often lazy. They give their parents nothing, she says. Just take. Girls quietly help their family, "give moneys and time," but they get no credit for it.

"But *we* are responsible for their room, their food," Mr. Xue Hai defends his sex.

If we're ever going to air all the other papers, we must postpone further discussion of this issue until a conversation class, although by that time they may no longer feel moved to talk.

Miss Chun Xu ends the two hours with her paper called "A Cripple Girl."

> My primary school classmate, Cheng Pin, was a cripple. Because of that, she could not play games with us fellow students. We thought she was different from us, and was not capable. She thus was looked down upon by many of her classmates.
>
> There was one thing that will never leave my mind. One afternoon, it rained heavily, and the ground was all wet and slippery. On the way home after school, I saw a group of students standing around a girl who was on ground.
>
> As I came nearer, I recognized that it was Cheng Pin. She had fallen into the wet ground and couldn't stand up by herself. Nobody there in the circle gave her a help. Instead, they all stood there, laughing at her.
>
> Tears in her face, Cheng Pin was sobbing softly.
>
> Though I wanted to take pity on her, I dared not help her to stand up. Because if I did that, I would be treated defiantly by other classmates. As you know, to a child, losing his (or her) friends is the most unhappy thing. So I just pretended I did not see that terrible scene and quickly went home.

The room sits in silence. Miss Chun has reminded each one of us of our own sins of omission and commission, whether we label them by that name or not. What we fail to do when we might have, what we did do that we now deeply regret.

"Perhaps your memories will help you be more sensitive to others' troubles when you're a teacher."

"I hope so." Miss Chun softly answers herself as much as me.

Sieg returns us to the present. "Is there a lot of prejudice against handicapped people?"

"Have you seen any lame people on campus?" Mr. Fan asks.

I try to recall. "I think I've seen one."

"Probably a foreigner," Mr. Fan says with a curl of his lip.

"But," Sieg asks practically, "how would the university know an applicant is handicapped?"

"You have to send medical records with your application."

"And they hold interviews for graduate students. They even look at such things as height."

"Height!" we both exclaim together.

"What does that have to do with acceptance?" Sieg asks.

"Height is very important," the students assure us. "In fact, if you are not very tall, you cannot enter normal school to train as a teacher. A teacher must be able to command students."

"Doesn't it matter that some seventeen year-olds haven't reached their full growth?" I ask.

The students shrug. They seem to accept the rules without questioning. "That's their bad luck."

"What about all those articles in *China Daily* praising the accomplishments of handicapped people? The ones who have struggled against such great odds?"

"The newspaper tells success stories."

"Handicap can keep a girl from getting a factory job," says Miss Lü.

"Or if she can get a job," Mr. Mao adds, "maybe she has no marriage prospects."

"Some things are changing a little." Mr. Zhuo Niannian is still thinking about the newspaper stories. "One of our leaders, Deng Xiaoping, has a handicapped son. So more attention is given."

Students from other classrooms clattered from the building five minutes ago. Our charges have stacked their books, papers, and lunch gear in front of them as a large, rattling hint. Problems of prejudice can't be solved in a single morning.

"Bye-bye," Sieg waves to the class.

"Bye-bye!" they chorus in joyful imitation.

They leap to vanish, dropping their papers on the lectern as proof of lessons done.

10 . Games and Graffiti

Autumn invades the campus. It's turned so cool in the morning that we can see our breath. A seemingly demented exerciser is still out every day on the hill opposite, bellowing, loudly thumping trees with his fist or his head, but the ranks of *qigong* practicers who gyrate gracefully on the cement plaza before breakfast diminish as late October dawns require jackets to ward off the murky chill.

Students come into conversation class shivering but soon warm to today's topic—childhood games. They tell us that, like American kids, Chinese children play Hide and Seek, using the same rules and moves. Cat Catches Rat is a slightly different version that involves blindfolding and chasing other running children.

Sometimes the students' explanations of a game puzzle our Western ears. Miss Bin Qilin describes "Eagle Catch Chickens." "The first person in line stretches out arms," she says. "That is the hen. The others are chickens. They all hold onto jackets in a line. You get as many chickens as possible. Then you try to touch."

"You mean there are two lines, and you try to grab each other?"

She looks confused. "No, just one line." Her English breaks down in her effort to make the game clear. If we've understood her correctly, one child plays the eagle trying to pick off chickens that the hen protects.

We frequently see long lines of tiny children, under teacher supervision, marching at curb edge on organized jaunts throughout Nanjing. We've watched snaking dragon dances on TV. Even with China's one-child policy, every year millions of heir-hungry couples, urged on by their parents, produce so many offspring in this country that lining up for school games, dances, or trips is as familiar to children here as bedding down for mass afternoon naps in their cribs at primary school.

We keep trying to get reticent members of this older class to speak up rather than wait to be called on, one student after the other, around the room. "Anybody think of any other group games?" Sieg asks.

Someone mentions "Seek and Hide." For this one, no matter which province it's played in, boys and girls split into two groups. One side are heroes, the other "bad guys." They each have their own "headquarters." If good guys catch bad guys away from their headquarters, they can "kill" them.

Before we find out what form "killing" takes, Mr. Xue Hai suddenly remembers a more individual game. "Glass balls!" he cries out.

"How do you play that?" Sieg asks.

"Dig a hole on ground," Mr. Xue says. "Try to throw a ball into the hole."

"Sounds like what we call marbles." Sieg chalks the word on the board. The students scribble down this American name.

"That's not the way we play," Miss Chun Xu counters. "Every child has a glass ball. You throw the farthest. If the farthest hits the brick wall, perhaps I give you a candy."

Miss Li Yanping remembers a game. She sits forward on her chair, her eyes snapping, as she gives directions. "Sit in a circle. One says, 'One, two, three.' You can't move, not even blink eyes. The person who can sit most still wins. If you lose, you must do a performance. Or else someone will scrub your nose with bent finger!"

Suddenly, as their memories flood, students have forgotten it's a class. They interrupt each other, arguing, comparing.

Boys played a form of mumblety-peg with a knife and did "cockfighting." In the latter, each of a pair stood on one leg, the other leg held up bent at the knee. Each "cock" tried, by aggressive body contact, to knock the other to the ground.

Both boys and girls, when they were little, liked to make a square sedan chair with interlaced arms and hands. Someone would sit on the "chair"; then two groups would "fight" by trying to pull the sitter from the seat.

They mention Drop the Handkerchief, rolling or pitching coins instead of marbles, skipping rope in groups, flying kites that they made themselves from paper, paste, bamboo, and string.

"You throw the kite up in the sky," Mr. Lao Sheng says with a gesture. "The wind brings it up. Sometimes we had to climb a tree and fetch it."

We tell them about Charlie Brown and his kite-eating tree. It amuses them to learn American and Chinese kites suffer similar fates.

"When you have a lot of players," I ask, "how do you choose sides?"

"You put your hands behind you, with either palm or back turned up. That tells which group you belong to."

"Do you have any girls who are tomboys?"

"Why not?" asks Miss An Ran. "They're called 'pretentious boys.' "

"Is that good or bad?"

"Maybe such girls are strong. But people talk about them." And that, her tone implies, is not good.

By their accounts, Chinese children Skin the Cat up a pole. They also kick a shuttlecock in competition for distance, height, and frequency without letting the shuttlecock hit the ground. They sew bags of rice three inches square, then toss them between two groups, trying to hit opponents and put them out. They make bows and arrows with "a willow string and a sharpened, featherless arrow."

"We can shoot at anything except men," says Mr. Li.

Maybe that explains why we have seen so few small songbirds in Nanjing trees.

Mr. Lao Sheng recalls a blackboard game. "You draw a face on the blackboard without a nose. Then you blindfold a child, turn him around, and he must draw the nose—if he can."

We share America's almost comparable Pin the Tail on the Donkey.

Mr. Xue Hai remembers two more outdoor games that require dirt and time. In the first, "we plant trees," he says. "Dig a hole. Put a branch in, water it, and see if it's alive." In the second, "find an interesting small picture. Bury glass in a hole and also the picture. Say to your friend, 'Let's go to see my secret.' Dig out the soil, and there's the picture under glass!"

And there's the campus loudspeaker music signaling noon break time.

The next day during class we discover, through graffiti, that the teaching honeymoon has ended, as it inevitably must.

Classroom walls at Hehai are anything but dull. There are no pictures to lend color, but past classes have left their marks—upside-down footprints (the higher the better) on the back walls, inked scribbles on the plaster beside rear desks.

One morning last week, between classes, we stopped to inspect one of these scribbles. Its form in Chinese suggested it might be an extended verse. We asked the nearest student, who happened to be Mr. Lao Sheng, to translate for us.

He bent over, peering at the characters. "It's a poem."

"What kind of a poem? What about?" Sieg asked.

"It's a rascal poem," Mr. Lao replied. That's all he would explain.

Graffiti impulses seem to run the same the world over. It interests us that Mr. Lao's strong sense of decorum would not let him translate the "rascal" jingle. It also tickled me to find a comparison I *could* read carved onto a desktop:

> Teacher—worker
> Student—you peasant.

Today I'm sitting in one of the seats toward the back of the room, listening to a series of presentations we've recently begun. Once a week, each student gives a talk on a clipping chosen from a Chinese- or English-language newspaper or magazine. The assignment is a stiff one: Students must choose an item in advance, summarize key points, expand on the article if possible with related examples or commentary, and respond to class questions on their presentations. All this in English, without burying their faces and reading the item verbatim.

Other assignments have also increased in difficulty. We keep building on what the students have already done, pushing them to incorporate suggested improvements. Writing criteria have grown longer and stricter. We've begun to ask for revisions when needed. Earlier this week, we dismayed the postgraduates by asking for an open-book, in-class essay comparing two selections we had recently read and discussed.

"We've never done that before!" several protested.

"Then it's something you need to learn how to do," we answered with maddening teacher insistence. When we collected the papers, we knew they were telling the truth about lacking experience. Many essays required further work. We had to ask one student to do a second revision.

With these heightened demands, I'm not too surprised when I glance down inside the open front of the desk where I'm sitting and see on its bottom surface a penciled statement: "The Muehls are hateful. All they care about is each other."

Since it's scrawled in English, the writer intends us to see and understand it. Is it the truth? Are we hateful? Self-centered? Uncaring?

I know what I *think* our feelings and motivations are, but which is more accurate—our own self-protective view, or what this onlooker perceives to be true? Or some of both?

For sure, whoever wrote this was hurting. Perhaps we have been asking at least of this person, too much too soon. As teachers, we can't stop demanding. But this bitter statement lands us smack up against an age-old problem encountered by those in our profession. How can we do this job better? How can we best guide students to find out what they can, through a lot of hard, discomfiting work, learn to do? Not all sessions can be as easy as talking about children's games.

After class, when our group has vanished, I show Sieg the sentences in the desk. He leans down to read them.

"Good!" he says. "That person is learning to criticize!"

II · Contrasting Viewpoints

It's raining this morning. The classroom has sprouted a garden of colorful umbrellas drying across vacant rear desks.

Today's writing assignment follows two recent readings in which American authors Maya Angelou and Gregory Hemingway had presented contrasting viewpoints and used dialogue to show conflict. We've asked the students, with their own variations, to do the same.

Mr. Xue Hai announces his topic: "An Argument Between My Parents and Me."

> It was an early summer day. My parents took me to go to Yin-Ze Park to have a walk. The weather of that time was not too hot, and the grass and the trees were growing flourishingly; many flowers were in their full blossom, which made us happy and have ease of mind.
>
> Suddenly my father said in a low voice, "Look at that young lady!"

"Where?" I said.

"It is over there." Father told me with his finger.

I stole a glance at her and whispered, "Yes, she is really fashionable."

She was almost thirty years old. She had a slender, graceful figure. She flowed her hair loose over her shoulder which swayed about as she moved. She had an oval face and a pair of beautiful, bright eyes. Conspicuously, she wore a pair of extremely high-heeled shoes.

"A dissolute young witch!" Mother cut in, "really like a roast chicken."

On hearing this, I shook my head as I said, "Mother, you are wrong. Everyone today has an inclination for beauty, even an old woman like you."

There was an unhappy appearance on my mother's face, and she never say a single word for a while.

Father jumped in, "What your mother said is right, I agree."

Because they were my parents, I dare not argue with them face to face. So I only murmured, "What ideas you have! You are too conservative."

As I murmured, I suddenly heard a flock of birds chirping noisily on the trees over head as if they wanted to join in our argument. I looked up my head and I've found the trees were green enough with dewdrops through which the sun was shining brightly. It was the first early summer of 1980's.

I thought, why did people—people like my parents—lag behind the reality? It was terrible that old people couldn't understand young people and the young people couldn't understand old people. That was the gap between us.

As I thought, an idea occurred to me: There is only one difference between old people and young people, the young people have a glorious future before them and the old people have a splendid future behind him, and maybe that is where the rub is.

Mr. Xue Hai's essay appeals to the listening class. They recognize their own generation-gap conflicts.

"We can respect our elders," someone up front starts, "but—"

"—we don't always agree," Mr. Fan finishes.

How I would love simply to accept Mr. Xue's essay for what it is—a vivid, revealing anecdote that captures the moment when an adolescent consciously diverges from his parents significantly, perhaps for the first time, on an issue involving awareness of the opposite sex. I thoroughly enjoy his tone, his frankness, the charm of his idiomatic Chinese-English, which the students sometimes dub "Chinglish."

But I can't stop with appreciation only. Briefly, for Mr. Xue's sake, for the class's possible growth, we discuss a few changes he might consider for smoother expression and organization.

Then we call on Mr. Zhuo Niannian. In his usual dignified way, he mounts the podium and launches into details that set us clearly in the decade of the Cultural Revolution. His title, he says, is "Let's Look at the Textbooks."

Time: 1974
Place: No. 2 Middle School
      A Senior student's classroom.

"In the last century," the political economy teacher said, "in the capitalist countries, there was an economic crisis every ten years. In this century, there was one every seven or five years. The intervals of the years without crisis became shorter and shorter . . ."

He saw a hand rising among the students.

"What for? Li Ming?" He knew Li was a son of an army officer. He read many materials about the current affairs in the world his father brought home.

"From some books, TV programs or films, we can see many capitalist countries are prosperous."

"Yes. But it's just a superficial phenomenon."

"But the people there have cars, we don't. They live in good houses, we don't. And they earn a lot of money."

"You should know," the teacher looked seriously, "the capitalist countries have a longer history than ours."

"Japan's economy, for example," Li Ming didn't stop, "in these twenty years has developed very quickly and became one of the richest countries."

When they were talking, the other students shifted their eyes between the speakers. Some of them were surprised at Li Ming's abruptness and boldness.

"We should see through the appearance to the essence. Don't be bewildered by the false phenomenon, Li Ming."

"I know, only socialism can save China. But I still don't understand why our economy doesn't develop so rapidly. Is it just because of the short history?"

There is a pause. Then the teacher said, "Your question is more than I can answer. Don't say any more now. Please sit down."

After Li Ming did, the teacher cleared off his throat. "Let's go on with our class."

Unfortunately, there is no chance for immediate discussion. Mr. Zhuo's paper has brought us to the first class break. After this introduction of circumstances during the Cultural Revolution, Sieg checks with several students, including Monitor Lüe Shi, clustered in the aisles.

"How do you feel about discussing more of your and your families' experiences during the Cultural Revolution? Is that too sensitive a subject?"

They confer among themselves in Chinese.

"No, it's all right." Mr. Lao Sheng, answering for the group, switches into English. "You know the government now doesn't like the Cultural Revolution."

"O.K.," Sieg says. "One of these days we'll schedule that as a topic for conversation."

After any break, it's hard to pick up discussion of an article heard in the previous hour. Students do agree Mr. Zhuo's Li Ming showed unusual courage to speak up at all.

"The authorities could have punished him as a Capitalist Roader." Mr. Xue Hai spits out the damning term.

But they have little else to say. We're aware that Mr. Zhuo's article could get us into sensitive current comparisons. Yet some response needs to address the differences he's raised. I settle for a written comment later when we return his paper.

> It is interesting to see the student's criticism raised. You probably know by now that although we are comfortable with many things in our country, we can also see many things wrong with the very softness and materialism this affluence produces. Example: In China, few parents have to worry about their teenage children being killed in a car accident. In America, too many parents face not only the fear, but also the reality. The truth is both systems have their weaknesses and their strengths. In future, perhaps we'll all learn from each other.

At present, it's Miss Bin Qilin's turn to read her essay. She calls it "To Learn Or Not for A Female."

> When I was going to have the entrance examination of the university four years ago, Mother hoped that I would give it up. She said, "You'd

better have a job and help do housework. As a girl, it is enough for you to finish middle school."

My elder sister, who was listening, and usually gave me much help, encouraging me to read books and subscribing to magazines for me, stood opposed to what Mother said.

"Why can't a girl be allowed to do as a boy?" she asked. "Girls are not destined to be shut in the kitchen. I also want to go to a TV university."

"I always regret," my sister said, "that I was forced to leave classroom when I finished junior middle school. Mother, you have destroyed me. Please don't do that again."

"What? I destroy you? You can't work? Or you can't eat? You are living a happy life without going to university. And I, knowing nothing about how to read and write, also lived to such age and also bring you up."

My sister replied, "I am sorry to say, Mother, but you are quite a poor woman. To you, the world is just your kitchen. You are blind to anything else. You always have to ask others to write letters to father. You only look at a picture book instead of read it.

"You often feel puzzled each time you can't calculate the sum you should pay to sellers. You often try to understand and to be interested in what father talk to you, but in vain.

"As for me," my sister continued, "knowing so little, I can't communicate much with others. My friends talk about Napoleon, who I don't know is a person; instead I thought a spoiled wheel (same Chinese pronunciation—*Po lun*). Yesterday I made an accident because I don't know those English words on my machine. What a pity. I always want to do better in my work, just the lack of knowledge limits me."

"But anyway," my mother said, "males are more clever and more talented than females." Mother couldn't change her mind. "Many things are for males to do. And those great persons are males."

"Oh, Mama, you are wrong. Females are the same intellectual as males. Yet males are given chance to study and encourage to do so. Thus they know more and can do more. If girls also given such chances, the situation is the same. In fact, Mama, many females are doing what males do in today's world. There are more and more female doctors, female lawyers and female officials. Females go to the moon like males. Females run for president like males."

"All go out. Who will look after the family, take care of children? Who will cook, wash?"

"You are hopeless, Mama. Why must females devote their lives to family? Why can't males share it?" My sister was angry.

Four years passed. They still can't agree with each other. Certainly I can agree with my elder sister, for if I had followed my mother's wishes, I wouldn't be here with you in the classroom today.

There is a buzz among the women students. Miss Bin has touched a chord of understanding.

Sieg guides the class in a heated discussion of conditions for young women in China today. Yes, things are better in some ways. Girls can compete for schooling—if the family lets them. Many families still forbid them to study, "especially in the countryside."

"But it's hard for men there too," Mr. Fan points out.

"Many men don't want an educated wife," Miss Zhuang Zi says. "He will be afraid she looks down on him, if she has more."

"Will this be a problem for you?" Sieg asks the exceptionally educated women in the room.

"Perhaps," says Miss Liu. There's that evasive, discreetly open-ended word again.

"Perhaps we will find educated husbands," Miss Chun says and giggles.

Mrs. Ching Chao sits silent. She is already married.

No one mentions the possibility of staying single. For most women in China, that is still not a desirable option.

We return to Miss Bin's essay.

"I like the strong way you presented your mother's viewpoint, Miss Bin." I repeat her phrases: " 'Who will look after the family? . . . Who will cook, wash?' "

"The men will," says Mr. Fan, resigned, and his classmates laugh.

12 . Grandparents

The assigned reading this morning is Joyce Maynard's essay "Four Generations." In it, she recounts the tangled, loving, sometimes impatient human relations between and among her grandmother, her mother, herself, and her own daughter. The essay starts and ends in a month when her grandmother, eighty-seven years old, lies close to death.

As usual, we begin by tackling words, phrases, and sentences, understanding them at the most superficial levels. Once again, student questions reveal, despite their adeptness in formal English, how widely our experiences differ.

"What is a nursing home?" they ask.

"What is Cracker Jack?"

"Is Shirley Temple," Mr. Zhuo wants to know, "a place to visit?"

Dulled by my own parochialism, I've never thought about Shirley Temple's name in any other context than the heights that film star achieved as child and adult. Her name suddenly acquires a new, worshipful possibility through Mr. Zhuo's assumption that any temple, just as in China, must be a venerable tourist attraction.

During our hour's exploration of the text, I'm reminded again how we must look at even simple English words through our students' eyes. When the author's grandmother lies jaundiced, dying of pancreatic cancer in the hospital, she says, "I always prided myself on being different. Now I *am* different. I'm yellow."

In a Western classroom, these words get a laugh. Here, where our students have stated they take pride in being yellow, that the yellow color on their flag proudly symbolizes the whole yellow race, this passage fails to convey Maynard's intended meaning.

We discuss another cultural difference in the essay. Maynard clearly values a girl child. She writes about her daughter, "I was offering up one more particularly fine accomplishment."

I get the students to consider this passage for its Western view of female offspring. Without belaboring the point, I trust what they read in these pages will reinforce Mr. Lao Sheng's genuine pride in his fifteen-month-old baby girl. I hope Maynard's pleasure in her own daughter will serve to shape their own attitudes, if any of them, once married, produce females in this still male-preferring world.

For a follow-up assignment keyed to today's reading, we ask each student to write about a grandparent or an older member of their family. They may use any kind of organization, dialogue, time, space, or sense details, flashbacks—all of which we've stressed—that they want to incorporate.

The results come at the end of the first week in November. From the opening paper on, it's obvious this family assignment has moved them. They know their subjects. They care deeply about them. Although on some days class attention tends to stray to private conversations while other students read aloud, unless checked by a head shake, this time the room is silent, attentive.

Mr. Fan Rui writes of a grandmother caught in a widow's grief, after his grandfather died suddenly of asthma. He ends his essay:

> I found my grandmother sobbing violently on her knees before my grandfather. I knew that for her there had never existed any other man like her husband who loved her so much and understood her so familiarly. And now she was just the mother of her son, the grandmother of

her grandson, but not any more a wife. She had lost a good partner who always helped her clean vegetables when she was ready to cook. She lost an intimate husband with whom she could chat whole-heartedly and freely in their spare time. And she also lost a companion with whom she sometimes quarreled over trivialities.

Miss Zhuang Zi's grandmother is still alive, having survived tremendous ordeals from a courageous past to a determined present.

In China, people usually think those who have kind-hearted grandmothers are happy and lucky. I am a happy and lucky one.

My grandmother was born into a rich family, in the north of China, in 1917. When she was young, besides being very pretty, she was particularly clever.

She loved to read and write although girls were not allowed to do so at that time. She was also good at sewing, and especially at paper-cutting. She could cut everything such as flowers, animals, birds out of a piece of paper. Some people said that no matter what was climbing on the ground and what was flying in the sky, my grandmother could cut them quickly and embroider them vividly in colorful silk as soon as she came across them. She was admired for her nimble hands.

In 1937, she married my grandfather and soon moved to the south of China. Next year, my father was born, so she became a worker in a textile mill in order to support her growing family.

During the so-called "Cultural Revolution," my grandmother met a lot of frustrations because of her family background. She, however, never gave in.

In 1970, we were sent to the countryside to "receive re-education" from the poor and lower-middle peasants.

What terrible days we had!

We were not familiar with the farm work; we had no money; not enough food; even no electric-lights at night!

At that time, everyone in my family was depressed except my grandmother. She was really a pillar. Miserable though our life was, my grandmother often encouraged us to cheer up and struggle against our fate.

At home, she united us as one and managed household affairs in perfect order; in the fields, she endured silently the hardship of the farm work and the supercilious looks of the others. In spite of these, she was kind to every peasant and often helped them. At last, she won the love and respect of the peasants.

Unexpectedly, she fell ill and had a major operation in 1975. In hospital, I couldn't help weeping when I saw my dear grandmother so thin and weak lying in the bed. She comforted me and said humourously, "Don't worry. The King of Hell refuses to accept me."

After the "Gang of Four" was overthrown in 1976, my family returned to the city. My grandmother was invited to be an adviser of the textile mill, but later she retired because of her poor health.

"Don't be lazy. Laziness is the greatest enemy of our life," she often says.

Now, people often see an old woman around 70 jogging in the park every early morning. This morning jogger is not very tall, nor very strong. She doesn't jog very fast. Her face, however, is full of self-confidence. From her face, people can see that she is an unusual and strong-minded woman. This morning jogger is my dear grandmother!

"Miss Zhuang, I hope you will give a copy of that to your grandmother," I say.

"She doesn't read English."

"Then translate it. She would be proud to know how much you admire her."

Miss Feng Yunxia has called her essay "Three Generations."

Last summer, my grandmother died. My mother felt faint with deep sorrow after hearing the sad news. I tried to be a mother to her for a moment, but my mother was so grieved that I couldn't help weeping either.

My grandmother was born in a poor peasant's family in 1910. She married my grandfather in 1930. They led a very hard life in the countryside. Their seven children were their centre as well as their problem. It was very difficult for such a Chinese peasant family to raise seven children at the time.

But my grandmother was a silent and resolute woman. She overcame all kinds of difficulties and gradually made her family rich. She married her five daughters honourably. She let her two sons receive education which was physically impossible for most peasant families at that age.

My grandmother, however, received no education. She knew the only successful way for her boys was to send them to school. My mother is a clever woman. She desired to go to school when she was a child. But the family couldn't support any more children in school. My grandmother felt compunction for her because of this.

When I entered University, my grandmother was joyful and felt somewhat relieved. She realized that my mother succeed at last: I have achieved the cherished desire of my mother—a dream of three generations in my family.

When I went home from college, my mother always asked me to go see my grandmother with her. We were very very happy when we were together. I told them everything interesting about my college. We talked, laughed and ate.

My grandmother fed us as she always did when we came. She prepared a lot of delicate food and when we went home, she always put in our bag sticky rice, deliciously prepared meat—the foods which my mom and I like best.

She usually walked with us for a long distance. She said she did not like to say goodbye to her favorite daughter and granddaughter forever.

After we persuaded her to turn back, she just stopped walking and stood there, with her white hair waving in the wind, watching us, until we disappeared in the distance.

Now, all this has gone. But my grandmother's love for us remains in our hearts. Today, my mother and I enjoy each other's company very much, and we love each other in an unreserved and unquestioning way, as my grandmother did for us.

The students seem eager to have their own essays heard. After commending Miss Feng for her skillful interweaving of the three generations, we move on to Mr. Xue Hai. He calls his simply "My Grandmother," pronouncing the word always with the emphasis on the second syllable.

One evening, both of my parents hadn't come back from their work. My grandmother was preparing supper. Suddenly she called me into the kitchen.

When I rushed in, I saw blood dripping down from her cut finger. I immediately got some haemostatic from the drawer and clumsily bandaged her finger. Then I noticed her hands which were like the dry bark of an old oak tree, rough and hard.

I couldn't believe that they were her hands, and I couldn't control my tears falling like pearls from a broken string.

I bent my head down and kissed her hands that I loved better than any softer, smoother hands I've ever met. Those hard and worn hands had done so much for me and my family.

I was born in the year of the "Great Leap Forward." My mother had to go out to make steel and iron from morning till night in answering to the call of "Striding Into Communism."

At that time, my grandmother looked after me carefully. She fed me with wheat flour porridge, like paste in the bottle today. Because in those years we had a natural disaster and a shortfall in our agriculture, people suffered from terrible hunger, and had nothing to eat. My grandmother, like many people, had to eat weeds, edible wild herbs and fruit, even tree bark and leaves in order to save a mouthful of food for me.

So I was very close to my grandmother when I was a little child. I often hugged her neck. She often kissed my cheek.

My grandmother was a kind-hearted, cheerful, optimistic and hard-working woman. She often did every kind of work in my family, such as cooking, knitting, sewing and laundering even though my parents advised her again and again not to do so.

My grandmother was a poor woman. She became a widow when she was only 27 years old. My father was her only son. The poor mother and the poor son depended on each other for survival. Really, she suffered a lot before liberation.

All that is in the past.

My grandmother is not alive today. She died of stomach cancer in 1969. Maybe, the main reason for her cancer was the hunger of 1960's.

Now, I am coming into my middle age and coming into contact with happiness in my own life. But I can't help liking to sit in a quiet place, recalling the image of my grandmother.

I think, in my deep heart, she is one of the great Chinese women.

What's going on in this classroom today does not need teacher intervention. It remains for soft-voiced Miss Chen Hong to bring the entire roomful to total, involved silence, as she reads aloud her tribute to her grandfather. She has trouble controlling her words, as her listeners have trouble controlling our eyes and throats before she finishes. Her title is "This Time I Cried."

Cried? Certainly I have cried before. I cried the time a bumble bee stung my earlobe, the time a brick in the street tripped me and dropped me to the ground, the time a dog in the neighborhood followed me and barked at me.

I cried when I was left alone at home and the time my elder brother, getting even for my locking him outside the house during a storm, chased me around the yard with a spider in his hand.

Crying as a little girl was a way of saying, "Hug me Mummy. I am hurt." It could help me get a candy from Mom and she would coax me to stop crying.

But it also earned me a frown from my grandfather, a thunderous slap on the back and a "What are you crying for? Girls at your age don't cry."

And thus gradually I learned from my grandfather how not to cry, keeping his instructions all through my teens.

Even when I checked grandfather into the hospital, I didn't cry. Even during his operation for cancer and awful suffering afterwards I held back my tears, only to learn crying again the day after he died.

With such good training in holding back my feelings, it was frightenly simple to stay near him, alone and dry-eyed every day, and, at home, to comfort Mom who was too frightened to see him.

In spite of all treatment, my grandfather's condition was getting worse and worse. As I stood at his bedside, the lids of his eyes cracked open. He squeezed my fingers and tried hard to speak, but it was impossible. His words hissed through a tube draining liquid from his lungs.

Prepared, I had brought pen and a sheet of white paper. My grandfather's hand scrawled out two words. I thought a tear was hanging in the corner of his eyes, as he handed me the note. It said, "I am afraid."

I smiled weakly. "Don't worry. Everything will work out fine, you'll see!"

I said the same words to Mum when I returned from the hospital as she sat in the dark kitchen, chewing her lips, drumming her fingernails on the wooden table. Each time I tried to speak, her eyes would fill with tears and she would turn away from my stare. At midnight, we got the news my grandfather died.

Next day, I went to the hospital to claim my grandfather's things: a paper bag and a wooden cane. That was all that were left! I held the warm wood. I saw my grandfather sitting outside telling us a story, poking his cane along the frozen ground. . . . In the bag there were some picture-story books. Even in bed, he was preparing the stories for my youngest sister.

Unable to keep in my tears this time, I finally collapsed onto a cold metal chair and sobbed miserably, the bag crushed to my chest. I cried as I thought of my grandfather's last words on that sheet of white paper. I cried as I saw Mom trembling in the large empty house. I cried for all the tearless pain and anger and frustrations built up inside me over the years.

I cried as I saw my youngest sister lying on the ground crying for her dearest story-teller grandpa.

Toward the end, Miss Chen Hong's words are so choked we have to strain through our own tears to listen. But we have heard. She—and every one of the other deeply involved writers in this room—have led all of us to care together.

13 · Exchanging Customs

One afternoon, Mr. Guo drops by the apartment. We trade pleasantries. Then he states his purpose in coming. "I wish you would teach the boys manners."

We're startled. The manners of our male students seem generally all right. It's true they don't stand back to let women go first through the door, but when they need to spit they either go outside, spit on paper on the floor, or— if there's no paper available—take care to grind the wet deposits, so common in this chill, smoggy world, into the cement with their shoe soles. Of course, no one honors the privacy of teacher record books or bookbags. Females more than males swap long confidences and have to be shushed during class, but mostly everybody maintains courtesy for classmates and to us.

Mr. Guo sees our surprise. "The students are rude. They push in line. They have no manners," he pronounces.

So we set up two sessions on the subject. In the first, we ask them to tell us what rules of behavior we might easily violate through ignorance in their country.

"Don't put your feet on the table," says Mr. Fan.

"Don't use your index and middle finger to point," they all agree.

"Why not?" Sieg asks.

"That says, 'You're degenerate,' " says Mr. Lao Sheng. "Two fingers pointed means you will kill. You can use them down or to the side."

With some chagrin, I remember all the times I've called on students by pointing. Let's hope they haven't misunderstood my habitual American gesture. In future, I'll have to try to omit that motion here or make it only palm up. "How about table manners?"

They have many rules. Where you sit is very important. Emperors, officers, and the most distinguished person by rank or age always sit to the south, looking north. Right side is more important than left.

Mr. Ku Qiu disagrees. "In some places," he insists, "the oldest person faces east."

"The host faces the door. Then he can see when guests come in," Miss Feng states.

Even in everyday eating, parents face the door. "Old-fashioned country chairs," they tell us, "were bigger for parents. And children let parents start first."

"If someone is absent," Miss Xi Yang says, "don't start until they get there. Or the host tells the guests to go ahead."

"That's very like U.S. custom," Sieg says. "What else?"

"You drink first," says Miss An Ran. "Then eat, drink, talk. It's impolite to have rice when drinking."

"That's true," Miss Xi agrees. "No talking at table, or don't talk too much. If you've finished, you can talk."

"One person pours drinks for others," says Mr. Fan. "They try to get you to drink as much as possible. Keep your glass full."

"What if you don't want any more?" Sieg asks.

"You can say, 'Sorry, that's enough,' " says Mr. Lüe Shi. "You're the experienced guest."

"Do you mean *older* guest?" I ask.

Mr. Lüe smiles. "Yes. Older."

"What do we need to know about chopsticks?"

"Put them on your plate," advises Miss An. "Use them for a little while, then put down. Watch the host. If most people aren't eating, don't eat."

"May I use chopsticks to take food off the turnaround?" Sieg asks.

"If there's a spoon, use spoon. If not, you can use your own chopsticks," says Miss Chen Hong. "Or you can use a second pair just for serving."

"But don't stand up and reach across the table for something from the turnaround," Miss An warns.

"Take only the food nearest. We serve food first to the most important guest," Miss Xi explains.

"Do not make your mouth too loud!" Mr. Mao, usually so silent, offers a tip. "Don't make noise when you chew. Use chopsticks elegantly." His voice caresses the last word.

"Elegantly? Tell me how!"

"Don't stuff your mouth," Mr. Li says.

"Don't take up plate and eat from it. You can pick up bowl, but at formal dinner you would not."

"Don't stir your food with your chopsticks."

"You can use chopsticks to cut food apart."

"What if I get a bone?" Sieg asks from experience.

"Use your fingers. Put the bone either on a small dish or on table in front of you."

So those rings of bones on the table around plates are polite in China!

Two students argue over when soup should appear.

"In Nanjing," says Miss Chun Xu, "soup is the last dish."

"In *my* hometown," Mr. Lüe Shi counters, "you can eat soup anytime."

Miss Chun whips her long ponytail around to stare critically at Mr. Lüe. "Nanjing people think it not good for your health."

We think we might be in for a clash between provinces, but Miss Zhuang Zi mentions her favorite "delicious dish"—fish. "Especially at Spring Festival," she says, "never touch the cooked whole fish. Even when it is on the table. No one eats fish until next day. Then you will be rich. The same thing for chicken. If the weather is hot, you can eat one side. The bride can turn the fish over."

"Only the bride?" I ask.

"It is her special privilege."

This reminds Miss Bin Qilin of another physical arrangement. "Keep the head of the chicken in one direction, or you will have bad luck."

"The cut on fish stomach should face the door!" cries Miss Lü Shu.

What a lot of niceties to master!

Sieg checks his watch. "Is there anything else we should know?"

"Tell others you have had a good dinner," Miss Liu Jie reminds us, "across rice bowl."

"And wipe your lips with your handkerchief," Mrs. Ching Chao says.

Miss Li Yanping clanks her lunch gear. All this talk of food makes her impatient to leave campus, to head for a nearby teacher's college where she and some of her friends feel the canteen food is much better than Hehai's.

"Next time," Sieg says, "we'll talk about Western-style manners."

The students cheer for the end of this class, and for shifting the burden of future talking onto us.

When they gather for the next conversation class, it's cold. Everybody wears jackets. In their smaller, split groups, they rush for the relative warmth and overstuffed comfort of the Guest House sitting room. Its furniture isn't in the usual wall-hugging rectangle. We've pulled a card table with four straight chairs into the center. The table holds four place settings—plate, knife, fork, spoon, paper napkin, and a bowl of bananas. Our biggest problem was finding forks. We brought none. The stores don't sell them. Luckily, our fellow teachers the Gravs, who brought six hundred pounds of household goods from Canada, had extras to lend.

The students can't keep their eyes off the bananas. Fruit is not a staple in their breakfast. Many of them skip that meal entirely for more sack time.

"What's this for?" the ever-curious Mr. Li asks.

"I'll explain when everyone gets here," Sieg says.

Mr. Mao picks up a fork, hefts it, turns it over and back again as if he had never held one in his hand before.

When the last straggler enters, muttering "Sorry!" Sieg begins. "We'll talk about our manners later, but today, you're in a restaurant. You've come here with a date to eat 'dinner.' "

"Oooh!" Miss Zhuang says with pleasure.

"We'll pair you up as much as possible," Sieg continues. "One couple at a time, you're to come through the door—remember, the man holds the door open for the lady. Then the man helps take her jacket off, hangs it on the coat tree, and pulls out her chair at the table so she can sit down, before seating himself."

A groan rises from the male students. The women sit forward in excitement.

"Lois and I will model it first for you."

We pantomime the admittedly old-fashioned but appreciated courtesies. It's so cold, even inside the room, I hate to give up my jacket for the few minutes necessary.

Once he's seated me and I've put a paper napkin on my lap, Sieg offers the bowl of bananas to me. There's only enough to give each student a half, so I pretend to take one, peel it, pick up my knife in my right hand, fork in my left, cut the banana in pieces, and eat, using the Western utensils.

I demonstrate both American and British ways to handle the fork. "When you eat your own banana, try both ways. See what's more comfortable."

"I don't like bananas," Miss Liu says.

"Then pretend to eat, as I did."

"Mr. Lao, you're Miss Feng's date," Sieg directs.

Laughing, they go out the door, then come back in. It's literally a touchy moment, when Mr. Lao takes Miss Feng's coat. It is still common for males and females to avoid touching each other in China unless they have entered into a marriage-destined relationship. For a man to remove a woman's coat seems totally foreign to their experience. Under these learning conditions, however, and especially since Mr. Lao is already married, Miss Feng is willing to let her coat be taken off.

As the first pair struggle with the strange moves, the others watch avidly. Their subsequent attempts encounter the same difficulties, with variations.

In his haste to sit down and get at the bananas, Mr. Fan forgets to pull out his date's chair. Mr. Xue has trouble with high-flying elbows, learning only at the last bite to force them down to his sides. Mostly, the women seem to prefer British-style eating, avoiding the extra American shift of fork back to the right hand after cutting.

All the men are awkward in helping women put their coats on again. They hold jackets either too high or too low. The women's stiff arms don't make the maneuver any easier.

Nothing has demonstrated quite so clearly how much cultural habits and expectations smooth our actions. While I'm washing and drying the tableware in soapy water between uses, I wonder if today's lesson has violated anybody's feelings.

I needn't have worried. More than one student leaving class says, "Let's do this again!"

But perhaps that's because they like bananas.

14 : A Discussion of the Cultural Revolution, 1966–1976

Monday morning, Mr. Li Jian comes into class sporting a handsome rust-colored wool sweater. Students appear so often in the same outfits that everyone remarks on anything new.

Mr. Li is very proud of his sweater. "Three friends knit it for me. One did the body, the other two did the sleeves."

Some of the women examine the results critically from the vantage point of their own knitting skills.

"Very nice!" they pronounce. Mr. Li accepts their compliments as justly due.

Today's conversation topic is the Cultural Revolution. We have general knowledge about that turbulent decade from 1966 to 1976. Last week's reminiscing papers about their grandparents taught us a bit more. But we look forward to this rare chance to learn from people who, though young, lived through the experience. As usual, we hope their fund of knowledge will make it easier for them to talk in English.

"Some of you are older than others," Sieg begins, "so your memories will be different. Just comment, from your own viewpoint, on what that period was like for you or your family. Mr. Xue, want to lead off?"

"I was in primary school in 1967," Mr. Xue Hai says. "My family suffered a lot. My father was accused of being a capitalist because he was a manager in machinery plant. They locked him in a room for ten months. They wanted him to confess his errors. They beat him! They read papers about his ideas. Sometimes, in front of brigade, he had to wear a dunce cap and a sign that said 'Capitalist.' He had no right to say words." Mr. Xue shakes his head, remembering. "All this time my family had no sustenance."

"What happened after the ten months?"

"My father had to go for reeducation for five or six years hard work. He was liberated in 1970s before the end."

"Miss Chun Xu?"

"I was in primary school. My family didn't suffer too much, but my family was separated. They had been cadre leaders. A year after my mother had my brother, she was sent to work in the fields. My elder brother stayed with my grandmother. I went with my father to the countryside to be reeducated."

"What do you mean by 'reeducated'?"

"The peasants were often teachers," Mr. Li explains. "There were classes and newspapers. You had to write reports about your thinking. They made you bow your head. They criticized, especially if you made a conscious or unconscious mistake—like tearing a picture of Chairman Mao. Sometimes they tied people's hands behind their backs."

"But if educated people went to the countryside, weren't they used as teachers for the benefit of the peasants?" I ask.

The group looks at each other, then back at me.

"Chairman Mao called on us to struggle against capitalist life." Miss Liu is patient with my ignorance. "Intellectuals went to the countryside to realize communism."

"So what kind of work did they do?"

"We carried fertilizer, cut grass," says Mr. Fan. "The peasants welcomed us. In autumn, we helped gather harvest."

"I worked in a camera factory," says Mr. Zhuo.

"I worked in a factory in the country," says Mr. Lao, "with no chance to go to school. If you had 'back door' ways, if your thinking was 'right' after two years' work, then you might go to school."

"That's why I studied ten years by myself," Mr. Zhuo says quietly.

Sieg glances around the circle. "Miss Xi Yang?"

"My grandfather died in 1966. He was a capitalist. He owned land. The whole family was looked down on. My uncle was paralyzed so he couldn't walk."

"We had a relative, an officer," volunteers Miss Zhuang Zi. "He was put in jail. Everybody was sent to countryside for reeducation. My grandparents couldn't do farm work, so they couldn't get money. My father returned to city in 1975. The government gave new house. In 1980, we all returned."

It's Mr. Ku Qiu's turn. "In 1974," he says, "my grandfather was seriously criticized. My mother's father had been an officer in Guomintang. My grandfather's brother was in Taiwan. My father was a carpenter, so he was considered a bourgeoisie—he could earn money by working for other people. The authorities wanted him to give all our money. They took pigs, bed, chairs. Later, they gave some money back at the end."

"I was in primary school," says Miss An Ran. "My second sister had graduated from middle school. If you didn't send a child to the countryside, the parents would be criticized by the factory workers. So she worked in the countryside for three or four years. She could come home, but she had to walk two, three hours on foot."

I look up from my notes. "What about your other siblings?"

"My first sister had a job. My third stayed in town. And my brother wouldn't be sent. He is the only boy."

Mr. Lüe Shi has maintained his customary reticence. Sieg calls on him.

"My parents are traditional peasants," Mr. Lüe answers. "They had some privileges. They felt glorious! Only peasants' sons and daughters and leader's children can go to college then. The peasants had charge. First workers, then peasants, then soldiers." He pauses, sensing the silence in the room. "Our agriculture was affected," he adds. "Very poor."

"*My* father," Miss Feng says grimly, "couldn't go to school. My grandfather was criticized by others outside family."

Sieg looks for some way to rebalance the discussion. "Wasn't it crowded for peasants to have all these people flooding in from the cities?"

"Big villages," answers Mr. Li, "didn't want Cultural Revolution people sent there. So they went to backward places. There was often prejudice."

"But some would volunteer to receive them," says Miss An.

"Didn't any intellectuals stay in the city?" I ask.

"At the end," Mrs. Ching Chao says, "I was in middle school. I continued to study and sit for exams for college. But if it didn't end, my family would be forced to go to the countryside. My father, who is a doctor, went to Anhui for reeducation with university. At the end, Father became director of hospital."

"I was in middle school too," says Miss Lü Shu. "The authorities demanded my parents to say they had some guilt in running a shop. They had to stay in factory all night and bow their heads."

The tones in which these young people utter the words "criticized" and "bow their heads" show what dread, what humiliation their families felt.

"Some of you have said your parents came back," Sieg observes. "What was happening to let them return from the countryside?"

"At first, my father was accused of engaging in antirevolutionary group," Miss Liu says. "He went to work in the countryside as a farmer. He could come home once a year. Later, he proved to be a revolutionary."

"In meetings," Mr. Lüe says, "they began to criticize the Gang of Four."

Mr. Zhuo stirs. "October 6, 1976!" he exclaims. "They arrest the Gang of Four! We were very happy! We celebrated in street in demonstration—'Down with the Gang of Four!'"

"And then," Mr. Mao says, "the exam system was resumed. The upper class could take exams for school again."

"Wait a minute," Sieg says. "Tell us more about the Gang of Four. Do you remember all their names?"

They spit out the names so fast I have to ask them to repeat to be sure I'm spelling them right: Jiang Qing, Wang Hongwen, Zhang Chunqiao, Yao Wenyuan. "The wife of Chairman Mao and three other vice-chairmen," Miss Xi adds.

"What happened to them?" I ask.

"All are still alive in Beijing," says Mr. Lüe. "The authorities keep them in a sort of prison. They are separated, one in each room. No political rights."

"Mr. Zhuo remembers that date vividly," Sieg says. "Do any of the rest of you?"

Most of them shake their heads in somber denial.

"What I remember," says Miss Bin Qilin, "after 1976 Cultural Revolution was over, I needn't write slogans any more or sing songs in praise of revolution!"

One factor in this massive human disruption still bothers me. "A lot of Chinese supported this," I say. "Wasn't there anything good about the Cultural Revolution?"

"No!" says Mr. Lao Sheng. "I lost ten years of my life!"

"Many graduates," Miss Liu says slowly, "were sent to mix with the peasants. Parents sometimes felt their children were honored to do such service."

Miss An disagrees. "They were crazy during that time. Mostly young people held the leading posts. After, if they weren't too evil, they were forgiven."

"How did people who had been punished view those who punished?" Sieg asks.

"Some themselves were punished, deprived of positions," says Mr. Li. "They returned to being ordinary people."

"If they did serious crimes, they were imprisoned. Or people criticized and shunned them."

"At that time," Mr. Ku Qiu offers, "some people were innocent. They just did what they were told."

Miss Liu leans forward with a glint from her lavender-tinted glasses. "Afterwards, we knew it was wrong. But then we thought it was right. China has a two-thousand-year history when people believed anything."

"Perhaps the only merit of the Cultural Revolution," says Miss Feng, returning to my question, "was to lead people to think. In China today, we use our own minds."

They sit silent a minute, almost drained.

"My stomach," Miss Chun Xu announces to end this long, memory-troubling class, "is impatient."

We let them go, with thanks for their information.

On entering our own dining hall, we find only one other occupant, a Chinese engineer we've heard is here to give two lectures.

It seems absurd to occupy separate tables in the otherwise empty room, to make our server take unnecessary steps. "May we join you?" Sieg asks.

"I would be delighted." The visitor speaks clear British-accented English. "You are visiting Hehai?"

We explain our role on campus. Sieg mentions the focus of this morning's discussion.

"Ah," the visitor says. "Your students were too young to understand." He looks down at his plate but does not seem to see it. "Those years," he says softly, "were a very bad time."

15 . Money Matters

It's so frigid today that students, who have been wearing hats, coats, and scarves throughout the first class hour, jump up and down in the back of the room at break time to get warmer. I jump with them, keeping gloved hands in my pockets.

Once everybody is slightly pinker cheeked, they settle back in their rows to share aloud their written responses to yesterday's reading. Our reading text has ten brief quotations, from Euripides to Frank Lloyd Wright, on the subject of poverty and wealth.

Money is a topic much on their minds. We know, by hearing both frequent jokes and serious comments, that they struggle from month to month on student pittances. Many feel ashamed because they remain dependent on their parents for additional support, when millions of other young people have finished their education and are already out working and contributing to the family income. Probably what they read from the lectern today will come informed by long contact with financial straits.

Mr. Zhuo Niannian starts us off.

WHAT DOES MONEY MEAN?

I was standing by the bookstall, turning over the pages of *A Principle of Social Psychology,* and hesitating about whether I bought it or not. I looked at the back cover: 5 Yuan 50 fen. Expensive, I thought. The description of the book was fluent and interesting. I wanted to read it. I had ten yuan in my pocket, but before going home I would go buy some vegetables for our supper. At last, I left the stall without the book.

I was reading a report in the newspaper. A young man, age 28, was arrested. He worked in a bank. His job was to burn the used money. He and his girl friend would marry soon. His future mother-in-law said he should buy all the major home electric equipments before their marriage. His savings were not enough and he was in debt already. He racked his brain and finally thought out a way.

One afternoon, the young man found no one beside him in the bank. He let a bundle of used money (1000 yuan) drop down to the floor and kicked it into the corner under a desk. When all the staff members went home after work, he picked up the bundle, put it in his bag.

I was talking with my colleagues. Yesterday, a worker in our factory, age 24, committed suicide. It was because several days ago, more than 100 cameras were stolen in the night from the assembly workshop. He was one of the suspected men. The security officers asked him to talk. They knew he often gambled with others. In the investigation, he denied he had stolen the cameras. That night, he left a death note and jumped from the window of the fourth floor and died, leaving thousands of yuan of debt behind.

Is money good or bad? I can't answer. The American poet Sandburg said, "Money is power, freedom, a cushion, the root of evil, the sum of blessing." Is he right or wrong?

Students agree Mr. Zhuo's examples fit with other tragedies they have read about or known. When he hands me his essay, I look again at that hard choice he had to make. Mr. Zhuo loves and values books above all possessions. Five yuan fifty fen, the price of that text he denied himself, equals about two dollars. When we leave next July, some of the books we brought are going to find their way into Mr. Zhuo's caring hands.

"Did anyone else respond to Sandburg's quote?" I ask.

Mr. Xue's hand rises.

"Let's hear it."

In his usual amiable, confiding, earnest way, Mr. Xue Hai begins by using part of a quotation.

> Money is capable of doing great good or great harm.
>
> Ten years ago, I went to the countryside to be settled down in order to get a better job in the state enterprises. Once, there was a chance for me to be recruited as a worker, because I had stayed there for more than two years. I was the only one qualified. However, a young man who came later than I was recruited instead of me as a worker.
>
> I was filled with indignation at that time. I didn't understand how this could happen. Later on, an informed peasant told me that the young man sent the chief brigade leader a box of refreshments in which he set 100 yuan. How powerful money is! As our Chinese proverb goes: "Money makes the mare go."

He gets halfway through the quotation in Chinese. The others join him. They also start to contribute greased-palm stories. Everyone knows one or more, it seems.

Miss Feng Yunxia is the next reader. She has been moved by a quotation from Emerson.

MONEY IS AS BEAUTIFUL AS ROSES

I like reading Emerson because he told the truth about Nature, the truth about human beings. He described money exactly and correctly: "Money, which represents the prose of life, and which is hardly spoken of in parlors without an apology, is, in its effects and laws, as beautiful as roses."

In China, it's true that an educated person hardly talks money without embarrassment, hardly speaks of it without an apology. I feel a little bit embarrassed now, since I want to talk of the happiness which money can bring to me.

Suppose, for a few minutes, I had enough money. Because I'm so tired of having lived in dormitories where eight or more than eight people live together for eight years, the very thing I long to do is get a home owned by myself. Its location would surely be quiet and beautiful. Within, the house would be well-equipped, beautifully decorated.

My next thing is to possess various books. I could buy any books I wanted for my private library. I dream of reading my favorite books in my beautiful reading-room.

One more other exciting use for money is travel. I dream of traveling all over the world. I'd like to see the sunset in the wide desert, the sunrise in the great sea, the green scene in the Alps, the white snow in Alaska.

Also, I'd like to help poor people.

All these could come true with the help of enough money.

Money doesn't mean everything to me, of course. But it could help me lead the life I desire. It can help me enjoy life more fully. Without money, all these ideas stay just part of a dream.

I know that stoics and puritans enjoy simplicity of life. Some of them even curse money, which, in their opinion, is the root of evil. I believe they are not right. Money itself is not bad at all. It's the people using it, owning it, seeking it, who may do evil things.

Money is really a victim of prejudice. It is misunderstood. Money "is, in its own effects and laws, as beautiful as roses."

Miss Feng waits on the dais to field questions from the class. There aren't any. Unless there is an argument involving home provinces, like whose local vinegar tastes better, the students still tend to sit silent.

"When you're out and teaching, Miss Feng, you'll be able to realize some of your dreams," I say.

"Teaching doesn't pay well!" The statement comes from several voices at once.

"But we can earn extra money," Mr. Ku Qiu quietly points out. He should know. On his own initiative, he has organized private English classes and earns a modest profit by teaching at night.

"Mr. Ku, which quotation caught your interest?"

Mr. Ku Qiu takes his place before the class and reads:

A Hmong proverb says, "The poor are happy. The rich weep." It tells the truth in some respects, but it's not always right.

If you're rich, you can buy beautiful clothes, enjoy delicious food, live in a comfortable house, and travel all over the world. If you're rich, you needn't raise a loan, worry about your tuition fees, work like an exhausted donkey, or try every means to earn bread for your family. If you're rich, the world is smiling to you; life is "as beautiful as roses," and you're really as happy as a skylark.

On the contrary, if you are poor, almost everything goes against you. You can't afford your education and just admire the rich in vain. You have to struggle for your living expenses. You even lose your friends. What's more, you can do nothing against some disasters.

Are you happy when the roof of the thatched cottage in which you live is taken away by a storm? Are you happy when your child is dying and you have no money to send for a doctor? Are you happy when you are out on business and you have to beg for a place to stay? Are you happy when others' children can go to college and yours have to stay at home to do miserable work?

People in the world are pursuing happiness. If the poor are happy, why aren't they willing to be poor? People in our country are trying to realize the four modernizations to be rich. If the rich weep, why are we doing so? Are all of us out of our senses? Not at all. It's just because the rich are happy, the poor weep!

A murmur of approving agreement runs through the entire room. I think Mr. Ku senses his listeners' strong responses. His lips form a rare half-smile. We can save our specific praise for later written comments. All I say right now is "Very strongly put! What are the Four Modernizations?"

"Industry, agriculture—" Mr. Ku pauses. He appeals to his classmates. With some confused discussion and variations in phrasing, they add, "science and technology, and national defense."

It's no wonder they have trouble recalling the exact terms. China steers its national course by numbered slogans with a special fondness for four. In addition to the Four Modernizations, there are the Four Cardinal Principles: (1) keep on the socialist road, (2) uphold Mao Zedong thought, (3) uphold the dictatorship of the proletariat, (4) adhere to the leadership of the Communist Party.

Right now, we have a cold group of nineteen who would rather be on their feet, stirring their blood, than huddling to hear another paper. With an extra tightening of their scarves, they rush down the stairs and outdoors, where the same chill temperature as in the classroom awaits us all.

16 . A Surprise

To celebrate Mr. Guo Kun's promotion to full professor (a rare advancement for someone not a Communist Party member), the foreign teachers host a luncheon for him at the Jinling. The Jinling is a fancy and, by Chinese standards, expensive tourist hotel in the center of Nanjing. As a native Chinese without hotel connections or the foreign exchange money the hotel courts, Mr. Guo cannot enter its doors unless foreigners bring him in as a guest.

We all settle around a table in its carpeted, table-clothed, view-on-the-garden ambience. After our toasts to his success, Mr. Guo fixes us with a smile so wide any dentist would welcome him to his chair.

"I have good news!" Mr. Guo spaces his words to heighten the surprise. "Students in the foreign teachers' classes will put on a performance at Christmas time. Plays, singing, dancing—two and one-half hours!" He beams.

Sieg gets his voice back first. "Where will this be? In the audiovisual room?"

"In Hehai auditorium." Mr. Guo sounds as if that were a special honor.

"How big an audience?" Rae Peters, a young Canadian who teaches secretarial classes, asks.

"At least a thousand. Perhaps eighteen hundred." Guo Kun continues to sip his Coke.

We flood him with uneasy questions. Yes, he assures us, we will have rehearsal time on stage. Of course we can have mikes. Throughout, he smiles and smiles, and goes on eating. The arrangements for this gala, coming up in less than six weeks, can all be made easily, he seems to feel—by us.

"And we will have a dancing party afterwards," he adds, with serene anticipation.

When we walk into the classroom Monday morning, the whole group vibrates in high spirits. Despite continuing cold, suddenly everything seems to be coming up holiday. Word of the command Christmas performance has percolated.

Sieg raps the buzzing class to attention. "Mr. Guo has given us a large order. Out of two and a half hours, this group is responsible for forty-five minutes. What ideas do you have?"

"Let's do a play!" Miss An says.

I chalk PLAY on the board.

"Are you thinking of any particular play?" Sieg asks.

"You suggest one," Mrs. Ching says.

"We'll check the library," Sieg promises. "If any of you have suggestions, let us know. Whether one play or two short ones, everybody should have a part."

They erupt into twitters, poking each other like grade school kids.

"C'mon, people," Sieg cools their excitement. "We need more ideas. Remember—forty-five minutes!"

"We could sing songs," suggests Miss Liu, who has a beautiful, though untrained, voice. ("No money for lessons," she told me once.) She, Miss Chun, and Miss An often warble soaring harmony during breaks.

"What kind of songs?"

"Christmas songs, of course! You can tell us what ones to sing."

Even in a brainstorming session like this, they turn through force of habit to the dictates of authority.

Sieg considers the word SONGS I've put on the board. "It would be nice to have some Chinese songs too."

"Mr. Fan has a good voice," Miss Zhuang reveals.

Mr. Fan blushes in an attack of acute modesty.

Miss Xi Yang volunteers Miss Chen Hong and Miss Lü Shu as "very good dancers." For her offering, she gets punched in the ribs from both sides.

DANCE joins the list.

"Any other ideas?" Sieg asks.

The class seems to have emptied the pools of its imagination.

Based on their expressed interests, Sieg assigns planning committees for each category. Then we get down to the day's "how to" speech assignment: With freedom to choose their own subjects, some come totally prepared; others have left it to last-second inspiration.

Mr. Li Jian explains how to make *jiaozi,* a boiled dumpling delicacy. "Roll dough with stick or round chopsticks," he begins.

Some students who chose sleep over breakfast this morning swallow.

Miss Liu Jie instructs us on how to behave when others are angry. "Keep silent," she advises. "Don't try to argue with the person. You can say, 'Since you are in disorder, I don't want to talk with you.' "

Miss An Ran's choice is "how to be a good teacher in middle school." "Be very strict with students in class," she continues. "Out of class, treat them equally. Be ready to answer questions raised by students. If you don't know the answer, then we study together."

"I'll remember that ploy next time this class stumps me," I say. "Mr. Fan?"

Mr. Fan isn't quite ready. He waves us to go on to another student.

Mr. Ku Qiu has brought to class a tangerine, which everyone here calls an orange. He whips out a knife and a handkerchief. He attacks the fruit to show us how to eat it "the etiquette way." After finishing his demonstration, he passes uneaten tangerine segments to his classmates.

Food seems to be a favorite topic this morning. Mr. Mao Yanyang teaches us "how to make pancake." "You need a very special pot—round, big, the center a little higher. You make it out of wheat, corn, or sweet potato. Add water, sometimes put egg, sometimes hot pepper. Hotten the pot, not too hot, not too cold. Use a stick to put liquid around pot. After it is done, roll it, put vegetables in it, pick it up, and eat it."

More swallowing from the students. I'm not sure they'll last the hour without bolting toward their canteen. Mr. Lüe Shi's fish recipe doesn't help.

When he gets to the final delicate details of the sauce, Miss Zhuang sighs. "What a delicious dish!"

Mr. Zhuo Niannian pulls everybody back to grim reality. His topic, he announces, is "how to eat in canteen."

The class groans.

Mr. Zhuo amends his title to "how to balance our food in canteen." "We live in university," he says. "We generally order one dish. Not all nutrients are in dishes. We may have two carbohydrates, two proteins. Too much carbohydrates makes us sleepy. Too many proteins make us agitated. We should decide color in food. Red color is protein with fat; white color, carbohydrates. Scientists tell us yellow-orange foods have vitamins and trace elements. Green foods also have this and fibers. We should eat all colors of food every day, if not at one meal, then at another."

"Tell that to the cooks," mutters Miss Chun.

Miss Xi Yang tells us "how to spend time every day": "Get up at seven o'clock. Make your bed. Put instant noodle in pot on electric stove. Rush to toilet room to brush teeth, wash face. Rush back to room, eat noodle, bread, cake, or biscuit and fruit, with plain boiled water.

"Walk to class. Have four periods. Get lunch at dormitory, talk and laugh at table. My parents said, 'Don't talk while eating,' but parents aren't here in college.

"In afternoon, wash, study, play badminton. After supper, also readings. At 10:00 P.M., sleep. After two hours, I get up, produce writing at midnight. Night is quiet."

Her schedule sounds exhausting. "Are we assigning you too much work?" I ask.

"Too much!" Mr. Fan jumps to avail himself of the sympathy in my tone.

"Just the right amount," Miss Xi says diplomatically.

Miss Li Yanping has a short bit of instruction especially for us: "Wear your Hehai badge on the left."

I grope for mine. It's on the right.

"In this country," Miss Li goes on, "left is more advanced than right. It's a political idea. I don't know if it's true."

"Left is also closer to your heart," Miss Chun points out.

Mr. Fan Rui is now inspired to a subject. "I will tell you how to sleep."

"You are good at that," Miss Chun twits him.

He ignores her. He knows he doesn't have much time. "How to sleep," he repeats. "Don't worry. Don't be very excited in bed. Imagine you're on the seashore, playing with your friends. It's very beautiful. Seagulls fly in the sky. Imagine mountains. Breathe regularly."

"Or count dull numbers," Mr. Li offers.

Suddenly everybody, fired up by Mr. Fan's subject, wants to talk.

"Listen to light music," counsels Miss An. "But I forget to turn off the radio. I sometimes wake alarmed and hear one girl grinding her teeth."

"Or take off your glasses," says Miss Liu, "and see a cloud of air."

On that note, this class period ends.

17 . Slow Progress

The next day, meeting as one group so everyone can hear, conversation class centers on plans for the Christmas program.

Sieg asks, "How about plays? Any specific titles?"

The students gaze back at us, unanimous in their benign, placidly expectant countenances. Sieg interprets their silence correctly.

"We checked the library yesterday afternoon and didn't find anything either. Mr. Younkin loaned us a book with three short British skits that could be possibilities."

Quickly, we run through a line reading of the three. The class likes two skits but rejects a third. "It's not funny," they declare. We'll have to find some more, somewhere.

Two days later, no new play titles have occurred to anyone. We're just five weeks away from the program deadline. This proximity gives Sieg, who always computes our income tax return months ahead of time, the jitters.

He announces that during Friday's writing class we will make time for each student to try drafting a skit for three or four people, based on realities of life on Hehai campus or in their own hometown.

They give a collective gasp. "We can't do that!"

"You can try," Sieg says. "We haven't come up with anything else."

"We don't know how to create," Miss Chen protests.

"Not true," Sieg answers. "Your papers show you have plenty of ability. You've had practice writing dialogue. This is a chance to find out what more you can do. So be thinking about possibilities."

They are not exactly in a good mood as they leave.

Friday, when they appear for writing class, they still look bewildered, blank.

"What shall we write about?" several implore.

We begin the hour with some group brainstorming. "Think about the things you know," Sieg says. "For instance, what do you find funny, absurd, irritating in your current scene?"

As usual, I chalk up their ideas. After ten minutes, their list contains

> disorder in rooms
> late waking up
> no breakfast
> breakfast
> laundry hanging outside windows
> upper bed problems
> washroom problems (including late night singing)
> disco dancing on floor above
> talking late
> radio left on all night
> canteen food with two cooked flies/hair/yucky (a recent slang vocabulary
>   word they've adopted eagerly)
> lack of sleep
> electricity/water problems
> mouse eating books

The number of ideas is dwindling. "That should be plenty for starters," Sieg says. "Use them or anything else you prefer."

They settle down to work. We had expected to break into small groups during the second hour, letting them exchange skits and hear peer criticism, but some students continue to write over the break. Most seem reluctant to interrupt their creative labors.

So we don't even collect the papers. Second drafts and exchanges with friends over the weekend may generate more substance or more sparkle in the skits. They're pleased with the prospect of extra time. They always like to polish before submitting their work, if possible. We're delighted to face a weekend unexpectedly free from papers.

"Just be sure to turn them in on Monday," Sieg says. "We'll read them all and discuss program possibilities Tuesday."

They barely hear him. Weekend euphoria plus the absence of a new writing assignment cheer them so much that they rush the doorway with no questions after class.

18 : Possible Scripts

Monday morning, it's bitter cold. During the night, a severe northern blast produced frigid winds that haven't abated. Although there's no thermometer to check, the frozen gobs of spit visible on every stretch of pavement as we hurry to class show it's below freezing even in sunny patches.

In the outer hall, we pass some engineering students jumping a long rope to get warm. You can see their breath.

"It's the coldest in Nanjing since 1972!" Miss Xi Yang exclaims.

Mr. Xue appears in the doorway. He must be wearing two or three pairs of trousers. His usually slim legs look fat. He moves stiffly.

Miss Li Yanping eyes Sieg curiously. "How many layers do you have on?"

Sieg glances down at his open jacket. He lifts his wool scarf and counts, "T-shirt, shirt, sweater, jacket. Four."

Mrs. Ching clicks her tongue in disapproval. "That's not enough. In weather like this, you must wear seven."

"I couldn't move!"

"We do. It is the only way."

Reluctantly, they take their seats and huddle shivering, pale, pinch-nosed. Miss Li rubs the beginnings of swollen red chilblains on her hands.

For both their and our sakes, we whiz through the morning assignments and collect their skits, cutting the last hour short so they can return to their dorms and at least pull blankets around them. We head for a warming glass of hawthorn wine and an afternoon's reading.

Everyone has turned in a skit. Some writers show more dramatic ability than others, but each piece reveals more than they have previously said about their campus and dorm lives.

Since we need to move beyond selection of line rehearsals this week, we choose five of the liveliest. With a minimum of editing, I type copies for us to read aloud and put to a student vote. Except for decisions, Tuesday's class will be an easy one for them.

Tuesday, Sieg begins, "Your job this morning is to hear and choose which ones we'll use for the Christmas performance. To begin, we'll read these without giving the author's name. The first one is called 'The Pretender.' "

Setting: Xiao Li's dorm room
Characters: Xiao Li, another boy, some girls

(Xiao Li *is combing his hair, and whistling cheerfully. A knock sounds on the door. At once, he musses his hair and begins to cough while bent over his desk.*)

Xiao Li: Come in, please!

Boy A: (*Enters, bringing food*) I've heard you're ill. What's wrong?

Xiao Li: Oh, a very high fever (*coughing*) and a terrible cough. Last night the temperature suddenly dropped, and I had forgotten to shut the window. I've caught a bad cold. This morning, I struggled to go to class, but I failed.

Boy A: You'd better stay in bed. I know you haven't had your breakfast yet. I've brought you some noodles.

Xiao Li: Thanks a lot. (*Begins to eat hungrily*) Oh, what's that? Is THAT a noodle? (*He puts hand into his mouth and pulls out an extremely long string from it.*)

Boy A: (*Sticks out his tongue in surprise*) I'm so sorry. I got your noodles from our canteen.
            (*Another knock at door*)

Xiao Li: (*Coughs again*) Come in.

Girl A:	Xiao Li, are you feeling better now? We've brought a box of moon cakes for you.
Girl B:	And some bread.
Girl C:	And some cookies.
Xiao Li:	*(Taking all the packages)* Thank you! I like them all! *(Coughs)* Though my appetite isn't quite up to everything. *(He puts his hand on his brow.)* I think I have a fever.
Girl A:	Perhaps we'd better call a doctor?
Xiao Li:	Oh no. No! Just by your coming, I feel better. Perhaps I'll try a bite of moon cake. Look! *(He picks up the package and reads.)* There are some words here. "Chinese traditional cakes. They taste sweet and delicious." I can't help eating a piece. *(He bites into it.)* Oh! Why is the cake so hard? Why does it hurt my tooth? *(He puts his fingers in his mouth and pulls out a huge screw nut.)*
Girls:	*(Cover their faces with their hands)* Oh . . . we're sorry!
Xiao Li:	*(Coughing and holding his hand to his cheek)* Thank you anyhow. Now I really must go to bed. I have a horrible headache *and* a toothache.
Boy A and Girls:	Perhaps you'll be better tomorrow. *(They leave.)*
Xiao Li:	*(Checks the door to be sure they've gone. Laughing, he takes out a letter from an envelope and reads aloud:)* My love. Could you wait for your sweetheart under the big gingko tree at 9:30 A.M.?

(Xiao Li looks at his watch. Then he holds a small mirror, combs his hair with a big comb. Peers out the door again, then goes out of room, whistling.)

There's a round of applause. Mr. Lao Sheng, the unidentified author, applauds his own work tentatively.

"Another possible title for that one is 'The Malingerer.' " I write the word on the board. " 'Malingering' is pretending to be sick when you aren't."

They grab their notebooks to enter the new word.

"This next one," Sieg says, picking up Miss Chun Xu's skit, "is 'The Case of the Hungry Rat.' "

He reads her directions: "Setting and characters: Xiao Lin, Xia Feng, and Xiao Tian are reading in their bedroom."

Lin:	Xiao Feng, I need to look up a reference to William Shakespeare. Please lend me your English Literature book.
Feng:	O.K., I'll find it for you. *(She goes to bookshelf.)* Oh no! Look at

	my book! It's all torn up! *(The others rush over to look.)* Yesterday I saw a rat walking near the shelf. I shouted at it, but it didn't even change its pace.
Lin:	Maybe it was too full of Shakespeare. But it was still hungry. *(She holds up one shoe.)* My shoe has been bitten by the rat too. See?
Tian:	You people are so careless. I'm glad none of my possessions have been ruined by the rat. I put mine away!
Feng:	You selfish girl. Someday I hope the rat will bite off your nose.
Tian:	Oh, don't say that! It frightens me! Here, I'll share some bread with you. *(She goes to fetch her bread and gives a shriek.)* That rat has eaten my bread! Only some crumbs are left!
Feng:	It serves you right. You left your bread out, didn't you?
Lin:	Girls! Don't quarrel with each other. Let's find a way to kill that pest.
Tian:	Yes, it should be killed. Last night, I was suddenly wakened. There was the rat, standing on the edge of my bed, looking at me. I think it was about to bite me.
Feng:	I've got a great idea how to kill the rat.
Lin:	How?
Feng:	While she's sleeping, we'll put some poison on Xiao Tian's nose. Then at night, the rat will bite her poisoned nose and die.
Tian:	You devil. How can you think up such a yucky idea?
Feng:	It's easy. You think about that rat. What does it like? Good bread, good shoes, and good books. Do you think it could resist a beautiful nose like yours?

Some of the women look over at Miss Chun Xu as they clap for this one. Our "unidentified playwright" device doesn't hold up because friends often exchange papers before class, but that's all right. We plunge into the next script, "A False Alarm." The author, Miss Zhuang Zi, looks down at her desk as she listens.

Time:	12 o'clock at night.
Place:	In a girls' room.
Characters:	Four girls, A, B, C, D
	One sound and prop man on stage with something to make a crashing sound.

Setting:	Everyone in the room is asleep. Suddenly something bangs.

A: *(Turns over in bed and murmurs)* Someone is knocking at the door. *(She takes a flashlight which the* prop man *hands her, and looks at her watch.)* It's twelve o'clock! What kind of a person comes knocking so late at night? *(Loudly)* Who's there? *(No answer)*

B: *(Impatiently)* Let him alone, A. It's much too late to let anyone in. We have classes at 7:30 tomorrow. Go back to sleep.

C: *(Suspicious)* Nobody knocked at the door. It sounded like someone threw rocks at our window!

A,B,D: *(Nervously)* Oooooooooooh!
*(*Prop man *waves* laundry*)*

D: *(The youngest screams, points.)* Look! There's someone at the window!

C: *(Frightened)* Maybe a thief or a hooligan. What shall we do?

B: *(Horrified)* Please speak in a low voice. Maybe he'll think we're not here.

D: *(Can't help crying)* Maybe he'll break in and kill us. I've heard some bad men do that before they rob a room.

A: *(The eldest and bravest)* I have a knife. Quick! Everbody grab something to protect yourself! *(The* prop man *hands* Girl B *a coat hanger,* Girl C *a mop,* Girl D *a feather duster.)* If he dares to break in, we'll give him the surprise of his life. Come on girls, follow me!

(All four of them, with their weapons, tiptoe toward the window. The prop man *drops another brick—or whatever crash is needed. All* four girls *scurry back to their beds and hide under the mosquito net. Just their eyes and the tips of their noses are out.)*

D: We're dying!

A: Nonsense. Let me turn on the light and see who it is.

C: No, don't! He'll see us more clearly.

B: C-c-can't we call the monitor?

A: There isn't time. Come on. We have four, and he is only one. *(She grabs her knife, turns on the light. Suddenly she points and laughs.)*

B,C,D: *(Putting their heads out from under their mosquito net.)* Why are you laughing?

A:	Nobody's here. It's just plaster that fell from the ceiling.
C:	Evil ceiling! *(They all wipe cold sweat from their foreheads.)*
B:	Then what was at the window? I know I saw something. *(She rushes over. So does* A.*)*
A:	It's just the clothes. They're waving in the wind. Who left their clothes out?
D:	*(Ashamed)* I did. I forgot to bring them back in.
A:	Never mind. Next time, I'll bet you remember.
D:	But—
C:	But what?
D:	But if I leave my clothes out again, it won't be easy for anyone to get to the window. *(Everybody laughs.)*
A:	Anyway, the false alarm is over for tonight. Let's get back to sleep.

The class likes this skit too.

"If we use this one," I say, "the characters will need names."

They aren't so enthusiastic about the next one we read. We take a break, then come back for the last student possibility. Mr. Fan Rui has written "Dark Conversation." Sieg introduces it by title only.

Time:	Midnight
Place:	Men's college dorm room
Characters:	Prologue; Mr. Sharp; Mr. Murmur; Mr. Sad; Mr. Wise, the Monitor.

Prologue:	As you know, dark conversations are an important part of college life. They take place after dark. They can be on any subject, but love is one of the most important topics. Let's listen to one of these dark conversations about love.
Sad:	*(Sighing bitterly)* From now on, I'll never believe in love again. I curse love!
Sharp:	Why do you curse love, Mr. Sad?
Murmur:	*(In a teasing voice)* I know why. His girl friend left him last week. *(Murmur waves at Sad as if saying Bye-bye.)*
Sharp:	What does that have to do with love? If women throw good men away, that's not the fault of love.
Sad:	*(Resignedly)* You may be right. But I will never again believe in

	true love. What we call love depends on appearances, social position, and family. These three win a girl's love, but not a deep feeling for the other person.
Murmur:	*(Whispering)* This guy is very logical about love.
Sharp:	And maybe a little cynical.
Wise:	*(Whistling cheerfully as he enters room)* My fine comrades, I see that you are all awake. Let's share the candy I got from my girl friend this evening. *(He hands it around.)* What have you been talking about?
Sharp:	We've been discussing the true meaning of Love. Mr. Sad thinks love depends on appearances, family, and social position. What do you think, Monitor?
Wise:	*(Sounding like he is giving a lecture)* I can't agree with you, Mr. Sad. Love is a pure feeling between a man and a woman. A man and a woman may be attracted to each other by beauty, but that is only a beginning.
Murmur:	Family—how important is that?
Wise:	Nowadays, most girls don't pay much attention to family. You can see this in daily life.
Murmur:	Then how about social position?
Wise:	That may be important. But a girl wants her boy friend, most of all, to be a capable person with a strong and independent mind.
Sharp:	Ya, ya, Monitor, quite right. You are a real Professor of Love. We are lucky to have such an expert here. How about your own love affair?
Wise:	*(Hesitating for a moment)* Oh, it mainly depends on my girl friend. I'd better ask her beforehand.
	(Everyone, even the monitor, breaks out in laughter.)
Sharp:	Where's your independent mind, Monitor?

This one draws the loudest applause yet.

Sieg lists on the board the titles of all the skits we've heard today plus the British ones we read a few days ago.

"As short as these are, we'll probably have room for five in the program, so check the five you like most."

He puts Monitor Lüe in charge of the vote. With notable consultations among friends, the students scribble their choices and pass the votes forward.

The tally shows we'll stage the four most enthusiastically received today and, from Dan's collection, one sketch about an old lady who connives in a London park to get a free chair from a park keeper by sitting stubbornly, illegally, on the grass.

"Thank you for your patience and your votes," Sieg tells them. "We'll get copies of these made so we can begin casting and line rehearsals Thursday."

19 . Folk Remedies

Yesterday, at the end of our skit-reading session, we held the students long enough to give Wednesday's writing and talking assignment.

"Last week we read myths and facts about the common cold. Tomorrow's assignment is short—"

"Good!" says Mr. Fan.

"Write a brief description of a folk remedy or cure you know about. It can be one you've heard or one used in your own family. Tell what was used, why people believed in it, and whether it seemed to work. When you share your papers, you can either read them or just talk informally."

Today, Miss Bin Qilin snares everybody's attention with her first sentence.

"To cure TB," she informs us, "decapitate a criminal. Take the fresh human blood, make a steamed bun, wrap it in a fresh lotus leaf, burn it. Patient eats all but the leaf.

"Perhaps the reasons were a lotus leaf is cool and antipyretic. Human blood is a kind of nutriment. A leaf is the symbol of life. Human blood means getting the criminal's life. The invalid who gets the blood will then live a long time."

"Do you know anybody treated with that remedy?" I half dread her answer.

Miss Bin smiles. "No. I just heard. But here is one in my own family. To cure hypertension, mix wood filings and vinegar together, bake the mixture, and wrap it in a piece of cloth. Rub the hot ball against the stomach. Since it is said my mother's hypertension is caused by a depressed mood, some obstruction of the circulation of vital energy exists in her stomach. Vinegar helps relieve internal heat. Wood filings help eliminate the obstruction. The warmth brings comfort. My mother took the remedy for some time. It was really effective. After the treatment, my mother felt her stomach light, her heart comfortable, and no obstruction at all."

"That one sounds much milder than your TB cure! Mr. Ku Qiu?"

Mr. Ku takes his paper to the lectern with his typically self-contained, quiet assurance. The students wait expectantly. He has already gained a reputation as a good storyteller. He begins reading.

Once I was playing hide-and-seek with two childhood pals of mine in the grass, when the ankle of my right foot was bitten by a centipede. Blood burst out from the bitten spot, and the venom caused my ankle to swell suddenly. It hurt terribly, and I cried out.

Hearing this, my grandfather and parents dashed out from the house, terrified. I told them what had happened. My parents were frightened, and didn't know what to do, but Grandfather calmed everyone down. He patted me on the shoulder and said, "Do not worry, child. It matters little.

"Catch a cock," he said to my parents. "Fetch a basin of clean water."

After these were done, Grandfather seated me in a chair, put my foot into the water and washed it carefully, trying to squeeze the venom out. He asked my mother to dry my foot with a towel while he took a pair of scissors and cut off a tip of the cockscomb.

Father helped him to turn over the cock and let the cock's blood drop down onto the bitten spot of my ankle. Then he covered it with a piece of sticking-plaster and put me in bed.

About ten minutes later, the aching stopped. Itching began. Next day the swelling was down. I had recovered.

"Any questions for Mr. Ku?" I ask.

No questions. Just the compliment of having two students reach for his paper so they can read what they've heard.

"Would you try that remedy on a child of your own?" Sieg asks, as Mr. Ku is about to sit.

"If I had a cock," he says.

Mr. Lao Sheng introduces the idea of brown sugar and ginger tea for a cold: "Take a piece of ginger half as big as a thumb. Cut it into thin slices. Put the pieces in a pot, add a bowl of water, and place it over a fire. When you can smell the ginger, remove the pot from the stove, pour the liquid into a mug, throw away the ginger slices. Add some brown sugar. Give it to the cold sufferer. How does it work?" He pauses dramatically. "Ancient Chinese medicine divides herbs into two kinds—hot and cold. Ginger belongs to the hot. If you have a cold, you should use hot herbs. Brown sugar is also classified as 'hot,' and it helps you drink the tea easily."

Two rows back, Mr. Li is taken with a violent fit of coughing.

"Perhaps you should prepare some ginger tea for Mr. Li. Does anyone else have a cold remedy?"

Mr. Zhuo (who has just asked us to change the spelling of his name to "Zuo") mentions vinegar vapor for a baby's cold. "You are supposed to breathe the vapor for half an hour every day for three days. It didn't work for us," he adds, "but a magazine reported that workers in a vinegar mill never caught colds."

Mr. Lüe Shi, never straying far from his Communist Party loyalties, attributes folk remedies to "the crystallizations of collective wisdom of the working people." "I had a friend with athlete's foot," he tells us. "The remedy is to get a cup of machine oil and some sulphur ready. Break the sulphur into tiny pieces. Put both in a bowl and stir thoroughly. When mixed, brush the foot three times a day for twenty days with the medicine."

"Does it really work?" Mr. Fan asks.

"My friend's foot was cured," Mr. Lüe assures him solemnly.

Miss Chun Xu describes her grandmother's "scald remedy." "When I was a child," she says, "I got in a fight with my brother. We knocked over the thermos flask and it scalded my foot. My grandmother fetched a small bottle from her bedroom and put some yellow liquid on my foot. Immediately my injury felt cool and refreshed. The pain disappeared.

"I asked my grandmother what magic liquid was in the bottle. She told me it was made out of rotten oranges. She learned this remedy from her mother. She did not know why it worked, but it always did."

"It could be the acid in the fruit. Or Vitamin C," I guess.

"Perhaps," Miss Chun agrees in that all-purpose, safely noncommittal rejoinder.

Miss Xi Yang keeps us in suspense about the purpose of her folk remedy. "Take black sesame seeds," she directs us. "Wash and clean them. Dry them in the sun, fry them in pot, and grind into powder. Add about one third white sugar into mixture. You can add pine nuts, walnuts if you wish. Eat. Folklore says this mixture will make your hair blacker too, but I tried it and tried it, and it didn't work."

"You don't think your hair is black enough?"

Miss Xi shakes her dark head wistfully. Alerted by her concern, everybody inspects her nicely cut, bouncy hair. Although we'd never noticed before, her hair isn't so glossy black as Miss Zhuang's. It is darker than Miss Liu's brown-tinted ponytail, which frequently attracts women students seated behind her to play with it.

"Looks dark enough to me," Sieg tries to reassure her.

"Women," Mr. Fan pronounces, "are never satisfied with themselves!"

"Men are," Miss Chun snaps back.

Quickly, I call on Mr. Xue Hai. His genial presence at the lectern is sure to give the students something less contentious to think about.

"My Grandmother and Black Balls," Mr. Xue announces. "Grandmother was suffering from flu that hospital doctors couldn't touch. We took her to traditional Chinese medicine doctor.

"The old doctor felt her pulse first. 'Pestilence!' he said. 'Spring is a pestilent season.' He wrote out a prescription as follows: 'The root of Chinese Bupleurum to disperse dampness, chilliness, and drafts; tangerine pith and ginkgo to stop cough; chrysanthemum and the achene of the great burdock to cure headaches.' Then the doctor wrote out another prescription: 'Two boxes of prepared Chinese medicine, also used to cure flu.'

"Grandmother took these two kinds of medicine. The following day she felt much better. Several days later, she had fully recovered. After that, 'black balls' were as sweet as candy in her eyes.

" 'Give me a black ball.' The hoarse voice of my grandmother seems to sound again in my ears."

I wait to see if any listener asks Mr. Xue a question. The class sits appreciative, but silent.

"I take it the black balls were the traditional Chinese prescription?"

"Yes."

"Do you know what's in them?"

"No, but they work," he assures me.

I turn to class members who haven't read yet. "Did anyone write about something that didn't work?"

Mr. Mao Yanyang nods.

"Let's hear it."

Mr. Mao keeps his chin down, his eyes on his paper, but words come clearly.

> Only once in my life did I try to cure an illness with folklore medicine. Afterwards, I made up my mind that I would rather suffer from a lifelong illness than touch that kind of medicine once more.
>
> It happened more than ten years ago. I had a bad cough. I coughed day and night. The whole family began to change their attitude towards me from sympathy to impatience.
>
> Since common cough syrup made no difference, mother began to go out in search of an effective folk prescription. She succeeded in bringing home a piece of alum.
>
> She put the alum in a pot and heated it into liquid, mixed in some hot water, and then filled a bowl. When it began to cool off, she passed the bowl to me and said that I would recover after drinking this medicine.
>
> Even to see it, I was frightened to death. Though very young, I had learnt a lot, so that I knew what it was to taste alum. I asked myself where she got such a damned way which, I predicted, would be more cruel than the cough.
>
> I insisted that she put some sugar in it, but she refused.
>
> "Sugar is an enemy of any medicine," she said. She threatened that if I wasted time longer, the whole family would all come to "help" me.
>
> Under this maternal pressure, I had to give in. I began the first mouthful and immediately spit it back, but the taste was there. It was a taste I had never had fully before. It seemed that my tongue, my teeth, my lips were all gone away, and all parts below the nose started to get heavier and heavier. Realizing that it would give me the same feeling to swallow it or to spit it back, I chose the first.
>
> So one mouthful after another. You can imagine how I felt. At last I finished this hard experience, but it was worse to cough again. Alum didn't work. I had been the most unfortunately experimental body.

He slinks back to his seat, melting into its comparative anonymity with relief. Mr. Li taps him on the shoulder, asking to see his paper. I'd like to comment on the effective use of English in his paper and on his vivid description, moving easily from specific to general. Although Mr. Mao, unless called on, says little in class, his papers always show he has one of the most complex minds and writes some of the most fluent English in this group. But in haste today to hear everybody (the more they write, the harder it is to get everyone up to the lectern), I haven't taken time to single out strong points. Best leave commendations—and suggestions—for later written response.

"Miss An Ran?"

She rises. Miss An is always very erect, deliberate, and businesslike in her approach to the podium. She lays her paper squarely on the lectern and glances up briefly from beneath her bangs.

> A woman who loses two husbands in a row is called a "comet," a symbol of bad luck. She will go to hell and her husbands will get her. Her soul can't rest unless she gives so much to the local Confucian temple that she "buys" the threshold. The threshold then becomes the incarnation of her body. As the threshold, she was supposed to "endure" patiently the trampling of thousands of people's feet. Then her husbands' ghosts would forgive her evil before she died. This was supposed to work in practice, but actually the woman would live the rest of her life lonely and unhappy, and die silently and miserably.

"A terrible fate!" Miss Lü Shu murmurs sympathetically.

I glance at my watch. "Time's up. People who've read today, leave your papers. We'll finish the unheard ones tomorrow and start our first rehearsals."

"Who gets the speaking parts?" someone asks.

"Wait and see," Sieg says, for once not answering a question directly.

20 · Preparations

We now have three and a half weeks to the Christmas program. I announce: "To speed up rehearsals, we've arbitrarily assigned parts. Everybody will get on stage in some way."

I turn to the monitor. "Mr. Lüe, you will be master of ceremonies. You'll introduce each part of the program. Once the exact order and numbers are settled, we'll get together to write your introductions. The rest of you have speaking parts in the various skits. And everybody will rehearse the songs."

Skit by skit, Sieg helps me distribute the parts. A nervous buzz and stir fill the room, as the students find out who gets major or minor roles. From my own acting experiences long ago, I know that mix of dread, exultation, and disappointment that can smite the members of a cast on learning their lots—or littles.

During the past week, Sieg and I have spent hours debating, juggling names, trying to slot students with the strongest voices and clearest pronunciation into the leads, and trying to assign minor parts fairly to those who will appear also in dance or duets.

Miss Feng, who had volunteered first for the drama committee and hasn't yet received her role, asks impatiently, "Where's my part?"

Sieg hands her the last script copy. "You're the old lady in 'Keep Off the Grass.' "

She clutches the pages to her breast and beams. It's a star role, full of potential humor. She scans it hungrily.

We manage a fast line reading of every script, working through a first stiff, ragged approach to unfamiliar lines. Their many problems in pronunciation, intonation, and projection are going to give all of us headaches before we're done. And the audience is supposed to be over a thousand?

The prospect leaves Sieg and me shuddering, no longer from temperature alone. But the students, leaving the classroom today, burst into that unrelenting cold warmed by their new theatrical challenges.

Saturday. We wake to a transformed world. Heavy snow fell silently, windlessly, during the night. Every branch on the dark pines sags under thick-frosted mounds. Palmetto fronds bend close to the ground. Students lucky enough to own cameras dash about, tracking through white expanses as they hurry to snap pictures of this relatively rare sight in Nanjing before the snow melts.

Sunday. We bus to a restorative breakfast of French toast, inner garden views, and quiet order at the Jinling. Mary Catherine Mooney, another American teacher at Hehai, and a friend of hers, both fresh from Sunday services, pore over pictures at a table near the window.

"How's your Christmas program coming?" Sieg asks Mary on the way out.

"Fine!" she says. "Got a lot of numbers in rehearsal. Good voices! What about yours?"

"We had the first line readings Friday," Sieg says. "What's with Rae Peters? We haven't seen her in days."

"No wonder." Mary rolls her eyes. "She's been up late every night, writing parts, copying songs for her Cinderella musical. She plans to involve all her students. Guo Kun's certainly sidetracked regular work!" She grins. "Have you heard he's invited a lot of other universities?"

"To come to the program?"

"To take part! He wants this a huge bash, sponsored by the Foreign Languages Department to make it better known in Nanjing."

"Where did you hear that?"

"Rae happened to run into somebody from his office this week."

Sieg shakes his head. "If that isn't typical! Information in China never comes direct. It just seeps around."

I do some calculation. "This program is going to run horribly long. Each of us has forty-five minutes. That's more than two hours right there."

"We'll just have to sing faster," Mary says.

I check with her to see which songs she's doing. No point in duplication. Fortunately, Mary's chosen mostly musical excerpts or religious carols. Our committee seems to be going in a more secular direction.

Monday. Still cold. Students write a vocabulary exam with gloves on. At the break, Miss Li Yanping bares both swollen hands briefly to rub them. Her chilblains now show in dime-sized red spots with pits at the centers. Yes, she has been to the clinic for salve to prevent infection. She shrugs.

"It happens every winter. My skin is sensitive. They will get better when it turns warm again."

We've observed that one of the male students consistently sits in class shivering, wearing only a thin cotton sports jacket over his sweater. He must not have any other. Privately, Sieg checks with Monitor Lüe.

"I have an extra jacket I recently bought and don't need," he says. "Do you suppose he would accept it?"

"I will see about it," Mr. Lüe promises.

Wednesday. The male student we worried about sits in class no longer huddled but erect, proud, in a smart new grey padded jacket equipped with many zippered pockets. Mr. Lüe Shi looks enigmatic in the back row. The student gazes at us blandly. Somehow, behind the scene, Chinese forces that will never be explained and that we will never ask about have moved to address the foreign teachers' "unnecessary" inquiry.

We continue to interrupt our usual lessons for more rehearsal. It stays spotty. Mr. Lao Sheng has begun to learn his lines, bless him, but when he declaims, while pulling an imaginary string from the canteen's specialty of the year, "What's that—a noodle?" the first two words emerge as "Wot's thaught?" We stop to work on his vowel troubles.

Miss Feng, playing her old lady in the park, requests a model for an elderly, cracked voice. Given my naturally aging vocal cords plus a persistent sore throat with hoarseness, I have no problem demonstrating.

Other actors still haven't freed themselves from their scripts.

"Come on, people!" Sieg says impatiently. "Do you realize we're now less than two weeks to performance? You've *got* to learn your lines!"

They don't seem too excited, although a slight quiver spreads through a nearby group when Mr. Lüe tells Sieg at the break, "The authorities will come see our program December twenty-first, from seven to nine o'clock."

"Authorities? What authorities?"

"Mr. Guo Kun. Perhaps the president, the vice-president, the Party secretary."

"They're all welcome," Sieg says gloomily.

In song rehearsals, Miss An Ran has worked out gestures to make the repetitive "Twelve Days of Christmas" seem not quite so long. We'll do the first four lines straight, she directs us; then men and women will dramatize verses variously. On "five golden rings," the ladies are to link their fingers with elbows akimbo. Even with the desk lifted off, our raised platform space is too scrunched to keep us from poking our neighbors. No matter. That auditorium stage is huge. Once there, we'll have room to spread out.

Miss An is unhappy. Some of us are putting our left hand instead of our right hand on top. Though she doesn't know it, Miss An covets the precision of a Radio City Music Hall dance line. We correct our unattractive inconsistency and move on to the next verse.

On "six geese a-laying," the women sing the line by themselves, and "lay" an egg by dipping down briefly. I think a broad, straddling squat would be more fun, but Miss Chun Xu models us into a graceful bob.

The men make a two-hand breaststroke motion for swimming swans. The women pretend to milk a cow as "eight maids a-milking." Men drum. Women pipe. Now we have a problem. If we keep on alternating gestures, the men would take the next line, "eleven ladies dancing"; the women, "twelve lords a-leaping."

"That is not right," Miss An declares.

So we reverse the order. Both sexes promptly get confused and sing out with the wrong group. This amuses all the onlookers who crowd both open classroom doorways.

We try the song once more, getting our parts slightly better this time.

"Just a minute." Sieg emerges from the back row before we take a third, presumably smooth run-through. "Miss An, let me see that milking gesture again."

She makes an open-fingered attempt that might start her up a large rope, but not very far. Miss Zhuang Zi pummels her fists before her like a boxer.

"No cow would ever stand for that!" Sieg demonstrates proper milking technique to us benighted maids. The women giggle, but all of us now curl our fingers, pinkie side down, and squeeze hard until we satisfy our critical instructor.

Then we run through the entire music program again. The period is almost over.

"Music's coming pretty well," Sieg admits. "What about the baby dance?"

"Another group is doing a masked dance," Miss Zhuang says. "We have decided not to do it."

He looks relieved. "Then we can concentrate on what we already have."

Mr. Fan and Miss Bin approach us after class. For their duet, they think they would rather do "Silent Night," instead of the Chinese folk song they've practiced. "But we don't know it," says Miss Bin. "Can you teach it to us this afternoon?"

I hesitate. It seems to me a community Christmas program, especially in this diverse country, ought to represent riches from different cultures and views. Mary Catherine's group plans to do at least one stanza of "Silent Night." Still, on more than one occasion here, we've heard the same song performed by different amateurs within minutes of each other. Miss Bin and Mr. Fan want to do the carol. It's their program. Why not?

"How about four o'clock?"

By that hour, my hoarseness has turned me into a bass. They have trouble picking up the tune. We have no written music to fall back on. They can't read Western notation and I can't write the Chinese system. Sieg and I both try to persuade them to stick with what they know.

"Your Chinese duet is so good!" Sieg says with genuine enthusiasm. "And it will give variety to the evening."

They look only half-convinced.

As they are about to leave, Miss Bin stops to inspect some evergreen branches I snitched at noon from Friendship Hill trees to bring Christmas into the apartment.

"They aren't big enough," she complains.

"I didn't want to break too much off. And these quarters take only small decorations."

Miss Bin seems very disappointed in my choices. She says nothing more, but I suspect the rolled red and green candy wrappers tucked among the twigs don't suit her notion of proper holiday ornaments either.

Miss An might like them. They're consistent.

21 . Student Journeys

Over the weekend, Mr. Guo Kun takes the post-graduate class to hear a Chinese linguistics professor lecture at Hehai's sister institution in Changzhou, a city halfway between Nanjing and Shanghai. It will be a four-hour train trip. We choose to remain in Nanjing.

Monday morning, they struggle into conversation class late.

"We are tired from our trip," Mr. Fan apologizes, as he sinks into the largest armchair. "No breakfast."

Just the same, their discussion of the events is lively. Tomorrow's in-class writing assignment grows out of their recent experience.

"Consider something about your trip," I tell them. "Search *all* your memories. What lingers in your mind? What did you see, or hear, or feel? It could be something major or something insignificant. Something very important to you, or just fleeting impressions. You'll have the first hour to write. We'll begin to share during the second."

Miss Bin Qilin stops to see us after class.

"My sister is getting married. I must be absent, if you permit."

"Of course!" we say together. "How long will you be gone?"

"Perhaps one, two days. But I cannot write the travel essay." Miss Bin's forehead puckers in distress.

"Then write an account of your sister's wedding instead," I say. "We'll catch you up on anything you miss."

She takes off happily to join her friends who have lingered outside.

With play practice and memorization of lines competing for the students' energies, we've begun to do more in-class writing. It frees the students to spend some time outside of class thinking about the preassigned writing topic. It helps make us available for questions as they work on their papers. We've encouraged them, if they wish, to prepare a draft before coming to class. One of us can read the draft and offer editorial comments before they write the final version.

Since they have other language and political classes beside our twenty hours a week, the students are grateful for this chance to get work done during the day.

The next day, after we collect the students' essays, written, then shared in class, we both reread what struck Mr. Zuo Niannian as significant during his trip:

A WINTER DAY ON THE RAILWAY

I was sitting on the train, leaning by the window and watching the scene outside.

Fields, hills, houses and little stations went by. Dry grasses were swaying in the chilly winds. The remaining leaves of trees were swinging as if dancing to warm up their bodies.

There is a middle-aged woman, wearing scarf and gloves, handing a meal box and hurrying on her way. She is going back home after work, I think, planning to cook supper for her husband and children.

A group of workers are there, unloading coal from the freight train, standing in a line. They are shoveling the coal and throwing backwards. It will soon be dark. They will overwork tonight.

No people in the scene now, just a few houses, the trees, grasses, fields, and little hills. Their color is brownish grey and it will soon be dark. The land and the light tell us it is in winter now. People at this time are in their warm rooms, having their warm dinners. And there are some who are outside in the cold, doing their business, and earning their money.

I was on the train, and I was one of them.

Sieg reads the short piece a third time. His eyes linger on its final line. "What do you suppose he means by 'I was one of them'?"

"I'm not sure. The group on the train? All those he watched? I do know one thing."

Sieg glances up. "What?"

"I wish I could write with Mr. Zuo's simple power."

When Miss Bin Qilin returns several days later, her composition becomes the basis for an impromptu conversation class. Miss Bin reads it aloud first:

My sister's wedding is going to be held today. The young man who is coming to be my brother-in-law is going to bring her to his house at three o'clock this afternoon. I am assigned to be bride's companion.

After lunch, we long for the auspicious time of the auspicious day to come. We are waiting unpatiently when suddenly firecrackers burst into cracking.

My elder brother sees the young man with his companion and two matchmakers coming at a distance and fires the crackers. My younger brother closes our gate quickly, not letting them in. Then the young man passes over a small red packet with money in, and my brother opens the gate.

The brown sugar tea with jujube (*zao-zi*—to wish bride and bridegroom to have a son in a short future) has already prepared for the four persons—two young men and the matchmakers—to drink. Then a bowl with six glutinous balls is put before each of them and my sister and me. I am told to eat only two balls. And I find everyone eats only two balls.

Before my sister comes out of her room timidly, my brother is asked to stay in her bed for a while and to fumble in her quilt; he finds another small red packet of money which she has hid for him.

The young man's home is not far away. We six persons walk through a crowded people, who come out to see bride and bridegroom. Before we reach the young man's house, firecrackers sound noisy, loud and happy. In the house, I am asked to drink brown soup tea with jujube and to eat another two glutinous balls as the other five do.

The young man's uncles and aunts give their red packets to my sister who gives her red packets to their children.

They are all happy. Only I am worried. I've eaten so much. How can I appreciate those delicious dishes of the evening's sumptuous dinner?

Miss Bin looks up to face the approving murmurs of her female classmates especially.

We are full of questions.

"Why must you eat only two glutinous balls?" I ask.

"It is important to leave four in the bowl because that is a lucky number."

"Is there a special meaning to that particular food?" Sieg wants to know.

"Glutinous balls," Miss Zhuang leaps to address our ignorance, "mean to wish bride and bridegroom happy."

That explanation doesn't entirely satisfy Sieg's suspicion concerning their symbolism, but he decides not to pursue the matter further. "What's in the small red packets?"

"They always have money in," Miss Bin says. "Twenty or thirty yuan."

"I'm not sure I understand all the going back and forth," I say. "Who gives the evening dinner?"

Several voices hasten to explain. It seems the groom's family prepares the first night's supper. The next day, the bride's younger brother goes to her new home and escorts her and the groom back to her former home.

"They do not have to do anything all day," Miss Bin says. "Everybody does everything for them. That night, the bride's family puts on another dinner. Then the couple returns to their home with groom's parents."

"Is there a honeymoon?" Sieg asks.

"If the couple work, each one, I think, can get ten days paid leave off. Some take trips. My sister and new husband didn't."

"And they live with the groom's family?"

Miss Bin nods. "In China, that is the custom."

"Then the grandmother can take care of the child while parents work," someone up front says.

"What about maternity leave? How long is that?"

"When baby is born, mother can get three to six months leave, perhaps a year off. They are paid for a time, but not too long. The pay may be cut off."

"Then what?" Sieg asks.

Miss Bin instructs him serenely in Chinese facts of life. "Almost every factory has a nursery."

22 . Proverbs

This morning dawns sunny, mild. In class, the students cheerfully start on their latest short essays. Yesterday we asked them to read in the textbook five brief quotations about the act of speaking and to choose one for response.

Today they strip off their gloves, zip open their jackets, then settle down to in-class writing. We hear the sounds of dictionary pages being flipped as well as a few whispered conferences with neighbors, who seem impatient to get back to their own creations.

Their work will produce a packed afternoon of paper reading for us, but that's good. With so much Christmas program rehearsal, skits and music both, this week their writing has made no progress.

After class, Mr. Lüe drops his essay on the desk. "There has been a change," he announces. "The authorities will now see the program on Sunday morning, the twentieth."

That word "authorities" is getting to us. Last night we asked ourselves, could there be anything in these skits the administration might consider censoring? Although the four novice playwrights treated their situations lightly, serious campus conditions like overcrowding, invasive rats, falling plaster, imperfect food, possible dorm intruders, and even that delicate subject—male-female relationships, however innocent—do turn up in their texts. These students are writing of realities present, we understand, on every Nanjing campus. The larger audience at that program will be primarily students. Could these "authorities" lose face because of the skits' contents? Or will the Foreign Languages Department gain respect by presenting original Hehai work? We'll find out on the twentieth—unless Mr. Lüe moves the date up again.

We attack the pile of class papers. Given five possible quotations, most students bypassed Oliver Wendell Holmes, Sr., La Rochefoucauld, and Pascal to respond to a Japanese proverb: "The tongue is more to be feared than the sword."

Miss Li Yanping observed succinctly in her essay that "saliva can drown a person."

Miss Liu Jie, responding to recent reports in Chinese newspapers about modeling careers for women losing their old miasma of shame, wrote:

> I don't quite agree with the Japanese proverb "The tongue is more to be feared than the sword." I think it all depends. To the timid person, the tongue is as vital as or even more fearful than the sword, but to a brave person, the tongue is not so fearful.
>
> In China we have recently some women models. They are looked upon as something mysterious and people talk about this newly emerging thing. Having been exposed to Confucianism for so long a time, irresistibly, some people in China simply can't bear the idea of women models. So they turn their sharp tongues on these women models.
>
> Some models can't bear the heavy burden of "Public Opinion," and get mental disease. Some even commit suicide. They are the prey of the TONGUE. On the other hand, we might say that they are weak-minded, and are not self-confident about what they are doing.
>
> Meanwhile, women models don't disappear in China. Many survive the deluge. They are strong-minded and believe that they are doing something for art. Now, more and more people begin to show respect to these women models.
>
> From this, we can get the conclusion if you are brave, you can stick to

your mind. Go ahead, never mind what the others are talking about you. Then, what can "Public Opinion" do to you?

Stimulated by the same quotation, Mr. Xue Hai called his essay "Tongues are 'Gossipers.' " He wrote:

> Tongues are very useful tasting-organs. We use them to relish meals three times a day. Furthermore, tongues are "microphones"; without them, we can't speak. But people sometimes abuse their tongues. They use them to spread gossip, flatter nobles, and even kill some innocent persons frenziedly. The Japanese proverb here gives us an excellent comparison: "The tongue is more to be feared than the sword."
>
> This is completely right! We can see swords in the open and we can dodge them, but we fail to see and guard against speaking evils behind. This reminds me of what I have experienced before.
>
> During the Great Cultural Revolution, one of my father's old colleagues was accused by gossips and slanderers as a hidden traitor, a spy and an anti-revolutionary. The main reason was that he had some relatives in Taiwan.
>
> Those so-called revolutionary fighters couldn't find any proof for his crimes. So they criticized him every day in front of large audiences. One by one, the chosen representatives from the audience criticized him with cruel and bitter words. Finally, this old man could not bear the inhuman humiliations. He killed himself by jumping down from a lavatory window of a high building. He was really killed by tongues. Although he was rehabilitated in 1978, his head could not be put whole on his body again.
>
> We young people should draw lessons from the Cultural Revolution. We should try to pay more attention to our self-cultivation, our own morality and practices, and not spread gossip against others.
>
> At the same time we should also try to get rid of the interference of gossips, because gossips flowing out of tongues are our natural enemies, which often sow revengeful seeds and stir up terrible troubles.
>
> As our Chinese saying goes, "Gossips are fearful things." So it's the best policy to keep our tongues honest.

"Evidence on the Cultural Revolution keeps piling up." Sieg puts Mr. Xue's paper on the stack we've both seen. "Did everybody use the same quotation?"

I hand him the last paper. "Trust Mr. Mao to go off in a different direction. But it still centers on the Cultural Revolution."

Mr. Mao Yanyang has written:

According to Joseph Roux, "Prejudices will become truth when orators and auditors share them." This truth makes me think of our "Cultural Revolution."

During that period of ten years, from 1966 to 1976, we Chinese, both leaders and common people, seemed out of sense. We only knew to listen to our leaders and follow them and never thought it possible for them to make any mistakes.

So when some of our leaders said that we should have class struggle, we thought it was absolutely right. When our former president, Liu Shaoqi, was wrongly accused of being a hidden traitor, we had the same hatred for him and firmly believed that it was a great fortune to our country to disclose and overcome this great enemy.

In our eyes, nothing was untruthful. It went quite naturally. However in our practicing what we believed was truth, we were playing an ever miserable tragedy rather unconsciously. So one prejudice after another brought our country nearly to the edge of destruction.

One thing I remembered most clear was the criticism of our present leader, Deng Xiaoping. When someone in the Central Committee said in the seeming eloquence that Deng was a biggest leader following the capitalist road in Party, and called the whole people to "break his scheme and drive him out," overnight Deng turned from a vice-premier to our common target of criticism.

Even I, an innocent Primary pupil who knew nothing about politics, was so excited and angry in my addressing at our criticism meeting. I even took the lead in shouting, "Down with Deng Xiaoping."

All this has become a joke now. But we ought to get something from this sad joke. Everyone should avoid prejudice for it may bring disasters to a person or to a nation. We must make use of more of our brains than in blind worship.

Sieg closes the class folder. "They're finding their own mature voices!"

23 . The "Authorities" Descend

I t's time we added props to rehearsals. Tuesday morning, along with papers for today's reading test, we lug across campus two small boxes, a bowl, one flashlight, a coat hanger, an umbrella, a mop, a feather duster, and a folding chair. Our unwieldy domestic loads make us the butt of many a laugh.

As we climb to the third flood, a building maintenance worker on her way down reverses direction. She doesn't laugh. She accosts Miss Zhuang Zi in the hall. They chatter in Chinese. Miss Zhuang comes in giggling.

"She thought you didn't like her cleaning!"

"Were you able to reassure her?"

"Perhaps."

After the reading test, we manage double run-throughs of every skit. They go much better, perhaps because we have props in hand. Then we practice a device to offset the lack of printed programs. In his introductions, Mr. Lüe gives each cast member's real name. Each person in turn steps forward and gives the part he or she plays. For instance, in "Keep Off the Grass," Mr. Lüe says, "Mr. Li Jian." Mr. Li steps forward and says, "I'm Danny." Miss Lü, Miss Feng, and Mr. Zuo do the same in their parts.

It's no substitute for elaborate Lincoln Center programs, but maybe the simple process will serve to highlight a little Western-style individuality, even while it moves these amateur actors past the first clutch of stage fright they all dread.

"Tomorrow we rehearse again during class," Sieg says. "Also in the evening." He turns to Mr. Lüe. "Where is the rehearsal for the authorities? Here? Or can we possibly get on the auditorium stage?"

"I will let you know later," Mr. Lüe promises.

Sieg chalks play titles with staggered times on the board. "We'll rehearse in this order, at these times. That way, the rest of you won't have to stand around. But please be here when your skit's due to begin!"

On Wednesday morning, trouble starts before dawn. For some unknown reason, the loudspeakers that normally rout everyone from sleep at 6:00 A.M. fail to blast off. We get up late, skipping exercises, and grab breakfast. Outside, the day looms dark, acrid to the nose.

Once inside our classroom door, right at 7:30, we find Mr. Guo. He wants a complete run-through of the entire program, music and skits both. Now. But the loudspeakers, whose silence has delayed some of the first scheduled actors, plus our staggered rehearsal times, which we try to explain, force us to wait.

Mr. Guo is furious. He smokes, in more ways than one. Cigarette smoke pours out the broken window panes, adding to the already foggy day.

At 7:40, we begin the British skit, "Keep Off the Grass." Its four actors, dressed down by a glowering Guo Kun for appearing late, are subdued. They muff lines, stumble over moves they've made smoothly before.

As their classmates arrive successively, we work through "Pretender," "Rat," "False Alarm," and "Dark Conversation." Each time, as we rehearsed yesterday, cast members step forward and name their roles, sometimes with a smile or a bow. When the entire class gathers, we sing the three Christmas songs. Mr. Fan and Miss Bin do their Chinese duet.

Mr. Guo is not pleased. He mutters throughout. Isn't it awkward to have the emcee introduce characters and then to have them identify themselves? Mr. Zuo isn't animated enough in his part. He should point his finger in the air when he gets an idea. The students haven't committed their lines to memory as they should. A Chinese song isn't appropriate, surely, to an English program?

In his tan trench coat, unsmiling, he strides up and down at the back of the room. One cigarette fires the next. Perhaps, he says, "Keep Off the Grass" is the best of the lot. "Twelve Days of Christmas" is okay. By the way, there will be a female emcee for the entire program. For Rae Peters' and Mary Catherine Mooney's classes too. We are to supply this young woman assistant with all of Mr. Lüe's cue cards and complete copies of every script so she can write new introductions.

I protest. Mr. Lüe's major part in the performance is those introductions. "Couldn't he continue to do just our part of the program?"

"Perhaps," he says again. Mr. Guo warns the class every single person must practice every single night from now on. "I will make my office available. And don't come late to class again!" He whips out.

We check with Mr. Lüe. It seems there will be no review by "authorities" tonight. Mr. Guo was it.

The afternoon proves raw, grey, cold, windy. Rae Peters, sick in bed with flu for the past two days, wraps herself in two coats and a huge scarf, and, for want of a better stage, rehearses her Cinderella musical for three hours outdoors in the cold wind on the dining hall steps opposite the Guest House. We watch her quadrilles. Her program, at least, seems to be flourishing.

Thursday, ignoring all other assignments, we work again. The casts are rehearsing at night by themselves. When we begin a fast, full, timed rehearsal on Friday, it's plain, one week to the deadline, that the students are finally getting serious about this performance. There's only one disappointment. Mr. Guo has sent word that "Dark Conversation," the skit focusing on talk about male-female relationships, must be cut. "Not enough action in it," he says.

At class break, Sieg goes to the office to pick up duplicated materials for next week's classes. He returns. I'm working with one student on his lines for pronunciation and projection.

Sieg calls class back into session early. He has an odd look, a rare tightening around the mouth. "If," he says, "*if* you could go with only one skit, which one would it be?" He chalks the four remaining titles on the board.

Eleven students vote for the innocuous British skit, the one most favored by Guo Kun, the one not written by any of them.

"Then that's it," Sieg says. "The *if* is true. Because of time restrictions, we now have one duet, two full chorus numbers, one skit. The skit will be 'Keep Off the Grass.'"

I am so angry—after six weeks of preparation, after all the original work done by these students, after such prolonged neglect of regular studies—that I cannot talk. I walk to the far back wall and lean against it. The students sit in stunned silence, their backs hunched.

Sieg spreads his hands. "I'm sorry. Mr. Guo tells me there was a meeting yesterday afternoon. Two other universities, Nan Da, and Nan Su Da, and the Red Army School in Nanjing are joining the program. We will have only forty-five minutes total for all acts from Hehai."

"Yesterday afternoon." That means all our students came from their dorms last night, some to the deserted Foreign Languages Office, and rehearsed without cause.

Mr. Chen Pingnan, the Hehai instructor and occasional class auditor, hovers in the doorway. He sidles through a row of seats, aiming to talk to me. I shake my head. I still can't find my voice. He scuttles back toward the office to report this strange foreign behavior. In China, it is bad form to show you're upset.

"Well," says Sieg, picking up the pieces, "we didn't bring your reading tests today because we thought we'd be rehearsing. We can have an impromptu conversation—"

Mr. Chen is back. He whispers to Sieg that perhaps, perhaps we could have one other skit—"The Pretender."

"What about it?" Sieg asks the class. "We'll still be under the gun of time. You could keep on rehearsing this and be cut at the last minute."

Mr. Lao Sheng, author as well as star in the skit, votes for dropping it. So does another principal actor in it, Mr. Ku Qiu.

"Perhaps in a smaller space," says Mr. Lao. "But it's hard to make ourselves heard from that big stage."

Is this Mr. Lao's diplomatic excuse to avoid special privilege above his classmates by having only his skit survive?

Mr. Chen Pingnan departs to convey the latest opinion from the classroom front.

We try to salvage some of the suddenly blank class time with "free talk." The students ask about U.S. Christmas customs, but it's clear their hearts aren't in either questions or answers. Neither are ours. We dismiss class early.

One of the women students waits outside. She drops into step with me along the tree-lined avenue. "You know," she says softly, "we Chinese are very used to sudden changes such as this. We plan, but our leaders make decision. So many things don't come to be. We expect it."

I stop in the middle of the street. "Is that why the class seemed to care so little about getting ready for this?"

"Oh, we liked it. But we do not expect."

"Thank you," I say with genuine appreciation. "You may have helped us put this more in perspective."

She smiles and darts off.

I catch up with Sieg, who thought we were talking about some private matter. I repeat her comments.

He frowns. "In effect, the class was trying to serve two masters. What a tough position to put them in! And what a frustrating way to do things!"

At the Guest House door, two of our fellow teachers are rolling their bikes inside. "Have you heard?" Marilyn Grav, teacher from Canada, asks.

"Heard what?" We aren't sure her news is our news. Or maybe fresh developments have surfaced since we left class?

"The whole Cinderella program for Rae's secretarial class has been cancelled. And her other program with Nan Da has been cut from forty to twenty minutes."

So much for Rae's outdoor rehearsals Wednesday in that bitter cold. Her second program is the musical medley of tunes she and a Nan Da teacher with a painfully bad back have been rehearsing in their spare time for two months.

"How is she taking it?"

"She's *mad*."

"Join the crowd," I say.

Sieg explains our cuts.

"Well, at least your class has some left."

Finally, finally on Sunday morning, we can get into the auditorium for one rehearsal. Everybody, including Mr. Guo, is there on time. The vast place looms cavernous, chill. It seems like acres and acres of cement, all refrigerated.

We've figured out a way to work every student (except Mr. Lüe who will do half the evening's introductions) into our one remaining skit. Since "Keep Off the Grass" has a park setting, each nonspeaking class member can stroll or sit in the background. Instead of "Sunday in the Park with George," the audience will see a version of "Keep Off the Grass with Postgraduates."

I hand out newspapers for some to "read." This is a big mistake. Several cast members become so engrossed in reading their or somebody else's previously unseen copies that they raise their heads only reluctantly to listen to instructions.

In our few allotted moments, we rehearse lines around several loud young men. They keep calling to each other while fixing and testing mikes on poles at three downstage points.

Mr. Li and Miss Lü have to adjust their entry to move rapidly across an expanse four times the width of the classroom floors where they've practiced.

Just in case the mikes should fail or a power blackout descend, I make all four principals try to project their lines to the rear of the balcony. Two can't be heard even halfway back in the aisles. The other two produce bouncing echoes.

We run through our songs, omitting the gestures practiced for "Twelve Days of Christmas." We're saving those for a surprise. The a cappella rehearsal seems to go well. A few listeners scattered around the hall applaud.

"You know," Mr. Guo says from the auditorium floor, "there will be a piano. Or an orchestra. You must give music sheets."

"Do we get a chance to rehearse with them?" Sieg asks doubtfully.

"Of course. We will move the piano here the day of the performance. Musicians should be onstage a few minutes before."

Too little, too late, I think but keep silent. It's not supposed to be a professional production anyhow.

24 : Second Thoughts

Tuesday morning, partly to distract the actors from jitters about tomorrow's performance, partly to nudge us all toward fresh ideas, we direct the students for three of the four class hours to new reading and writing.

Together, we look at a brief excerpt from Mark Twain's *Life on the Mississippi*. In three serious paragraphs, Twain describes that river's many beauties as he first saw them through naive, apprentice-young eyes; the warnings and dangers those same attractions signaled once he'd come to know them as a mature pilot; and the sad implication of this professional loss of innocence for doctors, pilots, or any persons who must inevitably corrupt their own aesthetic views through deepened knowledge and experience.

Once we clear up their misunderstandings of a few words and phrases, we propose a writing exercise for the next fifty minutes: Think, then write about an experience of your own where what you learned brought a sense of loss along with it, either immediately or with later realization.

Miss Feng stares out the window before picking up her pen. Mr. Fan makes several trips to the hall spittoon. There's the usual twisting around for a few whispered conferences and frequent flip of dictionary pages. Mostly, the students seem to forget the cold room and the bulkiness of writing with their gloves on, in the warming process of creation.

I look forward to our third hour when they begin to read their essays aloud. Taking over the podium and sharing their own work has become so normal a routine that tremors have vanished from their hands and voices. Most of them read calmly, clearly, presenting their own ideas without nervous fingers shielding their mouths.

Miss Zhuang Zi seems especially pleased as she smooths her paper on the lectern. She reads:

> Once a friend of mine asked me to have dinner. He just graduated from a medical university and now he was a doctor in a hospital.
>
> Being hospitable, he cooked many delicious dishes which soon worked up my appetite, so I took my chopsticks and began to eat.
>
> "Please help yourself." He pointed at a plate of pork liver and said, "This pork liver is quite fresh."
>
> I picked up one piece and chewed it with great relish.
>
> Before I swallowed it, he said, "Pork liver is easy to get a disease just like human beings. For example, hepatomegaly, cirrhosis and cancer. Some porks carry those germs so you must examine them carefully before you cook them."
>
> I didn't want to touch that pork liver again, so I began to eat pork gut.
>
> "Do you know pork gut?" he asked. "Since it contains a lot of dirty waste materials, it must be cleaned carefully before cooking. Otherwise . . ."
>
> Before he finished his speaking, my stomach revolted, so I stopped eating.
>
> "Excuse me," I said, and quickly ran to the toilet room and vomited.
>
> Since then, I daren't have dinner with doctors.

Everyone laughs. Some applaud.

"Right to the point. Nice use of details and dialogue!" I comment. "Any questions for Miss Zhuang?"

"Would you marry a doctor?" Miss Chun asks mischievously.

Miss Zhuang shakes her bangs in a vigorous negative.

Even though the next reader, Mr. Mao Yanyang, keeps his head buried in his paper, the class follows his words with rapt attention:

> Reading Twain's "Two View of a River," I can't help thinking how common but sentimental it is to lose one thing after getting another, particularly when what is "lost" is a kind of beauty we sense.
>
> Recalling my past college life always brings me a slight feeling of pity and sadness. There, for four years, we dozens of innocent youth seemed never to know what it was to lose or to part. We spent the most unforgettable and best years of our lives playing, studying, talking, and doing other seemingly simple and trifling things.
>
> Light-hearted, free of trouble and much care, we formed a close tie with each other and with our lovely campus by all our doings. Few of us predicted that one day we might lose all these. We even failed to see that this kind of life is a kind of bounty. We longed to go out to work, to put down all our burdens as students.
>
> It was only after we indeed went out that we began to sense a kind of loss, a loss that could never be restored. All the past scenes, persons appeared in my dreams more and more. Sometimes I was not clear whether or not the past four years were reality.
>
> Now we have to deal with all kinds of problems. We have to fill our brains with all sorts of thinking. Yes, I can get what I couldn't get in the past, practically, but I still keep asking myself why the same college or school life has managed to give me such two contrasted humours?
>
> Perhaps it's because I've got bored with this kind of life. Or I have grown up. Or the time has passed too fast and too cruelly. Or perhaps I can't see the really present beauty around me, equal to that of the past. Or there may be no beauty at all.
>
> What a pity it is that when I lived in beauty, I couldn't understand it. What a sorrowful thing it is that now when I have lost beauty, I could understand the whole of it.

The class does not applaud. They sit silent, reflecting, like us, on the depths Mr. Mao has touched. Postgraduate realities. Posthalcyon days (if halcyon days they ever were). Self-questioning, changing attitudes, not always for the happier. We each have to face them, whatever our stage.

Several other student papers reflect a similar theme. They express their

pangs at putting behind them, as one said, "the golden years of their mother
university."

Mr. Ku Qiu prefaces his paper by glancing back at us diffidently. "I hope it
is all right," he says. "In this paper, a loss becomes a gain." He begins:

> At the age of fifteen, I graduated from middle school. At that time I
> made up my mind to be a carpenter like my father to earn money for my
> poor family. However, when I asked permission of the head of our vil-
> lage, my idea was refused to do so because a carpenter was considered
> one of bourgeois at that time. I began to roam here and there because I
> was not strong enough to do tedious farm work.
>
> One day several months later I went to see my former teacher and told
> him my awkward situation.
>
> After a while of silence, he asked me to come back to school to study.
> At first, I just gave a bitter smile because at that time I thought it was
> useless for me to earn knowledge. I would be a farmer whatever I was.
>
> He talked to me like my own father. At last he persuaded me to refresh
> my studies. Two years later I took part in the National Examination.
> Fortunately, I passed the examination, and became one of the students
> at Yuezhang Normal School. Since then, I could further my study.
>
> I never thought I would be a postgraduate student now. . . . [If I
> hadn't been] refused to be a carpenter, I would be a miserable farm-
> er now!

There is a stir, a reaching of hands to see Mr. Ku's composition as he
returns to his seat. Time and discretion keep me from responding now in
ways I'd like to—to the power of Chinese village authorities, the happy intervention of a sensitive teacher, to Mr. Ku's modest assessment of his own
merits.

But my watch, the students' snuffles and shuffles, dictate it's time for our
last break of the day.

25 . Performance!

Miss An Ran announces after our last complete program run-through Wednesday morning, "There will be a full rehearsal with orchestra at four o'clock in the hall of the Management Building."

"Everybody must be at the theater at five o'clock for make-up," Mr. Lüe orders.

H'm. Shorter afternoon than we hoped.

At 4:00 P.M., we reach the Management Building. No students. No musicians in sight. It's not easy to mount the familiar littered stairs to the Foreign Languages Office. Workmen are finally filling in a gaping, unguarded shaft with an elevator. Construction materials and debris pile hazards in every hallway.

"Where is the rehearsal?" Sieg asks the office staff.

Mr. Guo Kun comes forward. He wears his usual reassuring smile. "Oh, that has been canceled."

I'm learning that in this country you never consider anything scheduled until it actually takes place. We needed a brisk walk this afternoon, right?

We thread our way back down and around the lumber. "This settles one thing," Sieg says. "No point reaching the theater before 5:15."

At 5:10, carrying Mr. Zuo's folding chair from the Guest House hall for the final trek, we take the dusty, brick-strewn campus road to the theater. An office staff member pulls up beside us. His bike is almost invisible beneath packaged rolls of colored crepe paper.

"For decorating the curtains. Good-bye!" He remounts and zooms off.

Curtain time is 6:30. We marvel again at the last minute scurrying, but why should they prepare early? Inured to a system full of abrupt cancellations, wise people here don't move until they're sure they must. The mounting evidence again explains why our students were so slow preparing for this program.

At the theater door, a young woman insists on taking "that heavy chair" from us. It must be unseemly for teachers, especially grey-haired ones, to carry any object but a scroll or a book. She ushers us past a couple of tootling musicians toward the equivalent of a greenroom backstage. Here, the greenroom is white. Or was. Dust and footprints over the years have added a palimpsest in brown and grey to its high plastered walls.

The room is so cold we can see our breath. It's packed with excited performers, all busy making up. Both women and men share one box of powder, one brush, one rouge pot, two lipsticks, two small hand mirrors. Everybody, including our class, takes turns.

Some linger over their makeup for twenty minutes. Others dash it on in fifteen seconds. Lipstick under Mr. Fan's mustache strikes me as a garish contradiction. Sieg looks weird after they've rouged both his cheeks into raw beefsteak blushes.

"You look much younger!" Miss Zhuang exclaims.

I can't stand the large flame rectangles painted on my cheeks. I hunt out a faucet in the women's restroom to scrub off half the gunk with a piece of wet newspaper.

In the wings, Mr. Zuo, a hitherto unsuspected literalist, is desperately searching for a mat, a piece of cardboard, *something* to provide "grass" in "Keep Off the Grass."

I try to assure him that the audience—assuming they can follow English—will accept the bare stage floor as greenery through the players' lines and actions.

Mr. Zuo's eyes glitter. They are almost fixed. He has never been on stage before. A quick peek through closed proscenium curtains shows we're going to play before a capacity crowd. Not the promised thousand. At least eighteen hundred. Who are they all? How many can understand enough English to follow the skit? Will Mr. Zuo freeze? On stage, I walk him and Miss Feng through their entrances and exits. Maybe moving about will help stem their panic.

Behind us, the eight-piece orchestra noodles around. In back of the orchestra, two crepe-paper hangers run up and down a tall ladder while they take turns clipping final touches to their festive letters and wreaths on the upstage blue curtain.

There's no chance for even a partial rehearsal with orchestra. The orchestra leader tells us for each song they'll give a two-line cue. Our group will sing the opening number. We hustle onstage.

We stand in two well-spread lines in front of the orchestra. Plenty of room now for gestures! The curtains part. The orchestra begins. Their instruments, almost pressing into our calves, blare so loud we can hardly hear our own voices. They play so fast our gestures doubletime like a revved-up film. "Twelve Days of Christmas" ends in the time it normally takes to sing six days. In "Jingle Bells," the one-horse sleigh doesn't trot or even gallop. It's a runaway.

Afterwards, Mr. Li pants, "I could hardly get my breath!" If the other twenty-eight groups listed on the single-page program maintain our speed, the show will be done in one hour.

They don't. Not all of them have the orchestra's help.

The next three numbers, a dance and two musical spots, stretch to fifteen minutes. "Keep Off the Grass" is supposed to be sixth. Suddenly, there's a cut. We're coming up fifth.

I run to the dressing room where Miss Feng, the skit's old lady, is turning from rosy to wrinkled grey under the hands of a makeup man from Nan Da.

"Come on, you're on!"

She jumps to her feet and ties a scarf over her head so her dark hair can't show. We dash to the wings.

The class arranges itself onstage. The curtain opens. Mr. Zuo, the watchful park keeper, makes his rounds. Danny and Norma (Mr. Li and Miss Lü) give their opening lines, although Danny has to pick up a mike and lug it with him as he strolls the acres to downstage right.

The audience laughs at his move. They also laugh in the right places, so the skit is being understood. Mercifully, it's short. Curtains close to warm applause. The actors run off relieved, amazed they've actually survived.

Happy congratulations all around. Their roles done, our students head for seats saved out front, or on the sides of the auditorium, or in the aisles, which are completely blocked by enthusiastic patrons.

We wait backstage to be sure Miss An and Miss Chun are set for their later Yankee Doodle duet—number fourteen on the list. They assure us they are, so we join the students in extra chairs set up so they completely block the side exits.

"What would an American fire marshal say to this scene?" Sieg asks.

"Plenty! If he could get through."

One number follows another—songs, dances, skits that can't be heard. The army's number, a late program item unscreened by Mr. Guo, proves to be a half-hour play. Even down front, it's almost impossible to follow. The mikes aren't picking up voices. Instead, every boot clump, every shoe scuff on wood amplifies perfectly. Three-quarters of the way through, the audience begins whistling, cat-calling. Enough of this play! On with the music!—seems to be the message.

We pass number fourteen. Our duet doesn't appear. We're up to number eighteen. It's now nine o'clock. Sieg checks backstage. Miss Chun's and Miss An's number has been canceled, he learns, because "Mr. Guo says the program is too long."

It certainly is. The audience grows more and more restless. They stamp their feet. There's been no intermission. "If we had one," an unknown student near us explains, "the audience might leave." There's supposed to be a party and dance for all the casts afterwards in the theater lobby.

As unobtrusively as possible, between numbers, we relinquish our chairs to two tired standees and slip out through the dark exit curtains into the drafty hall. If anyone asks what happened, we will plead tomorrow's lessons and old age, both, we're discovering, highly believable, versatile excuses.

Dan Younkin, an American teacher and our neighbor down the hall, who has been persuaded to play Santa Claus at the party, reports to us later. He sinks into one of the apartment's red armchairs. He looks as dazed as if he'd just survived a massive earthquake.

"I came down the lobby stairs with a big bag of candy. I started to distribute it, and they mobbed me, grabbing into the bag for everything they could get. So I just dumped it and retreated.

"The second I finished, the young woman who supplied the costume took it off my back. They must have been renting it by the minute." He shakes his head. "I'm glad that's over."

We are too. Considering the long build-up, the demanding preparations, the tense uncertainties all along the way, and the sharp disappointments before and during this evening, we wonder what Mr. Guo will plan for next year at this time?

"Probably the same thing," Dan says. "With different people."

26 : "Let Dragons Marry Dragons"

For today's conversation focus, the class happily settles to instructing us in Chinese courtship and marriage customs.

We're eager to hear what they have to say. Unless we're missing subtle cues, within this group of eleven women and eight men, sixteen of them single, no one has formed any romantic relationships despite nearly four months of close daily contact. We've seen no hand-holding (except, typically, between members of the same sex), no fond exchange of secret glance or touch, both easy to observe from this side of a teacher's desk. Although we've heard sparks of male-female discord occasionally, the group acts as a unit in an oddly asexual way, baffling for their ages.

Will today's comments hint why?

"Last week," Sieg begins, "Mr. Mao quoted a Chinese saying that praised the virtues of a maiden sitting silent. So how does she signal she's interested? How do young people get together here?"

"A shy girl may not express herself directly," Mr. Ku Qiu says.

"They can feel from their hearts!" Miss An Ran bursts out. "She can feel, 'He loves me.' He can write a letter."

"Perhaps the young man can give girl a present," Mr. Xue Hai says. "Not very expensive—a beautiful handkerchief, a branch of flowers. She might give gift in return to show her interest. If she refuses to accept gift, she isn't interested. It's bad manners to return a gift."

"Another way," says Mr. Lao Sheng, "you invite girl to go to cinema. If she accepts, she's interested. Then perhaps they go to park together. That will develop. At last, stay alone with her, express private thoughts. Or ask someone else to talk to her for you."

Sieg glances around the circle at the women. "You mean I couldn't be in a group with you—say in a class or a party—and ask you to accompany me to a movie?"

"Sometimes," Miss Liu Jie replies, "if you know it's an impossible situation. If Mr. Xue, for example, who is married, and his wife far away, wanted to go to movie with just a friend."

"But if girl goes out frequently with a young man," Mr. Mao Yanyang says, "then there's something serious between them."

"Are there sometimes misunderstandings about this?" Sieg is thinking of a Western teacher we know in Nanjing. In first-year innocence, this young man danced casually at a class party with one of his Chinese students, on request exchanged photographs, and held a student conference with her privately in his room, as he did by appointment with other class members. The set of events convinced the young woman her teacher wanted to marry her. She persisted in this illusion for over a year, besieging him with letters and calls, stalking him at all hours of day and night, much to his disclaiming embarrassment.

"Yes, sometimes misunderstanding," Mr. Zuo says. "The boy asks girl to go out, but the boy didn't tell the girl, 'I love you.' Just for something else."

"If there is intimate physical relationship, then what?"

"The girl thinks serious. Boy may not." Mr. Zuo pauses. "Or he may think he loves her, then may change his mind, love another."

"If there is something unpleasant, some scandal," Mrs. Ching Chao says, "the girl will not talk about it."

The room sits silent. Sieg's question has plainly touched delicate ground.

The silence seems to make Mrs. Ching nervous. "People a thousand *li* apart may be linked by marriage," she offers. "Perhaps it is their destiny arranged by gods. The old man of the moon who controls marriage takes a red thread and ties them together, so they're destined to marry. We say, 'Let beggars match beggars. Let dragons marry dragons. Let phoenix marry phoenix.' "

"Suppose two people from different backgrounds want to marry. Can they elope?"

The group looks serious. "Sometimes," Mr. Ku says, "without parents' permission, couple mustn't get married."

Sieg quotes from a recent article in *China Daily,* the official English-language newspaper published in Beijing. It cited two young people who, through elopement, lost their jobs and had their home set on fire, all because they defied community sanction.

Miss Li Yanping nods. "If they marry against parents' wishes, perhaps they can never again return home."

"This problem is more often rural," Miss Zhuang Zi explains. "In less-educated, poor area, the marriage is arranged for economic reason. So it is important to take place."

"Suppose everything goes smoothly?" Sieg asks. "The young couple like each other. They want to marry. They're of the same backgrounds. Then what?"

"First," Mr. Mao answers, "the boy gets his own parents' permission."

"Or the young woman asks the man to meet her parents," Miss An Ran cuts in.

"Then the boy goes to the girl's family," Mr. Mao continues. "Both sets of parents talk. They have a dinner engagement party for their relatives and friends."

"His parents and her parents will meet again to set time to be married." Miss An clearly knows the procedures. "The boy's parents send expensive gifts to the future bride—a bicycle, a watch, a camera. The girl gives the boy clothes. Later, the girl's family buys refrigerator, color TV."

"I didn't do that!" Mr. Lao Sheng interrupts. "I choose my wife. I didn't want an expensive dinner. This also avoids problem of friends being angry at not being invited. They don't have to pay. We had a travel marriage, after marriage certificate. Our parents agreed. They are very domestic—uh—demo-cratic!"

"But if you do go the usual route," Sieg persists, "after the engagement party, what happens?"

"They must buy furnitures, clothes, find a place to live!" Miss Lü Shu's eyes dance. "At least half of couples will move in with groom's parents. But before that—"

"Wedding ceremony!" Miss An exclaims.

"A religious ceremony?"

"No!" The chorus is convincing.

"You go to city office to get certificate," Miss Li tries to clear up our manifest ignorance. "But you cannot get certificate unless your unit leaders know. They give identification that you are single, of the right age—"

"Right age?" Sieg asks.

"The boy must be at least twenty-two, the girl twenty," Mr. Xue explains.

"But it is bad luck to marry when you are twenty-two," Miss Lü reminds us.

"Still, you can get marriage certificate," Miss Li goes on. "Here, at the university, you go first to personnel office. If they say all right and sign papers, you go to city office. Your photos are on marriage certificate. Then you are officially married. Then many people have wedding party."

It's the longest informal speech we've heard from Miss Li all semester. I wonder if she has checked this procedure out of personal interest?

"In countryside," Miss An picks up, "there are three days of relatives—aunts, uncles, grandparents, cousins—visiting and eating. In Nanjing, you go to a restaurant. I once saw a wedding of twenty tables!"

"The groom's family pays," Mr. Xue says. "It is *very* expensive. Sometimes young people help parents with costs. Sometimes, they borrow from friends or relatives and pay back. Wedding guests bring ten to fifty yuan for the couple." He draws in his breath. "Each month, if there are marriages of their friends, they must pay a lot of money!"

"Some families go into debt," Miss Lü says, "for a long time."

Mindful of his own economical solution, Mr. Lao sits relaxed, smiling.

Sieg still looks unsatisfied. "At the dinner, is there any exchange of vows?"

Patiently, students explain that before dinner there is a private ceremony. The bride washes the groom's hands and face, and chooses clothes. "The boy," Miss An reports, her voice charged with emotion, "puts gold ring on third finger, left hand. Girl puts on third finger, right hand. They keep on wearing rings."

"Few people," Miss Liu Jie disagrees, "give rings to brides."

They do agree the house may be decorated with flags and plants. The couple bows to both families, then to the guests, "to have a deep impression on their families," Miss An explains. Then the boy's family finds one or several cars to take bride and family to the costly restaurant dinner, where they circulate, hearing many toasts and jokes, and giving cigarettes to the men.

"Then the bride and groom move into their quarters that night," Miss Lü says. "Two or three days later, the couple goes to bride's parents' home. *They put on a party!*"

"This happens next day," Miss Chun states from Nanjing custom. She sees Sieg glance at his watch. "What shall we talk about next time? It is always good to know what words to look up."

"January first is almost here," Sieg answers. "How about New Year's Resolutions?"

"Easy," Mr. Li says in parting. "I don't make any."

"Try to imagine," Miss Liu advises him.

Today, on three counts, they are eager to clatter downstairs and out. Class is over, with lunch, however predictable, immediately ahead. Wednesday's topic will be as simple as this morning's. And suddenly winter's wretched deep freeze has relented. Outdoors it has mellowed into a bone-warming, jacket-sloughing sixty-five. Or rather, eighteen degrees Celsius.

27 · Winter Thoughts

Puffy snowflakes, dropped again by an erratic night wind, dust the plum tree this morning.

Mrs. Ching Chao gently lays a budded sprig, three inches long, on the lectern. "In Chinese literature," she says, "plum blossom is very ancient symbol of endurance."

"Thank you! We saw those, but didn't dare pick them. I never knew trees could bloom in weather like this."

"Don't you know Wang Wei? In Tang dynasty, he wrote a small poem, very famous, asking for news from home. He wants to know if winter plum outside his window is in bloom." Mrs. Ching's round face shines in delight as she remembers and shares from her own rich lore.

"We're reading some of the Tang poets now. I'll watch for that one."

The whole group works with unusual concentration on writing today. A few of them revise and polish drafts they've started outside class. Today's general topic, "Winter Thoughts," seems to spur them to longer essays than normal, but since our numbering system shows this is the twenty-fourth writing exercise they've done, maybe gradually they are finding they do have a great deal worth saying.

In the second period, as soon as they begin reading aloud, my vague feeling that they are developing a new confidence leaps into bloom like the plum.

Miss Bin Qilin writes:

> I got up early this morning at 6:10. It is a special case in this winter.
>
> I've been making my mind to get up early, and to breathe fresh air and to do some running. I always wish my winter happy and gay, but I often lie in bed.
>
> This morning, coming out of my dormitory, I found the sky was still dark with bright stars and the ground was dim with shining lights. A cold wind breezed. I shivered with cold, but I felt it fresh and clear. Many people were having physical training, running slowly or doing exercises. There was an energetic and steaming atmosphere in the chill morning. I was inspired and joined those students who were running. After a while I felt warm and comfortable, which reminded me of the comfort I used to get when I ran as a little girl.
>
> When I was a volleyball player at primary school, I ran every morning in winter. At that time, I used to get up early at 6:00 o'clock. The outside was still dark, and the chill wind blew. Yet I seemed never to have feared the darkness or have noticed the coldness. Our team ran along a wide road lined with rivers. How fresh the air was! How comfortable our bodies were! Running and running forward, we took off our cotton coats, and then sweaters. Yet we felt no cold at all.
>
> On the way back, the sky was somewhat bright. We saw clearly the trees, the houses and the water. They were all fresh, clear, and quiet.
>
> I remember those winters. I never got cold. During my primary school I seldom got sick. I got up early and lived healthy and lively.
>
> Yet this winter I have been to hospital several times. I put on a thicker coat, but don't feel warm. I sleep more, but still feel sleepy in class. It is an unhealthy and unlively winter. I feel sorry for my laziness. Though I get quilt warmth, I lose my lively life.
>
> Oh no, I can't be that. Tomorrow I will get up early again. I want to see the lovely winter morning.

Abruptly, Miss Bin stops. She raises her eyes to her audience.

"And to feel again the comfort of warmth from running like a child?" I ask.

She nods. "It is another New Year's resolution."
Miss Chun Xu takes her turn.

> I did not sense that winter had come until the morning my room-mates told me it was snowing. After hearing that, I really felt cold. I lay in bed wondering if my mother was worrying about me. At home, my mother always urged me to wear more clothes, to put more quilts on my bed, to eat more food to keep warm, if it was cold.
>
> Here, far away from my home, she still advises me again and again in her letters, although I tell her I can take care of myself. In my mother's eye, I am always her small child. If I said to her I could live independently, she would be hurt.
>
> As this winter came, I realized a new year would also come. I will be twenty-two years old. When I was a little girl, I always considered twenty-year-old persons as capable as grown ups. I admired them very much. How early I wanted to grow up at that time!
>
> Now, as I have reached my twenties, all my respectful thoughts have disappeared. There is no difference between me and a child except that I have mastered a little more knowledge. I cannot live independently without economic help from my parents. I am still cared for by mother. As yet I make no contribution to my family and to society. Thinking about that I always feel guilty.
>
> I wonder as this winter adds cold days to my years when can I be completely grown up?

"I hate to tell you," Sieg says, "but this same illusion continues as you are older. I always thought of people in their thirties, forties, fifties, and sixties as fully wise. It ain't so!"

"But you do learn to live with human imperfections." I wouldn't want Miss Chun's faith in the maturing process or her traditional respect for her elders totally undermined. What bothers me more is the guilty feeling she's voiced, a feeling shared by many of her classmates, that they are still shamefully dependent on their parents. I try to address her concern. "Miss Chun, you cannot see it now, but you are contributing by taking all this time and effort to become a better teacher. You'll soon put your gold mine of study to use."

"Perhaps. I hope," Miss Chun answers.

Miss Liu Jie, in her paper, amuses the class with: "In winter, you would always find me trembling around with shivering teeth."

After her, Mr. Xue Hai strides energetically to the lectern.

To my mind, winter is a cold and bleak season. Snow often falls heavily and flakes, driven by the wind, whirl in the air. Outside the house, the North Wind howls dreadfully like the screams of some wounded wild beasts. As soon as people mention it I am afraid of winter. Even in warm September, I often shiver with cold at the thought of cold winter.

Now winter has come, I feel terribly cold. This bad weather reminds me of "the cold winter" I passed in 1966, at the beginning of the Great Cultural Revolution.

My father had been accused as a Capitalist Roader. He was deprived of all his administrative powers in his factory. He was paraded through the streets to be exposed before the public with a big heavy board, "A Capitalist Roader," on his neck. Every day he was criticized by some "revolutionist" and forced to write self-criticism papers continuously. At that time, he could not even have the right to go back home to see me, his own son.

During that hard time, we had no money, no food. Poor mother and poor son depended on each other. Without the financial support given by our close relatives, we would have died of hunger.

Now everything has passed. That national disaster hated by the Chinese is gone. With the present economic and political reforms in China, the inland situations are getting better for many people, like a glorious spring.

I like spring. It makes me forget that "terrible winter" of my childhood. There is a Chinese saying, "Winter has come, spring is not far." Right! I miss spring and look forward to its quick coming.

"Along with the rest of us." I check my watch. Since he's mentioned the current economic reforms, it would be interesting to discuss with Mr. Xue and the class the suddenly rising food prices we've noticed recently in the market, but today the class seems especially pleased to read their work. "Mr. Mao?"

"Winter Thoughts," Mr. Mao Yanyang announces. He begins:

I was born in winter. I like winter. I like snow in winter. Whenever the first drop of snow swirls down from the boundless sky to the cool ground, I always run out and stand there, opening my mouth to receive the first pleasure winter offers me.

The cold but fresh white snow goes through my heart, clearing away all the resting sadness the autumn left, bringing me a new internal world.

I love to walk on snow. I like to hear the rhythmic cracking sound.

But when I turn around it is always a pity to destroy the originally flat and slippery expanse of the whiteness.

I'm fond of making the snowman, if not an expert. I hope this white man can bring a happier year to me for his body comes from heaven.

The most joyful thing in winter is our traditional spring festival. The whole family gathers together around the fire, drinking the best stored wine and eating *jiaozi* and other delicious dishes. On the midnight just before the New Year's Day ["I mean the lunar New Year's," he interpolates] the cracking of the fireworks constantly shocks the ears. At the moment after I finish my fireworks, I always go out and climb a tree to enjoy the colourful fire spread here and there over the sky. The night is not black any longer.

Every family is lost in the happiest atmosphere they seldom have usually. Who doesn't love this utmost happy moment?

Although sometimes I hate winter, for when it shows its asperity to me, yet it's only a momentary thing. Winter is like a strict father. He always brings the cruelty before the happiness to his children as if to test whether or not they deserve this happiness.

Mr. Mao scoots for his seat.

"Wait a minute, I'm not clear—"

Mr. Mao remains standing, waiting for the rest of my question.

"You mean winter is cruelty and spring happiness?"

"Yes."

"Happiness is also break time." I release them to their usual between-class bustle. It's varied today. Because there is a dance tonight, several women, giggling, practice ballroom dance steps in the narrow space between the last row of seats and the back wall. Mr. Fan Rui and Mr. Lao Sheng look on, trying to fathom this mystery.

One student drops off a delayed paper, written on the earlier topic prompted by Twain's loss-through-knowledge theme. For the minute, I can't do more than glance at its title: "Gain More or Lose More."

Back at the apartment, sitting on top of the desk by the window to absorb the afternoon sun, I read:

Christmas Day is coming. We have prepared our program for the Christmas Party for nearly a month.

I was surprised and a bit excited to be chosen to play [a main role].

After rehearsals, I got used to playing the role. I tried to express my feelings, real or pretended, by speech, gesture and even facial expressions to get closer to the part with the help of my teachers and classmates.

Since I hadn't played in a skit before, I found my acting enriched my life. I hoped my acting would add something merry to Christmas.

But the news came that all the skits except "Keep Off the Grass" would be cancelled because of time restrictions. I wondered what I had spent so much time in my skit for? I felt a strong sense of loss, loss of time. I lost so much time for studying during the cultural revolution that I feel I have to make up for it even in my thirties. If I had used the time for rehearsals to read I might have gotten more.

That's a waste of not only my time but also my teachers' and class-mates' time and efforts. In China, time is often wasted everywhere by the blind guidance. Unfortunately, in this instance, I am a victim.

Sieg looks up after his turn reading the paper. "And we thought they didn't mind!"

I touch Mrs. Ching's sprig of winter plum, in water now and opening its buds slightly within the room's shelter.

"Endurance," I mutter.

"What did you say?"

"Nothing. Just my own winter thoughts."

28 . Setbacks

When I first walk into class at 7:30 Friday morning, the room is cold and dark. I flip the wall switch. No response. I punch it off.

"We'll have to be our own lights," I tell Mr. Lao Sheng, who is always early.

He glances out at the hall lights. They are on. He steps over to the switch, punches it once, just as I did, except he waits. Sure enough, each long fluorescent tube flickers into bloom.

He smiles at me indulgently. "In China, you must be patient."

I guess we must. After class, we make two unsettling discoveries. The students are all a-buzz over a paper fresh from the Foreign Languages Office. It's the Hehai graduate students' newspaper, and Miss An Ran has a translation in it. She is too modest to mention it, but her classmates praise her accomplishment.

"What has she translated?" Sieg asks.

"Part of the article by Pirsig from the text," they explain.

We can't read the Chinese, but further questions reveal that nowhere in her translation does the original source, *Zen and the Art of Motorcycle Maintenance,* or the author's name appear. This is wholly consistent with Chinese publishing practices. In one magazine after another, works appear translated word for word, without crediting original sources.

Miss An, who is a very conscientious student, seems surprised at our strong protests. She hasn't yet connected what we've been modeling in our handouts or what we've been stressing about the need for acknowledgments in their frequent speeches with her "publishing" behavior outside the classroom.

Like sins of omission and commission, the arts of teaching and learning necessarily involve as much what you don't do as what you do. This semester is nearly over. Next semester, we must make renewed and stricter demands.

Before the morning ends, Mr. Chen Pingnan, the lecturer who occasionally comes as a working auditor to writing class, delivers what we at first think is a joke. He wants a grade and three hours' credit. In fact, he expects it.

"No joke," he assures us.

Although we have been responding to his papers, we thought out of courtesy to a colleague, this is the first we've heard of his expectations. If we'd known, it would have changed some of our responses from acceptance into more direct guidance, and we would have insisted that he attend class regularly.

Sieg tells him we need to think about this request.

I hear again Mr. Lao Sheng's words to me when the morning began. "In China . . . patience." Especially when confronted by surprise after surprise that grows out of too much noncommunication.

Over lunch on the coffee table, I look at the expensive blue vase Mr. Chen gave us for Christmas. At the time, we assumed it was an expression of appreciation. Was it intended in return for a favor, a bribe bestowed in advance?

29 · Painting through Student Eyes

Midweek, we schedule a field trip to the Jiangsu Provincial Art Museum. Most students say they've never been there. We feel it's essential to keep opening their eyes to possibilities in their own communities, to join them with worlds they haven't yet glimpsed.

We gather at the bus stop. Not everyone is here. Several, they tell us, are traveling by bicycle. We're taking not the route we know but an alternate they suggest.

"This one is better, shorter," Mr. Lüe says.

So we are in their hands in a pleasant, mutual exchange. Serene in their grasp of local language and terrain, they guide us. Rich in *renminbi,* we give Mr. Lüe, as class monitor, money to pay for bus transportation and museum entrance fees. By stuffing ourselves into the already crowded aisle, miraculously the fifteen of us are able to squeeze onto one bus. Students insist we take a vacated seat. As other seats empty, women students pile two deep into spaces meant for one.

A holiday mood pervades the group, even though their gloved hands grip notebooks ready to prepare for their next assigned writing. We've asked them during their visit to choose one painting they react to strongly, for whatever reason, describe the painting so any reader or listener can identify it, and comment on why they chose this one.

Inside the museum, a cold, three-story, poorly lighted but spacious building hung thickly with old and new works, the students at first cluster around us as if needing protection in a foreign environment. They want to know English words for depicted objects. We ask them to explain details we don't recognize.

Mr. Fan stops before a huge painting of birds. "This artist is very famous for painting eagles!" he says with excitement.

"And this one for horses! See? It is done by Xu Beihong!" Miss Zhuang pauses to admire a nearby painting of a stallion, its head lifted, alert.

Gradually, they fan out, absorbing colors, subjects, techniques, exclaiming over scenes familiar in their own provinces, exploring every floor. They take turns standing in a flood of sunshine in a windowed landing upstairs to warm up, then hurry back into the chill to take precise notes before their chosen canvas.

They're on their own now, lingering as long as they wish. Women guards have relaxed, seeing these visitors aren't touching the artwork or the row of miniature bonsai gardens set on temporary teak stands in the entrance hall.

Some students leave.

"I want to return here again," Mr. Zuo says.

"I have errands to do!" Her "class" duties done for the morning, Miss Li heads for the department stores in the Xinjiekou, Nanjing's main shopping center.

Several days later, when their museum visit papers come in, we're eager to see which painting each student chose.

Miss Bin Qilin calls her essay "Quietness."

> I seldom go to an art gallery, for I think I have no cells of artistic appreciation and can't enjoy the beauty of paintings. Yet this time I got enjoyment from a painting when I went to Jiangsu Art Gallery. It's a painting named "Village By Seaside," representing a small village surrounded by water with boats on it. I am attracted by the village's quietness. The quietness of the boats, the houses and the water reminds me of the quietness of summer evenings in my hometown.
>
> My hometown is as small as the village in the painting. It has many riv-

ers around it. When the evening falls in summer, people enjoy its beautiful quietness.

At my younger age, I used to go to river with my elder sister to wash clothes in the summer evening. Walking on a springy muddy path, while the wind breezed against my face, I felt as fresh and clean as the morning air. Houses were dim in the dust. It was quiet and hazy all around.

The river flowed quietly. It was smooth and soft. Little waves rippled against the bank lightly in harmony with the rhythm of the swaying willow branches. I couldn't see the waves or the branches, but I heard them whispering to each other.

I looked forward to see where the water flowed, but I found the water merged with the dark sky in the end. I couldn't make out where was the water and where was the sky.

Several small boats were in the distance, and singing could be heard faintly. The boats had lights like stars in the river. There were still many bright yellow beams flickering in the dark water, made by houses' lights nearby. The shiny moon hung in the sky. It sprayed its silver moonlight quietly. The water gleamed in the moonlight. A scent of quietness and mystery in the earth.

All these made a dim and quiet beauty of the night river. At this time I always got crazy and wanted to be with the water, the moon, and the light.

I am a silent girl and like quietness. I think quietness is fascinating and dim is mysterious. Certainly I also like red flowers, singing birds, these happy symbols. Yet I don't think their happiness belongs to me. Only the quietness, the quiet beauty can I enjoy, can I get.

It is the first time that I really get enjoyment from a painting.

We turn eagerly to the next paper. Will Mr. Zuo Niannian's be as simply revealing as Miss Bin's? Mr. Zuo calls his "Reflections of Appreciating the Paintings."

The traditional Chinese Paintings in the museum brought me to the life in the countryside. All I saw in the paintings were flowers, rivers, animals and mountains. I can't find a single car, a modern building and crowded people. I like the paintings. They evoked my memories of the past and my dream for the future's life.

I was city born and city bred. I only went to the country once. That was the year 1971. I was a middle school pupil. I didn't know many things. I was very young. I just found everything in the village was fresh.

We could shout in the vast fields, run on the path between two furrows, watch the buffalos swimming in the ponds and gaze at the stroke of cooking smoke rising from the farmers' houses. We could smell the odour of animal dung in the air and hear the bleat of sheep and cluck-cackle of hens. That was a quiet and a wide world, a world of a strange smell.

I couldn't help laughing when we ate there. Everyday we just had the same dish: the vine of sweet potato. In the city, that kind of thing was thrown to the pigs. At every meal, six or seven of us had one bowl of it and wolfed down the rice with it and were satisfied, because we were hungry after several hours' work in the cotton fields.

One of my favorite paintings is the "Sleeping Lotus and Golden Fish," painted by Xie Haiyan. In it, several lotuses are swinging, flowers are blooming, and in the clear water, golden fish are cruising. I recalled a prose by Prof. Zhu Zhiqing: "Moonlight Over the Lotus Pond." That's a wonderful place to go. Only too few in our city!

How I'd like to have such a place to rest after I'm tired of the noises of the cars in the streets, the sounds of TV from neighboring homes, and the smoke from the tall chimneys of factories. And in the night of suffocating summer, the cool and refreshing air carries away my sweat, the faint scent of flowers makes me intoxicating, and the peep of crickets, the croak of frogs compose the pleasant music. I'd just want to stay there and never want to move a step!

At this point, we aren't stopping to make corrections. We're too hungry for what they have to say.

Mr. Mao Yanyang begins, "I stood before the picture of the war horse and tried to see something in it without caring who the painter was."

In his long essay, Mr. Mao sees Xu Beihong's work and confirms with surprise that he does have some artistic judgment, because this painter is considered China's finest interpreter of horses. Mr. Mao continues:

I could imagine that the horse had been eating grass on the hillside and for a moment he thought of something and stopped eating, and raised his head.

But what was he thinking about? The first line of the poem which served as the title of the picture gave me the answer. It said: the war-horse recalling the past battles. Perhaps this was an old horse. For some reason he had retired from the war and was awarded a peaceful life for his great contributions to spend his last years.

Perhaps there was no war any more. He just strolled to this place which was perhaps the previous battlefield. But whatever it was, we may see that the horse couldn't endure this loneliness. He couldn't stand having nothing to do. With pride, excitement, but quiet sadness, he only thought of his past experience in the war.

What a hero he had been! What pride to his rider! What a dreadful enemy to all his own antagonists! Now all his glory had passed. What he could do was only eating, strolling, and thinking. How he wanted to re-live the past restless and severe life!

My imagination changed him from a mere horse to an old soldier, to several soldiers and generals, who felt, with one accord, a sense of loss, who couldn't get along with the present simple, easy life. When would the time come again for them to find their own values which had been lost? Where could they find them? And they hadn't forgotten that their time was getting shorter.

"He's got decades before he comes to that realization firsthand!" I add Mr. Mao's perceptive paper to the already-read-once stack.

Several writers relate what they say to current political ideas and ideals. Mr. Chen Pingnan, who didn't go with us to the museum but substituted writing about a separate trip to the Nanjing Historical Museum, concludes his account:

I was greatly moved by the revolutionary heros and their deeds after this visit. The exhibition told us one truth: revolution is the tendency of the development of China; the Communist Party is the guarantee of the socialist revolution and socialist construction.

Miss Chen Hong, writing about the painting "Thousands of Boats Full of Fish," ends her paper:

Looking at it, I could not help thinking about the kind of life the fisher-men led in the old days. They had no warm clothes, no well-equipped boats, and they had no food. And many died while fishing. But now under the new policy of our party they lead a happy life. They have enough money to buy TV, modern furniture, and even motor. They needn't worry about their life any more, no worry about clothing. They also made a great contribution to our country. They export the fish to foreign countries to help our country to earn more foreign currency to quicken the steps of building our country.

Although I couldn't see the fishermen in the picture, I was sure they were smiling from their deep hearts. I hope the smiles will never disappear on their faces.

Sieg reaches for yesterday's *China Daily*. "Listen to this article by Fu Houpu about the new look of China." Skipping, he reads aloud:

Gong Jianhua, 33, amateur photographer whose pictures are winning prizes at the First Shanghai International Photographic Art Exhibition, was in a western suburb of Shanghai. He saw several farmers sitting on a walking tractor and laughing happily. An old farmer was holding a pile of newly bought fine porcelain bowls with floral borders. . . . "The pile of fine china bowls shows that the living standard of the Chinese farmers is improving. Not long ago the farmers only used crudely made big bowls," Gong said. The photo, entitled, "The Happiness of Today's Farmers," won him a silver medal in a photo competition sponsored by *Shooting Pictorial*.

Sieg looks up. "It sounds as if Miss Chen could write copy for *China Daily!*"

"Look at the ending on Mr. Xue's paper." I hand him Mr. Xue Hai's description of a "Herd-Cow-Picture."

I like the happy life of rural areas. I hope that the Chinese people can lead a happy, sweet life like that cow boy in the painting in the coming years with the realization of the four modernizations. And I also truly hope the disasters like the Great Cultural Revolution will not come again!

"This one has a different tone." Sieg passes me Mr. Ku Qiu's essay:

It is absolutely right that art is the king of the world. It comes from life but it surpasses life. It not only reflects life vividly, but gives people boundless imagination and enjoyment.

This week our class visited the Art Museum of Jiangsu Province. The museum contains a vast field of beautiful and valuable paintings. Of all, what attracted me most is the work "Looking After a Buffalo" by Yan Jin, a very famous painter in the Qing Dynasty. It stays fresh in my mind.

On the painting I saw a buffalo, a cowboy with a flute, some trees on a hill, some birds in the sky, a river on the left.

As soon as the picture came into my eyes, my imagination arose. In the fresh air of a spring morning, a cowboy is sitting on the back of a buffalo looking after it. Pleasant tunes are coming from the flute. The breeze brings the tunes across the river and accompanies it far, far away. The river is murmuring cheerfully. The birds are singing sweetly. The buffalo is mooing sonorously. All of this forms a harmonious symphony. The grass is green. The trees are in blossom. The dew drops on the grass, flowers and leaves of the trees are shining like pearls in the sun. This brings people to paradise.

The cowboy is me. The buffalo is mine. I'm playing the flute. I'm smelling the fragrant flowers. . . . All of this happens to me. I'm the king of nature. I'm even more happier than a skylark. What a dramatically wonderful life I'm enjoying!

"Mr. Ku, we should be off now," came the voice of one of my classmates. I came back to myself. I had been lost in imagination and enjoyment!

Refreshed, I look up from Mr. Ku's paper. "I'm so glad we went! Do you think they'll go back again by themselves?"

"Perhaps," Sieg says.

30 . Into the Book of My Memory

We keep trying to introduce our students to more short examples of contemporary Western literature. A short selection fits neatly into one period for reading, understanding, and discussing. If modern, it lifts the class out of their deep immersion in traditional forms. If Western, it brings fresh appeal, penetrating those censoring walls that China's decades of isolation have built and maintained.

For all these reasons, last week we brought Donald Hall's poem "Ox Cart Man" to class. As usual, Sieg read the poem aloud once, while several voices muttered the words immediately after he spoke them. He's gotten used to this delayed antiphony. It's a kind of zigzag chorus that satisfies the students' hunger to improve their own pronunciation before they too read it aloud.

"Ox Cart Man" reminded Miss Zhuang Zi of a Tang dynasty poem by Du Fu about a charcoal seller. The class warmed to Hall's poem. "It tells about simple life in country," they said, "about the joy in harvesting."

This week, we bring in Gary Snyder's evocative "Plum petals falling. . . ." It has just twenty-three simple words.

We get the students to draw on paper their interpretations of the physical details or implications in the poem in order to understand it fully. At first they think this is a very odd way to approach a poem. Much hilarity. Some panic.

"I can't draw!" several protest.

"It doesn't matter," I say. "Just use stick figures. Put in any details you find."

They struggle over figures, over perspective. In disgust they erase, but the room quiets as they push their minds and pencils to interpret. After ten minutes, I call time. They stand their pictures along the chalk tray for a show.

Eagerly, they examine each other's very different interpretations. Everyone has included Snyder's landlady who, at poem's end, "comes out in the twilight / and beats a rug." Some put the rug on a line, some underfoot. Most students seat only one drinker at the table "in the garden." Others put two companions sharing a bottle. Miss Liu Jie makes the landlady the drinker. Mr. Xue Hai gives his seated man a cigar and puts a light outside his home to signal twilight.

Nearly all have carefully sketched in house and garden details, the falling plum petals, the "hard buds" on the cherry. Miss Chen Hong has added wind as the cause of petals falling. Mr. Li Jian's picture includes a dog, Miss Feng's a pig in the garden, although Snyder mentions neither in the poem. That's all right. A good poem can always carry its readers' freight.

Miss Lü Shu consulted her dictionary to get the cherry bud and leaf authentic. Miss An Ran, who in the art museum trip exulted over a large eagle painting for its "strong masculinity," has drawn her tree with vigorous roots and made her house behind the garden of sturdy brick, topped with a tile roof.

The students are delighted with their "show." Mr. Lüe Shi, ever the entrepreneur, says, "We should sell tickets!"

For our next writing class, the group brings in their own poems on any topic they wish. Because our first class assignment in poetry writing (not documented in this book) produced so much forced rhyme and wrenched nineteenth-century word order, this time we've asked them once again to avoid rhyme completely and to express their ideas the way they might speak them.

They read their poems aloud. There's many a buzz of appreciation. Later, we reread the copies they hand us, eager to see more clearly what was on their minds.

As these few unedited examples prove, plenty!

A DREAM

It has been one year
that we had to part.
At first I couldn't bear,
gradually I got used to the life without you.
Last night, I dreamed
you coming towards me with a smile.
I stretched my arms
to hold your hands,
but only touched the cold wall.
I woke up and you disappeared.
Did I miss the past unconsciously
or did the dream tell something about the future?
I wonder what hint
the dream gives to me.
    —*Liu Jie*

ZHONGSHAN LAKE AFTER SUMMER SHOWER

Gone the summer shower.
In Zhongshan Lake
a rainbow drinks water.
Densely grown lotuses
reluctantly give way to boats
that carry young ladies
picking seedpods of the lotuses,
but can't hold up laughter and songs
that fly out of the ladies.
Wild geese in the sky
glide down and tell the ducks
bathing in the lake:
"It is the ladies' sweet laughter and songs
that make smiles dance on the sun's face."
    —*Ku Qiu*

YANGTZE AT MIDAFTERNOON

Along the great trunk-like pumping pipe,
I came to the bank of the Yangtze River,
With a companion, my dear friend,
In the mid-afternoon sun light.

Standing at the end of the pipe,
Where it joined the water,
I looked passionately at my friend,
And pointed to the flowing direction of the River.

Great white ships loaded with cargoes
And ships of passengers moved
Up and down in the busy water
Like seagulls diving half-way in the River.

Fishing boats, back to the harbor, were full of prey.
The scales of the fish reflected the sunshine,
Giving off light from all directions
Like gigantic pieces of diamonds ornamented on the boats.

Fishermen chattered joyfully on the boats,
Forgetting the tiredness of a day's hard work.
Then I was intoxicated with their happiness of harvest,
and fancied their bright future.
 —Li Jian

WHERE IS THE FLOWER?

She didn't come tonight.
I don't know why.

The full moon in the sky
Reminds me of her charming smile.

Pairs of lovers go by.
It is the Mid-Autumn night.

The waves lap the bank.
They seem to me low cries.
 —Zuo Niannian

  Into the Book of My Memory

[Untitled]

The train started out.
The crowds left,
The clamour just now, suddenly
    Quiet, silent and dark.
The lights were gone one after another.
The station seemed to die in one minute,
Now a body without life,
Weighing the parents with its overwhelming force
Who still looked after the train with their son
    In the cold.
The platform is long.
Yet not long enough to lead their feeling.
The world is large,
Yet why can't it spare them a peaceful land?
    —*Bin Qilin*

LIFE

What is life?
You may doubt yourself.
Life is what you make.
You can make it easy.
You can make it hard;
You can make it enjoyful,
You can make it dreadful;
You can make it failure,
You can make it success.
So never complain of life itself,
Just check your efforts to life.
    —*Fan Rui*

SUMMER IS COMING

Summer is coming.
The wind is blowing.
It reddens the cherry
and greens the banana.

A young lady, as fresh as cherry,
walks home as light as a breeze
with a basket full of cherries
which she will sell or share
with her sisters and brother.
    —*An Ran*

ONE NIGHT IN WINTER

A crescent moon is in the sky.
It is cold and quiet.
Nobody is in the room
except me, at the desk,
doing some reading.

The word "warm" appears on the book.
The face of my mum occurs on my mind.
My mother is smiling to me.
I can no longer concentrate on the reading.
    —*Chun Xu*

TO MY FRIEND

If you were the front cover of a book,
    charming and pleasing,
I would be the back cover of it,
    natural and profound.

In the middle of the pages,
    all our stories;
    worries, joys,
    hopes, and chase.

We close together intimately,
Attractive, the story-book appears.
Once we are separated,
Lower, the price of it may be.
    —*Zhuang Zi*

SNOW

"What a beautiful snow!"
I can't help crying out.
Everything is standing in front of me,
Trees, fences, bushes, electric poles . . .
All at a sudden with white cloaks.

A row of young trees along the road
With the leaves, half-green, half-yellow,
Have been frozen into bouquets of crystal flowers
As Winter Grandpa's first gift to me
In the fresh and frosted morning.

Road coated with thin ice
Is playing a trick on a coward.
When I walk on it firmly,
The cracking of ice sounds musical.
The snow morning belongs to the brave.

Biting a baked sweet potato
picked up from a hot oven
I breathe out a long stream of vapour
That makes passers-by mouths watering
And brings me comfortable warmth.

In the first snow of this year,
I'm deeply touched by its beauty,
its colour, and its quiet.
I pick these up like leaves
And put them into the book of my memory.
   —*Lao Sheng*

THE MOON

"The moon follows me," you said.
"With me moves the moon," I insisted
when children.
So far away we ran in opposite directions,
and so long we quarrelled.

Now, old as we are,
under the moonlight, walking hand in hand,
clearly we find
following us is the moon.
  —*Li Yanping*

MY AUNT'S FACE

Wrinkles
Like tier upon tier of terraced fields,
Like a poem, too
Are graved on my aunt's face.
Wrinkles
Have written down the history of my hometown.
Wrinkles
Are full of the misery of the past.
Today
Smiles swim on her face.
Her face radiates the happiness of old age.
Her deep sight
Like limpid stream water
Flowing in my heart
Condenses her expectation of me.
  —*Chen Pingnan*

31 . Winding Down

January's calendar warns us we are moving quickly toward semester cut-off. New reminders surface every day.

With final classes meeting this week, the students are edgy. They've asked for each of our exams to begin at 7:30 in the morning ("so we can start studying for the next!"), but Monitor Lüe keeps informing us of changing schedules. No one knows yet what's happening just one week away.

Saturday morning, while Sieg is at the Foreign Languages Office trying to organize the miniature library kept sealed in a usually locked office behind locked, glassed-in bookcases, Mr. Fan Rui appears at the apartment door to turn in a delayed assignment.

I invite him in for a visit.

At 10:00 A.M., he has just had breakfast. He looks rested. With a glance at our blank, silent TV, he tells me about a current TV serial he likes to watch. "It is called 'Snow City.' It gives the story of young couples who come back from the countryside to make difficult way in the city." Mr. Fan watches TV whenever possible, enjoying a range of programs "including music."

"Do you play an instrument?"

"No. I'd like to study music from the beginning. I never had the chance when I was young."

We discuss types of middle schools. Only the best schools for the brightest students have music in their curriculums, he says. Mr. Fan didn't qualify for one of those schools.

I tell him about a recent evening drop-in visit when Mr. Zuo brought a friend to demonstrate playing the *erhu*, a traditional Chinese instrument. "I think he was self-taught," I add.

Mr. Fan cracks his knuckles. "Most young people think the *erhu* is old-fashioned. We want to play guitar."

Sieg comes in. He carries several books, including a brand new 1984 *Webster's Ninth New Collegiate Dictionary,* still sealed in its original plastic.

"I've been on my knees for an hour in that cold office," Sieg reports. "Good news! The departmental library is now organized by author. There are quite a few books we can use next semester."

In delight, I hug the thick dictionary. Small transportable paperbacks are all right, but for more technical terms, etymologies, Scrabble confirmations—

Mr. Fan laughs at my enthusiasm. "What time is it?"

"Eleven o'clock."

He gets up to leave. "I must go to lunch now."

"You just ate breakfast at ten o'clock!" I remind him.

"Perhaps I will eat a *little* lunch."

On the way out, he runs into Mr. Mao Yanyang, who stops just long enough to drop off his required revision of an earlier essay. It's nice when papers come in one or two at a time.

We turn to Mr. Mao's essay with curiosity and interest. Earlier in the semester, for the change-of-attitude essay, he wrote a long, rambling account of his experiences harvesting sweet potatoes in the countryside. His paper now reads:

UNFORGETTABLE YEARS

I have a bad digestive system, which is the result of having to eat too many sweet potatoes during my teenage period. At that time, I was a regular visitor to my grandma.

She lived in a village on the barren land on which nothing could grow except sweet potatoes. It was there that I experienced the life which still remains in my memory today.

I can clearly and exactly form in my mind the scene where all the villagers toiled on the field, digging potatoes out. The sun was about to set. A bloody ray hung over the field. Each face was red and sweaty. So many people, men and women, old and young, boys and girls, spades or pickaxes in hands. They struggled to reap their only valuable harvest—sweet potatoes.

In my family we had only two labourers, my aunt and I. My aunt, in the front, got the potatoes out. I, after her, piled them up. The work was boring. I managed to find some pleasure in this by now and then stopping work to look around at others, to listen to others. This man had just injured his feet by the pickaxe. That woman was cursing her potatoes too small. This baby was crying screamingly for nobody looked after him. That couple were quarreling as to who had done more than the other.

But I dare not stop for long. My aunt would abuse me as a lazy boy. She seemed never tired. All went so quickly, so naturally. When she dug all the potatoes out and was sure there was not a single one left beneath the earth, she, like the others, began the second step.

She cut the potatoes into small and thin cakes so that when they got dry under the sun it would be easier to store and make into powder. I arranged the cakes one by one on the field.

When all of these were done, it was entirely dark and the cool wind in the autumn began blowing. When I was on the way back I used to turn back to observe that land on which I had worked so hard. There in the distance, the land had become a stretch of whiteness. It seemed a special snow had fallen on the land, but it seemed more to me, to my young mind, that a crowd of people were standing on that deadly field, wearing the mourning dress. It was a horrible scene. I quicked my steps. It made me think of death, of ghosts in this cold night.

I had that kind of life for a few autumns. Although it was boring and made me constantly say to myself, "I'll never come back next year," yet the next year saw me again as one of the working people.

Today it has a mixed effect on me. The thought of it makes me happy—my proud hard-working experience—and yet sorry—my hardships and the peasants' miserable conditions. Sweet potatoes, their only satisfaction!

Sieg puts down Mr. Mao's paper. "Makes canteen rice with vegetables and pork seem like a banquet, doesn't it?"

"Yes," I say with renewed appetite—which doesn't hold up, however, when I confront the reality.

32 . Properties

No more classes for this semester! The students are "free"—to study tensely for exams, scheduled at last. We are "free"—to read and reread the four papers apiece they've judged their best, to begin the written summary ratings of each student that Mr. Guo has requested, to await those heaps of final exams in writing, reading, and vocabulary. Speech, bless the medium, leaves only notes to scan. We are also free to enter that agonizing fray of judgment-passing known as grades.

Wednesday morning, the day of the writing exam, my eyes open to a different sound. Like a rooster, there's a tenor on the loose outdoors. It's still dark. From his hillside opposite, the unseen singer salutes the distant dawn with slow arpeggios, long sustained notes, and a few abrupt bellows, as if he were inspiring troops into battle. I'd be disgusted with this form of early alarm clock if he didn't have such a beautiful voice.

It's cold and damp in the classroom. Students brace against more than physical discomforts, however. Without taking off their gloves, hunching in their coats and wool hats, they attack the dreaded exam question. It's based on an essay we have previously read and discussed at length in class:

> Apply your own thinking to E. M. Forster's essay "My Wood." What is your attitude toward property? Show how it is similar or different from Forster's. (You may use open books and dictionaries.)

Mr. Ku Qiu finishes first. He hands in his essay with a confident smile twenty minutes before the second period is over and hurries out to warm up.

Miss Bin Qilin is last. She is distressed just short of tears because she first misread the question. Failing to include her personal view, she started over once she discovered the mistake, but hasn't finished her rewrite. It's past time. Another class presses to enter the room. We have to pick up her exam.

"But I haven't finished," she wails.

"Give us both papers," we say. "We'll look at both versions as best we can."

After lunch, as we read their exams, we try to keep fresh in our minds Forster's brief essay from *Abinger Harvest*. In it, the British author analyzes with self-critical humor the negative effects of property on his own character. When he bought a small piece of wooded land, thanks to book royalties, he found his new acquisition made him feel "heavy . . . endlessly avaricious, pseudo-creative, intensely selfish." And how have the students responded to his ideas? Mr. Xue Hai writes:

> According to the view of "My Wood," written by E. M. Forster, "property makes one feel heavy." I agree with his view from my personal experience.
>
> I used to have a silver-gilt lock which was an heirloom of my family. It was made in Qing dynasty. It looked beautiful, elegant, and shiny. On its surface, there was a pair of carved dragons, which showed the cherished hope of my parents.
>
> My silver-gilt lock had been with me for nine years since I was born in 1957. There was a Chinese superstition that a newly-born child should be put on a "lock," usually made of silver, called a "longevity lock."
>
> The second day after I was born, my mother put this heirloom around my neck. I still wore this lock at the age of five, when I went out to play games with the other children. Sometimes neighbors, even passers-by, often stood before me and stared at my silver-gilt lock. I knew they were

very envious of my heirloom. Someone even wanted to buy my lock with three hundred yuan.

When I came back home, I told my parents all about this. My parents nodded and said, "Yes, it is valuable, but you are more valuable than this lock."

So I set a high value on my precious lock, but I began to feel it heavy, when I put it on my neck, because it was an heirloom of my family. At that time, I often put it inside my coat in order for it not to be lost and stolen. I held it tightly with my delicate hands whenever I went to bed.

One day, an old jeweller came to our home and consulted with my mother for the price of my silver-gilt lock. He wanted to buy it with one thousand yuan. Both my mother and I refused it. But he did not go and further rose its price. At this, I was very angry and drove him out of our home with a broken mop-stick.

After he was away, I took out my lock again from my drawer and kissed it continuously. It became even heavier than before when I put it on my neck.

I dared not wear it when I went out to play games with the other children. Even during the playing time, I often came back home and saw whether it was still in my drawer or not. When my mother saw my flustered look, she often said, "You are a crazy boy. Wear your lock and never put it off!"

It was a great pity when the apocalyptic visitation of the mysterious Cultural Revolution broke out in 1966. A group of cruel red guards searched our house and confiscated my silver-gilt lock. I lost my precious lock forever.

Having read "My Wood," I understand fully Forster's view. "Property makes one feel heavy." But I still long for my lock very much even though it made me feel heavy. Sometimes, I even cry out in my dream, "Where is my lock? I miss you very much. Can you come back again on my neck?"

Mrs. Ching Chao has no such second thoughts about property. She writes:

E. M. Forster says that when people own property they will become "endlessly avaricious" and "intensely selfish." I agree with his point of view about property ownership.

As a matter of fact, I have had such an experience.

Two years ago, I got married. My father-in-law gave me a set of furniture which was the first property I had owned. The furniture looked bright and modern. It did make my house appear new and splendid. At that time I felt happy and satisfied. Gradually, I didn't like the furniture as I used to do. I started to find fault with it. I thought the colour wasn't beautiful and I should have more pieces of furniture than just six pieces. So I wanted to get rid of this set of furniture and buy a set of new furniture which has 12 pieces. Nevertheless I wasn't rich enough to afford a new one. This worried me a great deal. My furniture made me endlessly avaricious.

Secondly, owning a property made me feel intensely selfish.

When I got married my mother sent me a dowry. They were beautiful sheets, embroidered quilt covers and some comfortable quilts. I liked them very much, not only because they were nice and expensive, but also because they had become my own property. I didn't want to share them with others. Yet, a lot of relatives and friends liked to visit us. Sometimes I must provide lodgings for them. When I had to let them use my new sheets and quilts, my unwillingness to do it made me feel so unhappy and anguished that I sometimes wanted them to leave my house. It's true owning a property did make me intensely selfish.

Dante says, "Possession is one with loss." In my case, after I own a property, such as furniture, comfortable quilts, I become endlessly avaricious and intensely selfish. In the same time, I lost the good quality of generosity and selflessness.

Not every student agrees so strongly with Forster. Mr. Zuo Niannian writes:

Ten years ago, I bought a "Forever" bike and that became one of my properties. Before that, I often envied some young men who rode their bikes, sitting erectly on them, jingling the small bells all the way, fast and quick, making other people's eyes follow them.

Now, I was glad that I had my own bike. Compared with E. M. Forster, I can visit many places with it, like lightning, while he felt heavy and had to refuse some invitations because of his wood.

I can't forget the day my wife and I rode to East Lake in Wuhan. We brought our food with us, appreciated the sceneries around the lake and took many pictures. We spent a whole day doing this. We were satisfied when we came back although a little tired.

I agree with E. M. Forster in that my bike sometimes brought me vexations. My mother often urged me at table to ride slowly and pay attention to the traffic. I thought I already rode very slowly, unlike other young men who rode like a hurricane. With this in my mind, I argued with her, and sometimes it made us have no appetite. Really, I rode with great patience in the rush hour, waiting for the buses and pedestrians to pass. I had much work ahead for me to do and I couldn't waste my time. So I had vexation, too, at that time.

E. M. Forster could taste his blackberries and he wanted to have his woods to himself, not shared with others. I am different from him in this respect. It is convenient to have a bike. I can load on it rice, liquefied gas pot, and needn't carry them on my back. And I could take my son to the near hospital with it if he were ill. Some of my friends or colleagues have no bikes. I am willing to lend it to them if they need it. And in return, I can ask them to do me a favor.

However, I need to do something for my bike. That is, I must take care of it. I must find a shelter for it, for fear that rains will rust it. I must see to it that it is locked well, for fear a thief might steal it away. And I often have to keep the dust and mud away from it, and put lubricant or grease on it. In short, I feel I ought to do something to it, just like E. M. Forster, to his wood.

Anyway, the "Forever" has been a "friend" of mine for ten years. I like it. I can't do without it. Now, it is rather old. Perhaps I'll get a new one. And I dream one day I can ride it around the world! My bike has brought me more happiness and convenience than trouble or vexation. So I can say, I am happier than E. M. Forster when it comes to property.

One writer waxes philosophical in part of his essay:

All readers should know the contemporary world is not the ideal communist society. Perhaps under the communist system, there is no use for personal ownership because materials to be produced in that society largely surpass the needs of all of the people. But the trouble is that our contemporary world is not what the communist system describes. So personal ownership will and must prevail a rather long time to make its own contribution to our society, but not make you feel so heavy.

Sieg holds out Mr. Mao Yanyang's paper. "Here's another that disagrees with Forster."

Mr. Mao writes:

Having read Forster's essay about property ownership, I began to find out my feelings towards my private property, a pair of glasses. To tell the truth, I have never realized that I have so many feelings toward this simple pair of glasses until after reading his article.

First, my glasses make me feel that they should be closely protected and watched and never should be stolen or lost or damaged. You can hardly imagine how reluctant I was when I handed to that shop girl 48 Yuan—a large sum of money to me at a time when I had to depend on my parents for financial support.

The same reluctance happened to me when others wanted to look at them and put them on even for a while, for fear that they might carelessly damage my glasses or take them away out of envy.

I always store them in a small bag, and take them out and dust them at least three times a day. I never wear them in class. Too much chalk powder may make them dirty, even when I can't see the blackboard clearly sitting in the back rows. I never wear them on the bus; the crowding people may squeeze them. The only time I ever wear my glasses is when I sit in a cinema because I feel safe there, and they are necessary.

Secondly, unlike Forster who wanted his property to be larger, I don't want my glasses to be more beautiful. The more beautiful they are, the more expensive, the more I should always be on alert. For me they are beautiful enough. I don't want to exchange them with any conceivable kind.

Thirdly, they bring me some satisfaction of vanity.

Among my former classmates I was the only one who bought so dear a pair of glasses. Because of others' admiring eyes, I felt proud. I was "rich." When I went home with my glasses on and a suit of elegant clothes, I seemed to sense others were looking at me and saying, "Look at that handsome boy with a pair of golden glasses. He has just graduated from college and now has become a postgraduate. Oh! What a boy!"

In other public places I put on my glasses and also put on airs, being knowledgeable, being a gentleman. Once I was on a train and was reading a novel in French in spite of understanding only a little. The surrounding people were farmers and workers. Some female students showed me their admiration. Later they became more admiring when they paid much attention in listening to me talk about foreign language and foreign countries. Perhaps I owe a large part of this proud experience to my glasses. They are my mask. They hide my innocence, my naughtiness, and make me look learned and mature.

My glasses don't make me feel the way Forster does about his woods. I just love them more than anything else. But they have become something beyond practical use. They can give me lots of spiritual joys.

So what is property? I think it is something you can enjoy both practically and spiritually. Forster's is not property. Mine is real property.

"And yours is a gift for honest writing!" I look over at Sieg. We've both finished our first rough reading of all the papers.

"They weren't writing like this at the beginning of the semester!" He taps the pile in front of him. "They're no longer afraid to use the word 'I.' "

"Or ashamed to admit to very human thoughts. Bless teachers like E. M. Forster!"

33 . On the Eve of Departure

You can tell it's warming up.

Spit gobs no longer freeze on the streets. The heat cycle of the air conditioner/heater sealed into our living room window, which refuses to operate on frigid days when we need it most, blows warm again. At night, a wild tomcat, regular visitor to garbage heaps outside our canteen kitchen, yowls amorously under the window.

Monday, when students take their reading exam, they write with gloves off! Spring is on the way.

Dan Younkin comes to our door with a dilemma. He is so upset he forgets to eat the tea and cookies we put beside him. He has received a formal inquiry from a young woman in his secretarial class, a go-between, who wants to know if he, the teacher, would be interested in marrying her friend, a student in the same class. It is a serious request. Other young Western bachelor teachers get such proposals. The willing fiancée is due for a private, individual language evaluation with Dan in the Guest House common room tomorrow morning.

"What shall I do?" Dan implores. "I can't afford even the appearance of being alone with her now!"

Sieg suggests he write a letter of tactful but firm refusal—providing he's so minded—and keep a carbon copy.

"If you want," I offer, "I'll sit in on your evaluation session. I could come for several students, so my presence won't look pointed just at her. I'd be interested to hear how you test your students' fluency anyhow."

Relieved, Dan accepts my offer. He dashes to his room to type the letter.

Sieg chuckles. "I'm glad I'm not young."

"Or single. See how much trouble I save you?"

Sieg has a date with Mr. Lao Sheng to look over English reading possibilities for next semester in the main campus library. We can't believe there is as little to find as our own previous searches suggest. Maybe, with a native Chinese speaker along to translate, Sieg can locate more resources.

On return from the library, he reports: "It's almost as bad as we thought. There's no Graham Greene. No Faulkner. They do have Hemingway's *A Farewell to Arms*."

"Is it true the catalog listing is only by title?"

"That's right. One librarian showed us a separate room, curtained off from student access, where the books are catalogued by author. But not even post-graduates can use that room. Mr. Lao talked to her, explained our need. She finally agreed to let a designated class representative come and look for what people want."

"But how do they know what they want until they look? And the stacks are closed except for library staff!"

"They'll just have to search for whatever's out on the reference shelves." Sieg sighs. "At least the encyclopedias there are fairly new. The *Britannica* is 1982. That will be some help."

Mr. Xue Hai appears at the door. Like his classmates, he's all a-hop to get home. Now that the last exam is over, students from distant places are scattering by train, beginning today, for their month's break from classes over the Chinese New Year. Mr. Xue is well padded for the long trip north to see his wife in Shanxi Province.

"You have your ticket?" Sieg asks.

"No. I will sit up all night on a clothes box pack." He smiles. "It is no matter. Every mile takes me home."

He tells us what he hasn't admitted before, that he is a lecturer at his own college and will return to teach there after he finishes this year-and-a-half course. His wife is a dentist. They are unusually well off because his status earns an apartment from the university. Even as a student here, he continues to draw his regular pay, which means he gets more than the other students with their basic stipends.

Proudly, Mr. Xue unwraps a pink photograph album to show us pictures of his wife on their wedding day. The young couple are dressed in elegant street clothes. They wear red badges.

Sieg studies the picture of Mr. Xue. He is staring at the ground, his large eyes masked by dropped lids.

"But I wouldn't recognize you!" Sieg says. "It doesn't look like you."

"Because I was nervous," Mr. Xue says. He takes his leave.

We forgo any further grade hassling today. Time enough tomorrow morning. With no more student visits likely tonight, with the Guest House oddly silent because some of our colleagues have already left on vacation, we turn to our customary postsupper reading aloud.

At present we have two books going, both pulled from the office library shelves when Sieg organized that collection. One is Edith Wharton's *House of Mirth*. The other is John Kennedy Toole's *A Confederacy of Dunces*.

To have New York's Lily Bart and New Orleans' Ignatius Reilly in a Nanjing living room on the same evening seems an unlikely combination. But it suits our present escapist mood and expansive tastes at the start of a vacation break that will find us traveling three thousand miles in China in a few days.

So I needlepoint. Sieg reads aloud. And our students, giddy in anticipation of reunions and delicious dishes, either relax in their local homes or take off north, south, east, and west through a sparkling Chinese night.

34 . Back into Action

One month later, at 9:40 on a February morning, we walk back into our new classroom just down the hill in Building Six. The students burst into applause. We applaud them for success in arriving on campus on time. And also because we're happy to see them.

Mr. Mao Yanyang, Mr. Ku Qiu, and Miss Bin Qilin are missing.

"Mr. Mao has a girlfriend," I suggest. "He doesn't want to come back."

The likelihood, however, is that all three are victims of crowded travel delays visible everywhere now in China.

The students, already reeling from their first two hours of a new linguistics class this morning taught by Dan Younkin ("He's *cruel!*" they pronounce after seeing his course syllabus and schedule), suffer further shocks when we give them their first writing and reading assignments.

Last fall, we explain, was an explore-and-get-acquainted semester. Mr. Guo and we agree that this semester they need to move to more complex, independent work, as much as possible. So, in their first full week's writing project, they are to produce either a letter to someone, an essay or short story about something that intrigues them (length, one thousand words or less), or two unrhymed poems of twelve to twenty lines each, or a one-act playlet. They are to arrive in class Wednesday prepared to discuss briefly which they want to do, and then they will share the completed results a week later.

Tomorrow, they are to come ready to discuss a short article from the reader. We add specifics. Friday, they should present short, written proposals for a two-week independent reading project that will result in a paper. Their reading and writing can involve wide-open explorations—we sketch a number of literary choices involving comparison, contrast, and analysis. Or they can come up with a proposal of their own.

To the students, it sounds like Too Much. Still half in the cradling arms of vacation, hung over from too much food and long travel, they sit dazed. Eyes glaze, mouths turn down, shoulders droop.

"We know it sounds like a lot," I tell them. "But little by little, you'll get it done. We'll give you some in-class time for writing. And tomorrow's conversation class has an easy subject—you'll be talking about the high and low points of your vacation."

They perk up. *This* is manageable. And Wednesday seems a world away.

Tuesday, we gather for small conversation groups in the Guest House common room. It's flooded with welcome sun and a slightly higher degree of warmth. Miss Li Yanping spreads her chilblain-swollen hands gratefully into the light. She has just washed them again, "to protect from liver disease." She shakes water from her hands onto the floor.

Sieg begins the rounds. "Okay. What were your best of times, your worst of times?"

"Until now," Miss Feng says with a twinkle, "no low point." She hurries on. "I like watching TV, visiting relatives, eating delicious dishes. And the fireworks. They were very beautiful."

"I like watching TV," Miss Zhuang Zi parrots, "visiting friends. I read novels and did housework."

"Was that a low point?" Sieg asks.

"Oh no. My low point was rain. Much rain."

Miss Li Yanping stayed with her parents, learned cooking, listened to music tapes. "I enjoy life!" she says. "But I went to see classmates and they weren't at home."

Mr. Ku Qiu's low point came when he tried to buy a ticket back late in February. People were " 'jumping the queue.' Students argued with police," he says. "I missed my train to Shanghai and had to take another train." He brightens. "But I enjoy good dishes."

Mr. Lüe Shi stayed with his parents in the Yellow River valley, "cooking, washing, feeding chickens. I visit my relatives." His low point was also the weather. "It was dry, piercing cold. Below zero degrees centigrade."

"So you come south now to warm up," Sieg says.

"I want it warmer!" Miss Li looks again with regret at her itching hands.

Mr. Xue Hai spent his vacation cleaning three houses, "my parents, my in-laws, our own. I am afraid I lost my temper. I also get very tired visiting back and forth. But the most exciting was the eve of Spring Festival. We watch TV, ate delicious dumplings. The fireworks at midnight promise a good future!"

Mr. Lao Sheng beams with recollection. "I met my daughter at the station. She is one and a half years old. I carried an orange in one pocket, a toy in another. My daughter just stared at me. Then a boy said, 'Your father has come back. Please call him Father.' I played with the helicopter toy. Finally she said in a low voice, 'Father.'

"My worst time was also at the station. I had to say good-bye. My daughter was happy, but my wife had tears."

Miss Xi Yang enjoyed eating delicious food and meeting classmates. She reports two low points. She saw her grandmother upset after a funeral of her neighbor. "Also, I thought I would go to Shanghai, but hepatitis epidemic there forbids."

Miss Liu Jie did some translations from Chinese into English for a friend "about social sciences and international politics." She and Miss Lü Shu each played mahjong with their respective families. Miss Liu lost. Miss Lü won "a few *jiao*."

Mrs. Ching Chao "did housework at home and hospital," because both her father and cousin fell ill. But they improved. She got to go to the wedding of a friend and saw the friend's new house. "This is a very good year to be married—the Year of the Dragon."

Mr. Zuo Niannian did a great deal of "cooking, washing, cleaning," he reports. "It is important to begin the new year with everything fresh. Even the windows." He seldom went out. He read very little. He spent a lot of time with his child: "He is dressed fatter than in summer. At Spring Festival, children get new clothes." Mr. Zuo looks proud.

Miss Chun Xu reports she did "nothing special—eating, watching TV, visiting friends and relatives. Always the same questions, so I just stayed home."

Mr. Fan Rui also chose to stay home with his two brothers. "I helped father do housework, cooking. During Spring Festival, my mouth is very busy eating and talking. After Spring Festival, my mouth is awkward."

The group laughs.

We know what Mr. Fan means. Already, we've noticed students are far more hesitant, briefer today in their English replies. Even their accents have slipped. No wonder. They've been thinking and talking primarily Chinese for a month. Miss Chun Xu claims *she* didn't give up English for the duration. As she left campus she used one word—"bye-bye."

Miss Bin Qilin helped her mother cook and decorate the house. "We put up new pictures on house wall."

"What kind of pictures?" Sieg asks.

"Lucky words!" Miss Bin says. "You know, couplets on door."

That explains all the red banners with black characters we saw during our long trip south to Hainan Island. The banners hung on the outside of peasant homes and flapped for sale in markets everywhere.

"What do the characters say?" I ask.

"Different things," Miss Bin explains. "For instance, 'The sunrise on the seashore is like fire.' 'When the sun rises, the red sun is like a flower.' 'When spring comes, the color of the water is aquamarine.' "

Sieg turns to our last two speakers of the morning. "Mr. Li Jian?"

Mr. Li shrugs. "I was home with younger brothers. One brother got married. His wife is pregnant, so he does housework. At home of each of my three brothers, we ate a feast. I also saw my eldest sister. I had to wait for a night to see one of my classmates." His face fell. "We quarreled. That made me feel bad."

"Maybe you can write him a letter and patch things up. Miss Chen Hong?"

"We had nine persons," Miss Chen answers. "My grandfather, my uncle spend Spring Festival with us. My grandfather is deaf." She dimples. "I had to shout! But really, I didn't eat much, didn't visit much. I caught cold doing the washing."

She does sound hoarse. And we've all been working for four hours. We let them go.

In the afternoon, Ding Feng, a young assistant in the Waiban office, drops in with an English article he is translating into Chinese: "Secrets of Managing the World's Top Hotel," by Joyce Rainat.

I run my eye over the text. I'm not sure how this English article was communicated to the December 1987 issue of *FAR EAST Business*. Could it have been dictated over the phone? That might explain several departures from the author's original intent.

One is a description of a huge Bangkok hotel complex: "It's a living, breathing orgasm."

We help Mr. Ding correct this to *organism* in his copy before translating. English is such a hazardous tongue.

35 . Progress

March seems to be running on fast forward.
We put in a crammed week of classes—reading, writing, conversation, vocabulary. Students explain their intended two-week independent projects. Just like inexperienced students in the United States, given a chance to read whatever they choose, some of them present sprawling first proposals. Mr. Li Jian sets as his fourteen-day goal "understanding international relations." Miss Feng Yunxia chooses "American and English women writers."

We delve into ways to focus their interests. We also hand out copies of a documentation chart with examples. They ask suspiciously, "What's it for?"

Knowing we're up against entrenched Chinese publishing practices, we try once again to explain about responsible attribution, footnotes and bibliography. The students get that "I'm-being-worked-too-hard" glaze. We stress the documentation sheet is the kind of material they don't have to memorize.

"Just know how to use it," I urge. "Consult it whenever a specific need comes up."

They take the sheets reluctantly, as if they might explode in their hands at any second. I don't blame them. Documentation kills many a scholar, for a range of reasons.

Part of this week's reading is a Jeff Greenfield article originally published in *Esquire* in 1975. It's called, "The Black and White Truth about Basketball: A Skin-deep Theory of Style."

"Don't worry about trying to understand the Americanisms or game tactics," I warn these hyperconscientious dictionary hunters. "We'll talk about those. Just watch mainly for comparison/contrast techniques. You'll be using both a lot in your writing this semester."

They're slightly cheered to be reading about American sports.

When we discuss Greenfield's article, the students ask the meaning of "lay-up shot," "doll-house space," and "liquid grace," among other mysteries. Sieg cautions them to avoid adding phrases like "son of a bitch" to their formal vocabulary. He describes the American scene in the 1970s to explain the author's final words, "a fusion of cultures that seems more and more difficult in the world beyond the out-of-bounds line." He has time in today's class to comment on later progress in black-white relationships.

"I hope we read more articles like this," Mr. Li says.

On March 8, the normally quiet, stolid Miss An Ran bounces into conversation class looking pleased.

"It's International Women's Day!" she proclaims.

Mr. Mao turns a sour face to her. "You should cancel it."

She scowls. "Why?"

"Women's Day promotes women several levels—for one day. Women are looked down on other times of year. Tell me, why is there no Man's Day?"

"Every Sunday is Men's Day," says Miss Chun Xu.

"Not so!" Mr. Fan Rui sputters. "They share work. Many do most of the home work!"

"Mr. Fan has a point," Sieg says. "Last week, when you were talking about what you did over vacation, several men here said they cleaned house and cooked."

"But my mother," Miss Bin Qilin says, "is a traditional woman."

"In my family," Miss Chun jumps in, "there are no such problems because my grandmother does much of the work. She likes to, but she is getting older."

Mr. Mao looks across at Miss An. "What is the purpose of Women's Day?"

"To promote women's rights!"

"But the day doesn't have original meaning," Mr. Li protests. "Now it celebrates liberation. You have already been liberated."

"There's still a long way to go." The class stares at Mr. Fan. He seems suddenly to have switched sides.

"I know for a fact," Mr. Li says, "some women don't want this day. Mother's Day, Father's Day, but then the rest of the year, no attention."

"The person first," Miss An insists stubbornly, "with own rights."

Throughout this unusually heated exchange, Mr. Zuo Niannian, the one married man in this small group, has remained silent.

"What's your opinion?" Mr. Li asks him.

Mr. Zuo smiles. "We didn't discuss these matters before marriage."

"In China, before marriage," Miss Lü Shu observes, "some young men pretend to do more housework."

Miss Chun looks at Sieg. "We have a saying about how they change—'from slave to general.' "

Mr. Fan turns to Sieg who, as discussion leader, has been more silent than usual this morning. "The Women's Liberation Movement in America," Mr. Fan says, as if announcing a speech title. "Could you say something about it?"

Sieg looks across at me. "We *both* can say something about it."

We bring up goals of equal pay, equal opportunity, respect for self, and some of the social, economic, and psychological problems stemming from equal job opportunities. "China faces some of the same changes we're going through," Sieg finishes. "Miss An, you certainly introduced an important issue today!"

Wednesday, they bring to class for sharing their first independent writing. Mr. Fan Rui has chosen poetry as his medium. He reads one of his, untitled:

> In the eyes of my mother,
> I seem always a child,
> never going to be grown up,
> though I'm over twenty now.
>
> I try to act like a gentleman,
> visualizing myself a future husband,

but her hearted exhortation
and meticulous consideration
often put me at a loss.

I dare not meet my mother's eyes
when having to say good-bye.
Her tender eyes always shake
my seeming firm heart. I don't know:
should I go or should I stay?

We take a few minutes to discuss his final lines. Is this a poem about his growing independence? The class thinks yes. Mr. Fan, the author, disagrees. "It's just a poem about having to say good-bye," he insists.

In Miss Xi Yang's short story called "Love Experience," she describes a succession of young women a matchmaker brings to try to suit a young man and his family. Miss Xi characterizes the bachelor and his eligibility:

> He was unnecessarily afraid of being single. He was both handsome and rich. He had many valuable things, a flat, a color TV, an excellent portable recorder made in Japan, a refrigerator, a washing machine, a new type of furniture, etc. The only thing that he didn't own was a wife.

"Own a wife?" Like a piece of furniture? No wonder Miss An was so excited yesterday about International Women's Day!

When her turn comes, Miss Li Yanping carries several pages to the lectern. She looks briefly at her audience. "A short story," she announces. "It's called 'Snowy Night.' " She begins:

> It's a cold, overcast afternoon. I sit at my table to finish the assignment given this morning, in order to have a full enjoyment tomorrow.
>
> "What a queer question! How strange he should think of that odd topic!" I murmur, and doodle on the paper. Then I erase it and throw that paper away. The heavy task, the silly question, the depressing day make me miserable.
>
> My mother comes back from work. "Look, Wen. See what I bring to you this evening!"
>
> They are Jiaozi (dumplings) which I was eager to eat last week. But in my great unhappiness, I just have a look and say, "I'm not interested."
>
> "What?" My mother looks disappointed. She turns angry when see-

ing my unpleasant face. "What's wrong with you? Why are you always making me trouble now? Why can't you be good like your elder brother?"

My elder brother works in Beijing. He is too far away to give her trouble. For years at home I am my parents' apple. Being the youngest, I'm spoiled and self-willed, they tell me.

"I don't know. And I don't want to eat anything," I say unreasonably. In order to show my anger, I slam some books into my bag.

"Where are you going?"

"It's none of your business," I say obstinately. Thinking that sounded too rude, I add, "I'm going to the classroom."

"It's going to snow. Take an umbrella."

"I don't care."

I stride forward without turning back to look at her. But I can guess she is seeing me off.

What an awful temper I have! How deep I hate the books, but I carry many. How eager I am to watch TV this evening, but so many heavy books force me to go nowhere but to the classroom. How warm to stay at home eating, but now I've no choice but to go to the cold classroom hungrily.

I enter an empty classroom in low spirits and find a seat in the back. I sit down, take out a novel entitled *Family* written by Ba Jin.

It's the weekend. The campus is bustling and full of life. So the whole building is very quiet. Calming down from my regrets I begin to read. Soon I am involved in the story. The fates of Ming Feng and Jue Hui attract me. Their pure love moves me a great deal. I feel pity when reading how Jue Xing has to obey his grandfather and marry a girl he did not know before. I feel lucky for him because the girl he marries is nice and gentle.

I forget time and even forget myself when the sound of the door opening interrupts me. I look up and see that several students are reading in the classroom.

"Is it raining or snowing?" I murmur. "Why do they carry umbrellas?" I leave the room quietly to have a look for myself.

"My mother is right. It is snowing, and snowing heavily. How can I go back without an umbrella?" I start to worry. "It's 8:55. Maybe it will stop soon." I try to console myself.

Returning to my seat, I find I become absent-minded. No matter how hard I try to concentrate on my book, I fail to. I have no wish to read any more. It snows on and on heavily.

I look out of the window, see the falling of the snow, and hope sincerely it will stop. Gradually other students tidy their things and leave. I sit still at my seat, waiting eagerly and patiently for the snow to stop. But I am in vain.

It's 9:45. The snow gets thicker. I become afraid. How wonderful if my mother comes to meet me. But it's impossible. She has no idea where I am. Sitting near me is a boy who is still reading as if nothing is happening.

"How can he keep so calm?"

"How can he not? He has an umbrella." I look at him enviously. "Mother and father must be worrying about me. And the light of the building will be turned off automatically at 10." I hate myself very much now. But regret is useless.

"How happy to go home with an umbrella," I dream.

Suddenly, a male voice interrupts my dream.

"Hello."

I look up surprised. It is the boy who was reading so long. He has put away his book.

"If I don't make a confusion, you didn't carry your umbrella."

"Mm, mm . . ."

"O.K. Let me take you home. I've one and we can share it."

He is indeed a very ordinary boy, the kind you can find everywhere on campus. Ordinary hair style, ordinary glasses, not very tall, wearing a jacket without fastening the zipper.

"Oh, no no, thank you, I can go back." I suddenly find the words, and pretend to be very brave.

"How can you? It's snowing hard." He pauses and continues, "You don't trust me, do you?"

That's the point. On a snowy evening, a strange boy accompanies me, sharing one umbrella. That's unthinkable. I won't. I make up my mind that I'll return home by myself even if it snows stones.

I lick my lip and give a smile. "No, no, how could you think that?"

The boy looks steadily at me. "I know you, really. You're Nanjingese and a freshman in the Chinese Department. I'm a senior in the same department." He puts his hand into his bag and takes out a card. "Look. Here's my student identification."

Just at that moment, the lights are turned off.

"Listen to me. Don't hesitate. Come on, I'll lead you out."

Though in the darkness, somehow I can still see his frank and honest eyes. My determination collapses and I can't restrain myself. I stand up and follow him out of the classroom.

Everything is white outside. Snow jackets everything, every branch, every twig. There are few people on the street. How beautiful the world is!

We walk slowly. I share more than half of the umbrella. When we enter our alley, I say to him, "It's not far from my home. Let me go."

"Oh no. It's too dark. Let me help you to your door."

When we reach there, I stop. "This is my home." I look at the snow covering half of him. "My parents are in. Come and have a warm," I invite.

"I appreciate it, but it's too late."

"Next time, OK? Thank you very much."

"It's me who should thank you."

"Why?"

"Thank you for your believing me, your believing a strange boy," he answers, and turns back, finding his way in the snow.

My mother opens the door. "Whom are you speaking to?" she asks. "Why not invite him in?"

"Mum. Excuse me for the way I behaved this afternoon. Isn't the snow beautiful?" I say affectionately.

The class, which has followed in attentive silence, stirs at the end. I have to restrain myself from giving a loud cheer. Miss Li, whose work was somewhat uneven last semester, has gone all out to make her efforts count today.

36 . Contrasts

Whenever Shui Jing, the Guest House maid, comes down the hall carrying our clean laundry, she walks with beauty in her arms.

She is a small, slender but sturdy woman, about twenty-four years old. Today Shui Jing has been hard at work since 7:30 A.M. She has collected our bundle (each teacher or family has an assigned wash day every week) and processed all the sheets, towels, and personal clothes through the miniature automatic washer that crowds the boiled drinking water heater in that tiny, sunken, often steamy cubicle under the stairs.

If the day isn't rainy, even though it's grey, Shui Jing hangs her loads out on long lines strung above high weeds, uneven ground, and scattered rubble. If there is a sudden downpour, as frequently happens now, she carries the wet, heavy masses the length of the building to our cold kitchen. There, she poles each piece up onto ceiling-high lines to hang and dry, sometimes for two days. Then she poles every piece down and hauls the lot back to quarters near the washroom that she uses by day and Mr. Miao, the building super, uses by night.

It's there, hidden behind close-curtained doors, perhaps watching a small TV set, that she sorts and folds the laundry. She always folds it with extraordinary care. What at last she sets the high pile down on a chair outside our door, each sheet and towel has its corners squared, evened with the next item. Every pair of socks is neatly matched and rolled, Sieg's shirts and T-shirts lie as if newly taken from their wrappings, and his shorts—they could make a drill sergeant believe he'd finally discovered perfection in ordered ranks.

Sometimes, Shui Jing brings her two-year-old son with her for the day. We hear quiet noises in the room next door that houses only occasional visitors. Or we see him trying to pedal a tricycle the Gravs keep parked in the hall for their daughter's use.

We can't hold much of a conversation with Shui Jing. Language barriers keep us apart, but that doesn't stop us from communicating. She longs to learn English. We use the hall blackboard to teach her names for numbers, days of the week, months, expressions about weather. In return, she gives us Chinese equivalents and the word for "little boy," *nanhaizi*. She is better at remembering than we are. But she evaporates from the hall whenever Shi Changmei, her Waiban boss, enters the front door.

The season's first dandelions brighten the grass under Shui Jing's laundry lines. On a south-facing slope, a tiny bluet of some sort nods in the wind. In one protected corner, a white magnolia has budded. The weather prods us into some needed spring cleaning. Sieg manages to bang loose rusted fasteners that have gripped apartment window screens in place, probably for decades. Using the cold-water hand shower in the bath, we hose those screens clean as best we can, then mop an inch of red topsoil from the tub.

Sieg goes outside. With a bucket of water and a Chinese rag-strip mop, he reaches the top panes of the highest windows and scrubs, sloshes, then scrubs again to remove thick, grey grime.

We can see out again! The result is so pleasant, we tackle hall screens and windows too. Shui Jing catches us. Never having been able to pry off the screens herself, she brings a brush and enthusiastically takes control of the bathtub hose. She is not satisfied with our window polishing. She finds a cloth. From floor level, she applies vigorous elbow grease below, while we work higher.

We appreciate her cheerful help and companionship. It's a pleasant joining of forces in a good, if not academic, cause. More than in teaching, we can see immediate, gratifying results.

I take back that last sentence. This morning, in class, the students wrote papers responding to our preannounced assignment:

> Make a comparison/contrast between any two people about how they do something. Examples: yourself and another person; any two people you know well (how they walk, or talk, or act, or cook, or make decisions, or . . .). You might prefer to contrast groups. Whatever you choose, comment, if you can, on what might make these people behave so differently.

This afternoon, we read their responses with increasing excitement.
Mr. Fan Rui heads his paper "Contrasts between American and Chinese."

1. Most Americans are white people, except for blacks, Mexicans, and other minorities. Chinese tend to be yellow people, so they like yellow better than any other colours. But both are proud of their respective skin colours.

2. Most Americans are taller, stronger than Chinese because of excessive nutrition and intentional physical exercises.

3. Americans are more humorous than Chinese. Humour is one of the outstanding characteristics of Americans. They like to employ humour to face embarrassment, disappointment, and to enliven a serious atmosphere such as an important meeting, or a gathering of strangers. But Chinese are too formal in everything. This is mostly caused by the traditional Chinese education.

4. Frankness is another major characteristic of Americans. Most Americans show their likes and dislikes, hatred and love, happiness and sorrow directly. They admit the mistakes they make immediately, if they know these, and show their success proudly. But that is not the case with Chinese. Chinese always prefer modesty, even though they make great achievements. Psychologically speaking, they are not so willing to admit the mistakes they make. Sometimes they even hate the man who points out these mistakes. I don't think it is a normal state of inner heart.

5. Jealousy is another demerit of Chinese. Sometimes they can't view the achievements of others fairly and reasonably because of narrow mind.

But most Americans can be proud of the progress of their colleagues and share the happiness of success with them.

6. The above-mentioned points come from my own observation and reading. Maybe they are not completely right.

Sieg reads Mr. Fan's paper twice, as I have. It's fascinating to see ourselves as others see us. Mr. Fan Rui's view of Americans leans, perhaps from tact, toward the rosy. We need to add a note in the margin that Americans, as human as the Chinese, can also be prey to hatred, jealousy, and other worldwide flaws.

We turn to the next papers. A paragraph from Miss Chun Xu's story goes:

In Wang Lin's family, there are two children, Wang Lin and her brother. Her parents hold to the feudal thought that boys are more valuable than girls. So they take little care about Wang Lin. Growing up in such a family, Wang Lin has a sense of inferiority. Her parents seldom pay attention to what she thinks, so she always keeps quiet. She is not good at expressing herself [. . . but she does have] the ability of concentration. Her specialty is playing violin.

I look up. "Maybe we should talk more in conversation class about male and female roles as the students see them right now. The old ways seem so persistent."

"Maybe." Sieg passes me Mr. Ku Qiu's paper, which has no heading. Mr. Ku Qiu plunges directly into his story:

There lives a family of three people, the husband, the wife and the four-year-old son in Guangzhou. The husband came from Hunan Province. The wife came from Jiangsu Province. The son was born and has been brought up in Guangzhou.

Now people from Hunan love their food cooked with salt and pepper, while people from Jiangsu prefer their food cooked with sugar and vinegar. So incongruous things have followed since this couple got married. It is the very question whether their food is to be cooked with salt and pepper in the favor of the husband or with sugar and vinegar in the favor of the wife.

They often argue for a long time before their food is cooked. As a result of the argument, the husband cooks his food with salt and pepper. The wife cooks hers with sugar and vinegar. But it doesn't matter to the son whatever happens. He is the product of his parents. So he has a favor of the mixture of his parents.

Once the family was presented a fine fish. The question of which way they would cook the fish raised a big argument.

"I'll cook the fish with sugar and vinegar this time," the wife said. "My dear, will you agree with me?"

"Not at all," the husband said and pulled a long face. "On the contrary, you must agree with me this time. I'll cook the fish with salt and pepper."

"Nuisance!" the wife cried out.

"Wait!" The husband had an idea. "You cook half the fish with your favorite. I cook the other half of the fish with my salt and pepper."

The wife calmed down. The problem was settled. They cooked the fish according to their own wills. Fortunately, it was a big fish.

At table, the husband was having his fish, the wife was having hers. The child, a natural mixture of his parents, sat between them. His chopsticks went sometimes to his father's fish bowl, and sometimes to his mother's.

Unable to stop smiling, I put down Mr. Ku Qiu's paper.

"Isn't he from Hunan?" Sieg asks.

"I think so."

"Do you suppose that's an old folk tale from his province that he's retelling? Or is it autobiographical?"

"Does it matter? Look how well he's put it into English."

Sieg scans the story again. "And to think the department office almost ruled him out of this program because of his strong peasant accent from the south!"

37 . Effects of Spring Weather

March continues to move March-like, showing fickle moods. One morning we wake to a strange saffron dawn, followed by thickening dark, then a prolonged thunderstorm and heavy rain. The lightning isn't close, I'm glad to notice. Our hilltop location, with pines lashing high above the Guest House, seems an open invitation to Leigong, the thunder god. But the thunder spreads distantly across the Yangzi's broad valley in fretful, grumbling rolls. We watch cyclists and pedestrians, rain-caped and umbrellaed, splash along in the swimming street below.

Another morning, we find three inches of wet snow coating every tree. Trunks are plastered halfway around, witnesses to how much the wind veered during the night. Students pour from dorms, a few carrying cameras, to catch this transient beauty. It's gone by noon.

We collect our students' first independent reading projects. They hand them over, complaining "how hard it is!" It's true the results lack the zing of their usual writing. They're a jumble of pasted-together excerpts with a minimum of original thinking. Despite the handout of examples, students still can't seem to get the hang of documentation.

We bring in a Ray Bradbury story called "I See You Never" to share with them. They like his story. It's short. The language is simple. They find drama they can understand in Bradbury's tale of an immigrant about to be deported.

Talking far more than we wish, we go through the story slowly again, analyzing with them the techniques Bradbury used to get his effects. It's a shame to dissect such a lively story, but I want them to know how to read deeply, how they can find in other people's work writing techniques to use freshly in their own.

Miss Feng stops by the desk after class. Her eyes shine. "Please give us more work like that! We can really understand from a class like today."

Perhaps. Perhaps not. If they can only learn, somehow, to discover for themselves, without a leader present.

Mr. Xue Hai has been absent all week. He drops in at the apartment on his way back from the clinic where he's been getting two penicillin shots a day for flu. He explains he won't be in class again tomorrow, but he wants to leave an earlier writing assignment with us. We urge him, for everybody's sake, to get back to his dorm quickly. He hacks and coughs his way down the cold hall. Being ill, however, hasn't drained his fluency. If anything it's given him more time than usual to develop his thoughts.

He heads what he calls a short story "Spring Rain."

The Chinese season for Rain Water has swiftly come as the Spring Equinox is over. You see, the continued rain keeps on and on outside the window, which makes me feel both sleepy and happy. Through the window I see that pitter-pattering light rain. Like a piece of soft veil, it flutters before my eyes without stopping. It washes clean the distant mountains and vallies. It moistens the soil. It also draws a half-clear picture on the pane.

Listen attentively, I've heard the hubbub of a stream faraway, the twittering of swallows in the sky, also a beautiful song from the loudspeaker of our school, "Tomorrow, tomorrow . . ." On hearing this, I can't help putting down my pen, walking towards the window and opening it. "What composition shall I do?" I seem either to ask myself or turn to the rain for help. But it is still dripping and does not answer my question. Staring at the cow-hair-like dripping and spring in the air, my thought flies swiftly to unforgettable things which happened ten years ago.

Then I had to settle down in the countryside to receive the education from the low-middle peasants. During those years, the "Gang of Four" played the tyrant in China. They called on people to wage class struggle and the struggle between the two lines. They didn't allow peasants to keep their own family's private plots, or to engage in trade.

In those years, Grandpa Chang, an honest peasant, was an old debtor to our production brigade. Once, our production brigade gave each peasant ten *jin* of peanuts. Grandpa Chang sold it to a worker passing by in exchange for some money to buy his son a coat because the Spring Festival was coming.

But the honest and pitiful Grandpa Chang did not know "The Movement for Cutting off the Capitalist Tail" was being launched in the countryside. Those revolutionary leaders of our production brigade had a mass meeting and criticized Grandpa Chang.

Then they paraded him through the streets and exposed him before the public as a living target. At that time, I could not forget his gloomy face with its heavy frown and the angry biting of the lower lip. He wore a cotton coat with some "white flowers" on it because it was too old to wear. He also wore a straw rope tightly tied around his waist which served as a belt. Everything was difficult for this pitiful widower. People seeing this situation at that time turned their faces back and wept silently.

I still remembered the young production brigade leader—Xian Sen, also an honest young man. Every evening, he called people door to door to go to the meeting-room to listen to the wired broadcasting attached to our commune, which was called "the education of class struggle." I knew Xian Sen was a kind-hearted young man. I knew that he was forced to do this.

At last, there were only a few under-adult young people who came to the meeting-room. Regardless of the loud voice of the loudspeaker, these young people studied "the No. 54 Document" attentively under the light. (That means they played the cards.) This showed that the people also knew the policy being carried out by the "Gang of Four" was not correct, but they dared not criticize it directly. They could just resist it by taking a passive attitude.

When the heavy snow dam of this time broke down with the fall of the "Gang of Four," the sunny spring came back with the twittering of swallows. Our Central Party Committee carried out its newly-made rural policy—the economic policy especially for the countrysides, which was like soft dripping of spring rain moistening the dry hearts of peasants continuously.

During the recent Winter Holidays, I paid a special visit to the village I used to work in ten years ago. I met Xian Sen, now a father with two children. I also met Grandpa Chang, and had a good talk with him in his house.

His house was newly built, with a big courtyard. In the centre, there were some young apple trees. Hundreds of hens were happily eating in one corner.

Grandpa Chang told me that the life of peasants there was getting better and better since the rural policy made by our party had been carried out. He was now a specialized trade producer in eggs. Last year, he made 2000 Yuan [about $525]; he bought a new bicycle, and also asked the carpenters to make a set of fashionable furniture for him.

Three big tile-roof rooms which had the decoration of these newly-made furniture looked spacious and bright. Grandpa Chang's changed condition really left a deep impression on me: he was a microcosm of millions of peasants in China today.

Rain is dripping much heavier now. It flutters into the window by the soft wind. I feel it cool when it touches my face. I taste it sweet when it flutters into my mouth. Suddenly, an idea comes into my mind. The spring rain this time is just the reappearance of our rural economic policy. In this drizzling rain, I am sure, once the seeds of hopes have put forth leaves, they will grow with vigour with each passing day.

Pitter-patter! Pitter-patter!

Standing before the open window, staring at the tree toads on the ground, I seem to see a colourful picture of harvest a long distance away.

38 . Women's Roles

One of our readings this week is a poem by Czeslaw Milosz called "A Song on the End of the World." Sieg reads the poet's name and the poem's title aloud. The class bursts into laughter. He ignores the reaction. They're probably unfamiliar with such a cluster of consonants as he's written on the board. But when he refers to "Milosz" again, the whole class roars.

"What's so funny?"

They are so broken up, they sputter, trying to explain. One of the most popular Western figures on TV is Mickey Mouse, known in China as "Mi Laoshu." Sieg tries to go on, but when they howl again at his third use of "Milosz," he shifts over to the poet's first name. Since this doesn't raise any hilarious associations, the class settles down to considering what the poet has said.

This semester, students are responsible for introducing their own topics of discussion in conversation class. One morning, Mr. Lüe Shi, who often sounds as if he's speaking in capital letters, says, "There are three characteristics in modern business success: Ability, Chance and Opportunity, Personal Contacts in Society."

"In China, opportunity is more important than ability," Miss Feng snaps.

"Why?" Sieg asks.

"You have to have special ways."

"What 'special ways'?"

"Back door," Mrs. Ching says. "For example, if daughter-in-law of mayor is on good terms with leaders, perhaps flirting, then she may get place. Or a not very well-qualified woman teacher goes to U.S. There is gossip, because she is beautiful."

"I don't agree," Miss Zhuang Zi says. "Women work hard, finally succeed. Some women's ability is superior to men."

"But there are really differences," Miss Li suggests timidly. "Women are good at housework."

"Men can lift a car off the ground," Miss Xi affirms.

Sieg waits to see if anyone here will counter this old physical strength argument today.

"Women's ability," Miss Liu starts, "is focused on housework and children. Women are more weak, kind, timid, so they can't take part in politics. Men are more aggressive. So success depends on luck. Everybody needs chances."

"Feudal society doesn't give them to women," Mr. Lüe points out.

"Even when they get chance," Mrs. Chang argues, "women run into difficulty in household because their success interferes with home."

"I read an article." Miss Zhuang leans forward. "It said 95 percent of men want wives gentle, only 5 percent want them ambitious."

"I don't think there's a contradiction between ambition and gentleness," Miss Liu says quietly.

"But if wife is better trained than husband," Mr. Lao says, "husband will be considered useless."

Mr. Lüe, unusually voluble this morning, says, "All of us males want a wife who is tender."

This provokes a storm of discussion. Group A is still arguing with each other when Group B asserts its right to take their places next hour. They want to know why everyone went out talking so loudly. We explain. Apparently, the issue stirs them too.

Miss An Ran pounces. "Women are tied by housework, so they don't have time to succeed. In China, with education, women have more freedom to choose."

"But any woman who succeeds," Mr. Li Jian insists, "has help from her husband, her family, or friends."

Miss Bin frowns. "A woman may succeed without being married!"

"Perhaps." Mr. Li's doubting tone drives her into a pout.

"There is prejudice in China," Miss Chun Xu observes. "If woman gives too much time outside her family, she is considered an unqualified wife."

"And over a certain age," Miss Lü Shu says, "it's hard to find a husband."

"What age?" Sieg asks.

"Thirty."

Mr. Mao Yanyang smiles across at Miss Lü. She hasn't reached that dread year yet, but she *is* a postgraduate. "In China," he reminds her, "there is a saying, 'Every girl can find a husband.' "

Mr. Xue Hai appears on our doorstep again. After ten days on penicillin, two shots a day, his throat is no better, he explains. "And I'm spitting blood. The x-ray shows no lung trouble, but I'm going home to my wife. She is a dentist. With her care and some traditional medicine, I hope to get better."

"When do you leave?" we ask with concern.

"At midnight tonight. It will be a long trip home. I must sit up all night in a hard seat, but I will be there tomorrow."

"Does your wife know you're coming?"

"Oh no. She would worry."

Mr. Xue's wife is in for quite a surprise. We trust that with her tender coddling, in between her work as a dentist, Mr. Xue will soon get well.

39 . Bean Curd and
Other Facts of Life

During the last classes in March, students share, then hand in a second round of independent writing projects. Mr. Lüe Shi calls his essay, "The Little Tailor."

> I wonder why I so often think of the little tailor in our street. It is not because I want to have my garments made. It is just because what I remember bothers me.
>
> The little tailor was hired by our village the year before last. He was a short, thin young man, and a little handsome. He was very kind and gentle. While speaking to others, he usually smiled.
>
> His sister was a little fat. Her eyes were just like the slits cut by a pointed knife. These two came to our village and set up a tailor shop.

Because the village provided them with sewing machines and they brought only electric irons and pairs of scissors, they charged the villagers twenty to thirty percent lower than the ordinary level.

They also brought with them several copies of books on clothing styles. They could make every kind of garment according to the books, and the garments made by them were very fashionable. They spent less time on the garments, and the quality was high. Thus, many people went to the tailor's to have their clothes made.

They were very kind and enthusiastic with the customers. Being industrious, they often worked hard far into the night. Their business became extremely prosperous.

Just at that time a few villagers wanted to throw mud at them. They said that the little tailor and his sister charged the villagers too much, took possession of the other's cloth, and changed the good parts of the sewing machines for bad parts. They also said the little tailor was kind only to flatter the villagers.

This kind of rumour was widely spread among the villagers. From then on, many villagers began to be unfriendly to the little tailor.

Hearing this kind of rumour, the leaders of our village dismissed the little tailor, and immediately organized another tailor shop.

The little tailor and his sister went away unhappily.

The workers in the new village tailor shop were some of the villagers themselves. In this shop the sewing machine ran smoothly as before, but the village tailors spent too much time on clothes and they were not punctual. They charged too much, and the quality was not so high as the little tailor's.

During this winter holiday, my mother asked me to go to the tailor shop to have my garments cut out and made, but I did not go there, because I had no confidence in the tailor shop run by the villagers.

I often thought of the little tailor. If only the little tailor were still in the tailor shop! Almost all the villagers thought of the little tailor in the same way. We all realized that what we had lost was really precious, but the loss could not be regained.

Miss Li Yanping has switched this time from a story to an article, which she calls "Winter Nights."

Snow in winter always makes me think of bean-curd.

When I was a child, my family at least one time each week would gather, sitting by a fire, and enjoy the prospect of this family-made dish.

The water would boil in the casserole, in which bean-curd was quivering slightly, looking white, pure, smooth, delicate and delicious, while the fire in the stove burned just at its best.

My sisters and I were the most active and interested in the bean-curd. We usually carried our stools and sat around the stove far earlier than the bean-curd was ready. We frequently ordered our parents to serve it. After they refused, we then waited eagerly and stared hungrily at the bean-curd, sending out its fragrance and filling the room with its sweet smell.

When at last the bean-curd was ready, my mother used her spoon to fill our small-sized bowls one by one. Occasionally being too impatient to wait, I tried in vain to do it by myself, but the stove was a little tall for me to reach the pot, so I just had to wait for my mother to serve me. We often enjoyed the ready food.

This wasn't our main dinner in the evening, but just something extra and special for fun. "It's cold outside," my mother would say. "We can warm up from eating some of it."

One evening last winter, the moon was very fascinating. My friend accompanied me to Xue Wu Lake. We found a seat near the lake and sat down. The moon reflected beautifully in the lake, quivering elegantly like a white circle of bean-curd in the flowing water. The reflection of the mountain, the stars and the branches of trees surrounded the moon on the surface of the lake. It seemed that they all came together like a happy family with the moon as the most important member. Many streams came down from the moonlight like bands of silver, flashing.

My friend and I sat quietly, appreciating the beautiful cold night. Gradually, my imagination seemed to rise to heaven. I drifted into sleep until my friend gave me a slight push. "Are you sleeping?"

While visiting my home this winter, I came back into the house from out of doors. Opening the door, I found my family seated around the stove. When I entered, they turned and greeted me with tender smiles. The bean-curd was again in the casserole. The fire was burning. I suddenly felt that I had stepped back into my childhood. It seemed the city was empty, but for just our family. The world was empty except for my family.

No matter how cold it is in winter, I feel warm in my mind whenever I think of these unforgettable moments, especially when we gathered around the stove to eat that wonderful bean-curd.

I will never look at bean curd in the market again without recalling Miss Li's responses to it. Eagerly, we turn to Miss Chen Hong's chosen form of writing, a letter.

March 26, 1988

My darling,

How are you getting on with your work? For some reason I didn't write back immediately. I am sorry that I have kept you waiting for such a long time. I was in low spirits for some reason. And I had to think about many things.

In your eyes I am always a girl never grown up. You are four years older than I, and you always keep saying, "Let it alone. I will do that for you." I take your view for granted. Sometimes I'm even proud of being young. But now it upsets me a lot. Because I am young, my classmates do not acknowledge me. They keep saying, "She is young, she can't do that job well." How can they know? They didn't give me a chance to have a try. Yes, I am younger than they; it doesn't mean that I can't do my job as good as they do. They always want experience people to do a job. Where do they get their experience? Practice, of course. I have no chance to practice. Where can I have my teaching experience? If somebody says I am young again, I will quarrel with him. So don't take me as a young girl any more, but as an adult. And let me go my own way.

You always say that you like my sweet and soft voice. At one time, I was very glad to hear that. But now I long for nothing if only I can speak in a loud voice. You can't imagine what happened to me here the first time I stood before the blackboard, with all these eyes staring at me. My face turned red. My hands were trembling, my legs were trembling, and my voice quivered. I suffered a lot and also made the teachers and my classmates suffer a lot. I don't know the reason, but when I was in University, things were not like that. What worried me then?

But afterwards, things became even more difficult for me. Every time when I stood before the blackboard, I could not help thinking of the first time. Although I tried my best, my voice still quivered. My heart was trembling. I was ashamed of that.

You are right. After graduation, I will be a teacher. How can I be a teacher with such a low voice when my students listen to me? With microphone in pocket? I can't think of that. The most thing that I need now is self-confidence, not a loud voice.

Yes, I still can remember every word of the story that you read to me on a shining day in the park. "Fishing with the President." That is about a girl who wanted to be a drummer in the children's musical of the neighborhood. But the children and the teacher were afraid that she wouldn't play the drum well. She was so angry that she ran away from home. On the way, she met a man whom she called "Big Man" and later she knew that the "Big Man" was the former American President Grover Cleveland. So she went fishing with him, and forgot all the unhappy things. When she told him all her troubles, the president smiled and told her what had happened to him when he made his first speech.

"I remember the first time I made a speech. I was afraid too. I wanted to make that speech, and I knew I could if I could only get started. Because suddenly I thought: Why, those people sitting out there don't know I am afraid! So I tried to look as though I were not. Before I knew it, I got started and went right on talking without any trouble at all."

He told the girl something no one else knew. That night at the rehearsal she played those drums beautifully.

I was deeply moved by the story. I am just like the girl in the story. Yes, the very thing that I need now is self-confidence. That girl could play her drums so beautifully and I also can speak loudly, fluently and clearly. Right? You wouldn't hear my sweet and soft voice any more, but a loud firm voice. Can you bear that?

So next time when you see me, I will have changed a lot. Perhaps I am no longer a shy, timid and taciturn girl. So be prepared to bear my loud voice. And please write to me as soon as possible.

Best wishes!

Yours,

Chen Hong

I look up at Sieg. "We've put her through such pain!"

"But she's learning," he says.

40 . Signs of the Season

Spring is breaking out in all sorts of ways—pleasant and unpleasant.

Canteen food has seemed so boring I've been sprinkling raisins on the rice for variety. Today the cook cuts dark frilly mushrooms, the texture of seaweed, into the usual greens. "Delicious," as Miss Zhuang loves to say.

With the return of milder weather, with more people outdoors, campus authorities have revved up the decibels on the loudspeakers again.

Near Hehai's main gate, a Nanjing nursery crew has been busy planting a line of trees along Xi Kang Road. First, workers appear. Every few feet for a mile, they lift fifteen-inch square blocks of cement near the curb, stack these blocks as an extra, temporary challenge to pedestrians, and dig holes. Trucks full of young trees arrive. More workers plunk magnolias six feet tall, alternated with another tree I don't recognize, into the holes. The crew's combined efforts bring grace to the noisy street.

"They will provide much shade in summer!" Mrs. Ching predicts.

"*If* summer ever comes." Sieg confesses we both feel exposed this morning. For the first time in months, we've tried coming to class without our winter underwear. Students must have done the same. They look remarkably thinner.

"It will get hot. Too hot!" Miss Zhuang Zhi promises. "Nanjing is one of three furnaces in China."

I'd like a yuan for every time we've heard those words. Mention Nanjing to any Chinese, here or at home. Three times out of five, their instant association is "furnace"!

What will happen in class when it really does heat up outdoors? Right now, there's a rising incidence of absences. Mr. Mao has some kind of eruption, probably shingles, on his back. It hurts him so much he can't lean back against the seat; he doesn't want to go out during the break into this morning's warmer sunshine. I check his vocabulary sentences early and tell him to head to the clinic.

Miss Zhuang, who doesn't have her sentences with her, also leaves for the clinic because of a sore in her mouth. In great earnestness, she peels her lip back to show me how much she's "suffering."

Mr. Lüe's girlfriend has come from the north to visit. He has been missing from class for three days. Mr. Lüe is certainly not alone in his drop-everything-for-a-friend response. Mr. Li and Mr. Fan have previously demonstrated identical reactions to such visits. Our own work-oriented ethic is so entrenched we find ourselves impatient with this Chinese custom. Still, spring makes us back off and ask, who is right? These young men and women invest the Chinese word for friend—*pengyou*—with far deeper passion than I've ever heard from fellow Americans. Perhaps, as they claim, Westerners *are* more superficial in our friendships, quicker to say "friend" without the deep sense of commitment that Asians honor.

Another seasonal symptom appears among students who sit, at least bodily, in class. One gazes out the open window at a prowling cat. Another reads a book under her desk, although she's supposed to be following Mr. Lao Sheng's news item at the lectern.

In a conversation round, Miss Liu's question for the group is "When can we have a picnic?"

Miss Li Yanping says: "I'm worried. I've run out of things to say. So heavy work surrounds us in our bedroom, my imagination doesn't work!"

This week's formal vocabulary handout contains the word *deleterious*. On checking the sentences where they use the new words, I find several students echo Miss Li's feeling. They each produce a version of "Too much homework is deleterious to health."

So we trim down our assignments. After all, these students face three teachers' demands in English alone, while late March insists there's more to life than books and papers.

41 · Some Absent, Some Present

It's Saturday morning. April, in all its early glory. Mr Guo, after a final pro forma meeting of teachers called to ask, "Can I do anything for you before I go?" has vanished for his anticipated half-semester in Texas.

While we linger over a postbreakfast cup of coffee, Mr. Lüe Shi and Mr. Lao Sheng appear, all smiles, at the door. I assume Mr. Lüe has come to turn in his reading report delayed by that three-day distracting visit from his girlfriend.

Wrong.

"We have come to tell you we won't be in class for two weeks," Mr. Lüe says. They both radiate abandon.

It seems that a Hehai faculty member is working in Guangzhou, frantically preparing an English-Chinese sports dictionary for this summer's Olympic Games in Korea. He needs two proofreaders. Mr. Guo's acting replacement has picked, naturally, Mr. Lüe, a loyal Communist Party member, first. Plum-rich Mr. Lüe has been delegated to choose his coworker. He has asked Mr. Lao, the current class monitor.

They'll miss two packed weeks of increasingly complex classes. "Maybe more," Mr. Lüe hints.

They leave this afternoon for a two-week experience that could start them on the way to further textual involvements. Their transportation, lodging, and meals are paid. They expect no money—just the privilege of learning by doing plus the luxury of traveling at no cost other than their own labor.

We certainly aren't going to say no, but we ask them to catch up later with missed assignments. Class discussions, of course, will be impossible to make up. In addition, will they talk to the class about their experiences?

"Of course," they both promise readily.

"By the way," Sieg asks, "do you have your current reading project done, Mr. Lüe?"

Mr. Lüe laughs. "No. You see, I was very busy last week."

Mr. Lao chuckles. "His girlfriend was here."

They depart, heading down the hall to explain their coming absence to Dan next. They are like two kids let out of school. Which, officially, they are.

Monday, we face a very small class. Mr. Xue Hai still has not returned. Mr. Mao, with his shingles, is missing. Mr. Zuo Niannian is gone too. The students flock to tell us why. He has received a telegram from his wife. Her unit leader commands her to come back to work following her pregnancy leave after the birth of their son. If she does not, she will lose her job. Mr. Zuo must take the long trip home to find a babysitter for their child.

With so many absent, we postpone our week's reading plans, which were moving toward Plato's difficult "Myth of the Cave." We substitute some easier, more modern material.

Today, we read and discuss a short story called "A Question of Blood," by Ernest Haycox. The plot centers on a disagreement between a frontier white man and his Native American wife over how to raise their son.

These students side with the father. They insist, "The wife is only an Indian and uneducated."

We protest their "only an Indian" and argue that she too has her own valid culture in which to raise her son.

The students are not convinced. They remain totally biased toward "education."

Wednesday, we're happy to see Mr. Mao back in class again. He says he feels much better. I chalk the day's two-hour in-class writing assignment on the board:

Chekhov, in his story, "The Wicked Boy," wrote: ". . . in this earthly life there is no absolute happiness. Happiness usually carries a poison in itself, or else is poisoned by something from outside." Reflect on your own or others' experience for evidence to support or argue against this seemingly pessimistic view.

The students settle to write. The classroom seems quietly absorbed. It is so cold Sieg tells me to take my raw throat back to the slightly warmer apartment. I'm glad to go.

Among the papers he brings back with him are the following.
Miss Xi Yang:

[UNTITLED]

I'm neither a complete pessimist nor a complete optimist. My attitude towards life is now a mixture of these two kinds, but mainly on pessimistic.

In my childhood, everything in my eyes was beautiful. Even during the Cultural Revolution, I was very young and ignorant. My grandparents and parents had no interest in politics. They didn't take part in any political group or argue with each other. Therefore, our family life was comparatively peaceful.

My parents often took me out for a walk. At that time the streets were clean and quiet. There were no large restaurants, no modern shops and no colorful lights.

When I went to primary school, the first sentence I learned to write was "Long live Chairman Mao!" Beside this, we were still required to learn Chairman Mao's works for half an hour every morning though we were too young to understand what they talked about.

I read them carefully and didn't forget to take notes afterwards. When a poor peasant was invited to give us a lecture on how the landlord had deprived him in a cruel way in the old society, tears were in my eyes. I took pity on him and hated the landlord very much. The school often gave us such a meticulous political and ideological education. We took all of these things for granted. They were all serious things.

After the smashing of the "gang of four," our Central Party declared that the so-called "Great Cultural Revolution" was ended and that it was just an upheaval. What a surprise! Everything was upside down. White became black. Right became Wrong.

With time passing, I grew up. I learned to see with my own eyes, then to think about some things.

Reality is not so beautiful as what the newspaper says and what I imagined in the past. Though I haven't yet got any job in society up till now, I still can see many serious social problems around me: the divorce rate is increasing; prices are constantly raised; juvenile delinquency, the "back doors," and the bureaucratic style of work are all problems in contemporary China.

I'm shocked at my discoveries and I don't know what to do with such wicked phenomena. Refuse to be contaminated by evil influences, or go along with them in their evil deeds? I agree to the former. So the more and more disenchanting feeling with our society and future will accompany me.

On the other hand, life for me has a bright aspect. I also own my happiness. I have many close friends. It's a great pleasure to have a chat with them. I like music, which can make me excited, or sentimental. I like walking slowly at dusk as well as playing games with children. Most important, I love nature—the cloudless sky, the brilliant sunshine, the blue sea, the green trees, the colorful flowers, the free birds and the quiet stream. I enjoy all of these!

Miss Chun Xu:

UNHAPPINESS-SWEETNESS

There is an old Chinese saying, "A loss may turn out to be a gain." This is based on a fable.

Long, long ago, an old man, living on the frontier, owned a group of horses. They were all strong and muscular. They could run one thousand miles per day. The old man was very proud of his possession.

One morning, he found that one of his mares was missing. He asked all the neighbors if they had seen it, but he got no answer. He was very depressed.

Several days later, when he was having supper, he suddenly heard a horse neighing outside his house. He quickly went out. He was pleasantly surprised to see the lost mare standing in front of him, with a colt.

The old man murmured, "When I lost my mare, who could have guessed it was a blessing in disguise?"

So I'd rather change what Chekhov said in this way: ". . . in this earthly life there is no absolute happiness. Unhappiness usually carries a 'sweet' in itself, or else is sweetened by something from outside."

No matter what other people think about my change, I absolutely believe in it myself. Every time when I meet with a difficulty, I never lose my heart. I face the unhappiness with a smile. I manage to find the resolution. I have the self-confidence that I can change the situation. When I succeed, I will have the chance to taste sweetness.

Once I got a low mark in an exam. I did feel ashamed and unhappy when I was told the news. But that was just a minute. After that I thought I was as clever as those top students. If I had worked very hard, I would have gotten a good mark too. Then I did what I had thought. For the next examination I studied even harder than those top students. I really got a good mark. I tasted the sweetness. How happy I was! The sweetness became more delicious to me after I had experienced bitterness.

Mr. Mao Yanyang:

POOR MAN

Whatever happiness people can find is usually accompanied by all sorts of anguish or trouble, either practically or spiritually. When you have got, by any means, a great fortune, you will always be led into thinking of how to deal with it, and be forced to remember the constant self-warning against theft or robbery.

You may have a beautiful girl friend or have married a fairylike wife. You will be too happy to believe whether it's true or not. "Does she really love me?" or "Does she have some malicious plans by marrying me?" Such problems always pull you toward unrest. Even if you believe her and her action as firmly as a rock, you also will be in doubt whether there is a man around you who is trying every means to induce her to love him. What an agony!

I'm no exception. More than twenty years' experiences have made me a qualified speaker to tell what it is like to have this contradictory state of mind.

For years, I have been feeling happy to receive others' blessing words concerning my success of career and also see their admiring eyes, but I also see something else.

They also have their own happy world, the world beyond my reach, the world seeming to me a long-wished-for dream. They live a comfortable and quiet life. They have happy families. It seems to me that they have no worry at all.

I have to struggle in the piles of books. I have to seek a future domicile. I have to deal with all the things that need me but don't interest me. I am the one who according to a Chinese saying, "finds it difficult to get down once riding on the back of a tiger." I have to go on and on to see what my future will be.

So do I feel happy? Yes, I can feel happy only when I receive others' praise for me. "You do well." I can feel happy only when I receive the credentials—the award for the loss. But most of the time I am sighing, sighing for loss of a quiet life, sighing for abandoning myself into constant fierce competition.

One word. Human beings are the most avaricious creatures in the world. We always seek for perfection, but there is no perfection. So when we can't get our increasing needs satisfied, we label ourselves as "poor" or "unfortunate." So happiness is an agony. A little happiness is a great agony, and a great happiness would produce a greater agony.

42 · Love, Sanitation Workers, and Rebellion

Mr. Xue Hai is back! He returns in rosy, restored health, thanks to traditional Chinese medicine and the ministrations of his dentist wife.

He comes to the apartment to check up on past assignments. He has brought us a bottle of aged vinegar, "a specialty of my province," and two new Seventh Party Congress commemorative stamps from his wife.

"They are new," he explains. "Some day they will be very valuable. Not everybody in China can buy such stamps. My wife has a certificate to buy. She has been collecting for more than five years!"

From the desk, Sieg pulls a folder of items we brought to China as possible gifts. He gives Mr. Xue an 1888 Chinese stamp watermarked with a yin-yang symbol, part of his own childhood collection.

"It's nice to see stamp collecting alive and flourishing in your country!" he says.

The next day we try out the vinegar on some greens. Mr. Xue is right. His province's glory is *very* distinctive.

Midweek, we take tangerines into class to distribute at the break. The students rarely get fruit. It's not served in campus meals, and rising market prices (2.30 yuan for a half kilo of tangerines) are way beyond their means.

This morning is another in-class writing day, with a difference. The first two hours give students writing time for their independent projects plus a chance for editorial suggestions from us if they choose.

Miss Liu, Mr. Li, and Miss Chun keep on visiting in their adjacent seats despite Sieg's "TO WORK" sign on the board and the model presented by less garrulous students. When they don't respond to glances, I separate them —just like junior high school kids. Mr. Li wipes off his second seat of the morning and peers at the assignment schedule on the board. Miss Liu opens her pencil box. Then they settle down to work.

Later, when they get their fruit, some of the students spend the break pelting each other with tangerine skins. Spring!

Miss Lü, Miss Li, and Mr. Fan finish drafts of their writing. They take turns joining us in the back of the room for individual conferences. We read, raise questions, and give suggestions about idioms. Then they go back to their seats to revise, add, and delete in final copies. We hope others will adopt this practice, as they discover it does help to have editorial response early on.

As usual for our independent projects, writers were free to choose their preferred genre. When we start our reading of today's papers in mid-afternoon, we find Mr. Xue Hai has written a poem he calls "Love."

> Lying on the bed with your eyes open,
> you argue with yourself again.
> You say:
> "She is not so beautiful!"
> But your mind answers:
> "It doesn't matter!"
>
> You sleeplessly turn this side and that,
> thinking without stopping:
> "Which is a real feeling?

Which is a lie?"
You say:
"She is not so intelligent!"
But your mind answers:
"It doesn't matter at all!"

Miss Xi Yang writes in her essay:

In our society, there is a kind of prejudice against the sanitation workers. They are looked down upon by some so-called high-class citizens. They are thought to be persons of lack of knowledge and of no elegance in both speech and manners. Middle school students, after graduation, don't like to be street-cleaners. Parents often instruct their children when they play too much outside, "Go back home! Work hard! Or you'll be a street cleaner!"

Sieg passes Miss Chen Hong's paper to me. "I don't know whether it's an essay or a story," he says. "It certainly comes directly from her experience in this setting, but she's invented names for her classmates and given it an earlier date."

Whatever it is, Miss Chen calls her piece "Gloomy Monday!"

Spring comes in March, the flowers are in full bloom, the grass and trees turn green. Everything comes back to life after the long winter sleep. But March is dreary for me because vacation is over and school has fallen on me. Today, a windy and rainy Monday, is part of the burden.

What makes it even worse is that I am forced to sit in the classroom to write a composition without anything in my mind. No doubt this shadow of gloom hangs over the cold classroom and over some of the people around me who sit with their heads down.

As I look around, all the teaching equipment seems old and depressing. The three-legged blackboard stands unsteadily in the front of the classroom. The teachers dare not write anything on it. It seems that as soon as you touch it, it will crack down. The teacher's desk is covered with dust. The teacher never puts his book on the desk but just holds it in his blue hand. Used pieces of chalk are scattered everywhere on the desk. Nobody collects them and puts them in the box.

Through the open window, the wind brings a tantalizing smell from the canteen not far from our classroom. It makes my mouth water and my stomach growl.

Aside from the unattractive surroundings, the people in the classroom also show their tension and impatience. Xiang Wang sits at my right, her hands under chin. She stares at the blackboard as if there were something on it that she could write about. At my left is Xiao Lin. He is chewing his pointer finger. On his desk there are a few black words on a piece of white paper. But from the way his brow knits I can see that he is also having trouble. His mind is wandering.

In front of me, two students talk in a low voice. They are lost in their private talk. They don't even notice that the teacher stands before them, frowning.

As I look down, this ugly desk of mine is filled with holes and scratches because other impatient students, when they lost their tempers, took out their anger on the wooden surface. I rub my hand across the desk. It feels rough and cold.

These last few miserable minutes make me wonder whether what my former classmates said about college is true. Where are the happiness and joy? Where are the freedom and relaxed atmosphere? I am not happy at all. I am supposed to be enjoying myself instead of suffering. It is spring now. We should go out to have a picnic, to smell the colorful flowers, to touch the green trees, and to sit on the warm grass.

But I have to sit in this refrigerator, racking my brains to write a composition. Oh, what happiness I will have without all these assignments!

"Poor Miss Chen!" We have been crouching over this heap of papers for so long that I sympathize with her fully. "Join the crowd."

43 · Territories

A warbling yellow-billed blackbird wakes us at six o'clock this morning. We gaze at him through hazy blue folds of our newly installed mosquito net that dim everything. Sieg has thumbtacked its voluminous cascade to the wall at the head of the bed, trying to get it out of our faces. Through a fold darkly we watch a second blackbird join the first, swell and preen its feathers, then sidle up to the first bird, which flies away.

A pleasant way to wake up!

In reading class, we finish discussing Alexander Leighton's long 1946 essay titled "That Day at Hiroshima." In a previous class, we cleared up vocabulary questions and looked closely at the essay's structure as well as its use of facts, images, and words skillfully chosen to convey the author's attitude toward his grim subject.

Now Sieg leads the students to compare Chinese feelings about the Nanjing massacre with their judgment of American actions in Hiroshima and Nagasaki.

Even though these students weren't born in 1945, their residual bitterness wells up in furious condemnation of individual Japanese atrocities that took place in many provinces in China. They describe the American killing in Hiroshima as "scientific," "clean."

Miss Liu says she read our pilots didn't even "realize what they were dropping."

The class gets so excited arguing they start to shift into Chinese and have to be brought back to English.

Mrs. Ching Chao exclaims, "If China had a bomb at that time and could drop it on Japan we would have done it and had no guilt!"

Their emotions lead them to ignore that innocent civilians, including children, died horribly in Hiroshima as well as in Nanjing.

"The Japanese bombed Pearl Harbor, attacking it without warning," several insist, "so they got what they deserved in return."

Clearly, these young Chinese don't share either Leighton's or our sense of regret despite justifications at the time for what we did.

At class break, Miss Zhuang Zi gives another current reason for resentment. "The Japanese are still invading us economically," she argues. "They send their better products to the West and send poor quality products over here. Like TV sets and tape recorders."

I'm startled by her claim. "What's your reason to believe that?"

"I've read it in the newspaper." Her tone suggests that's all the proof necessary.

Students leave class still talking vehemently about the differences between Hiroshima and Nanjing.

Next hour, during a vocabulary lesson featuring the students' own sentences, I get a lesson in my mother tongue. This week, one of our words is "spurious." On the dittoed handout, I had defined spurious as "false; not genuine" and used it in a sentence about counterfeiting ten-dollar bills.

Miss Feng Yunxia reads her original sentence aloud. "The spurious child was looked down on because his parents weren't married."

"But the child is real," I object, "even if illegitimate."

"Our Chinese-English dictionary gives that meaning," Miss Feng rejoins.

I'm delighted to see her willing to argue for her viewpoint against a teacher's! Last semester, Mr. Ku Qiu subsided into immediate, polite silence when I assumed his use of the word "steelyard" for a weighing device at markets was wrong. Only later, when I checked a large dictionary, did I discover my provincial ignorance. At that point, I went back to Mr. Ku, praised his accuracy, and chided him for not challenging me.

Miss Lü Shu passes me her *Webster's* for a quick check on "spurious." Miss Feng is right. The original Latin word *spurius* meant "bastard," and apparently Chinese dictionaries emphasize that sense.

Friday, we tackle a short story, "Truth and Consequences," by Brendan Gill. It's about a young girl and a young boy. She's lame, somewhat foulmouthed, but vigorous. He's dedicated, mostly by his mother's imperious wishes, to becoming a priest. The story captures youthful awakening and defiance of authority.

In some ways, I wonder about the mischief of introducing such material to these young postgraduates already chafing under various forms of cultural and institutional restraints. Literature has recognized power to open readers' eyes to previously undared possibilities.

But if I hesitate over changes this story could start in our students' lives, I delight in its holding up a handicapped heroine who is attractive in body and spirit. Too often in China, our students have said, anyone who differs in any way from the norm gets ignored, laughed at, passed over, or rejected. The exception who struggles to some form of success and recognition draws high praise. But for the few who beat the odds, there are countless flawed others who remain uneducated, unmarried, unemployed, and cannot succeed so long as there are millions of "standard" people around.

The class warms to "Truth and Consequences." They marvel at the idea of teenagers being able to own and drive cars. They think the girl's hand is "cool and unmoving" in the boy's hand when his furious, about-to-be-defied mother approaches because "the girl wanted to help the boy be calm."

Their questions about the girl's profanity and the boy's transformation lead to a discussion of Western ethical behavior. Sieg chalks a brief version of the Ten Commandments on the board. The three that especially appeal to the class are "Honor your father and mother," "You shall not steal," and "You shall not bear false witness against your neighbor."

"People did that," Mr. Fan says about the last one, "during the Cultural Revolution."

Several days later, for his next independent writing project, Mr. Li Jian chooses this story for comment. He heads his essay "A Reflection on 'Truth and Consequences.'"

In Brendan Gill's short story, "Truth and Consequences," Charles, the hero, was an eighteen-year-old boy and a would-be priest under the strict and didactic instructions of his mother. He had never got in touch with any girl of his age until a lame girl with blond hair and a red mouth came to him, pressed her hands on his, and finally changed his belief in his vocation.

After I finished reading the story, I could not help recalling my strict and stiff relation with a girl deskmate at elementary school. Due to the feudal tradition of relationship between male and female in China, the influence of aged parents, and the fear of being criticized from old-fashioned teachers, boys and girls drew a clear line between them no matter what they did at that time.

At our school, pupils could not choose their own deskmates. Boy pupils could not sit together because they did mischievous things like making faces, and talking to each other in a low voice in class. The teacher arranged the seats for all the pupils. Usually a boy sat with a girl. (At the time a desk was for two persons.)

At the beginning of first term, several days passed peacefully. Gradually some quarrels began to occur between deskmates about the "territory" on their desks.

Having seen this happen to several classmates, some of us boys thought of an idea: to draw a line on the desks, which divided the surface into two equal parts.

Because March 8 is International Women's Day, we used "March 8" to indicate women, and called the line drawn on the desk the "March 8 line." Whenever our opponents, the girl deskmates, "invaded" our "territory," a war would break out. If it happened in class, the war would be silent for fear of the teacher's punishment; if it took place after class, it would be noisy. The boys and girls would have sharp and nasty words for each other.

I still remember what I did with her when my girl deskmate put her arm across the line. When I had classes, I often kept an eye on the dividing line. Almost every five minutes I glanced at the "integrity of my territory." Once she moved her arm over the line no matter consciously or subconsciously, I moved my elbow bit by bit toward the "front." As soon as my elbow hit hers, she immediately drew back. Sometimes, though, she did not move at all. We elbowed each other silently, still facing the blackboard. The stalemate continued until she found that she was not my rival in strength.

Sometimes girls sitting in front of boys reclined against the boys' desk. The boys would smear the front edge of the desk with blue or black ink. Whenever a girl in front leaned against the desk, she would get a stain on her jacket. Then she would learn the lesson not to recline against the desk again unless she wanted another blur.

Just like Charles in the story, we were very sensitive to anything about girls at that time, but we never thought about being a priest as he did.

44 : A Mixed Bag

Spring comes on at a gallop. So does the last week in April. Students act frantic, tense, anticipating Dan's linguistics midterm to be held Friday. To give them more time for study, we ease off on outside assignments. During Monday's reading class, we renew English pronunciation practice in the now familiar Hiroshima article.

Each student reads several paragraphs aloud. While one solos, others mutter the same text in muted accompaniment. This patient, mass production of sounds feels comfortable to them as a normal Chinese way to learn. When we hit difficult words, like "buttes" and "incendiary," I stop the person reading and model the word. Everybody then tries the word out on his or her tongue.

Wednesday is another talking day in reading class. We've asked students to choose authors or subjects they want to look up in the library's encyclopedias and to talk about their extended project involving reading, writing, and speaking so that class members or we might make suggestions to help their search.

Thursday afternoon, as prearranged, both Sieg and I go to the library to guide any of our nineteen who want help locating materials. Several sign into the reference room.

We have to keep our voices low because engineering faculty and students are working near the encyclopedias at the few tables available.

We had anticipated our group might have a little trouble finding their way between the *Britannica*'s recent Macropaedia and Micropaedia sets. We're staggered to discover even the most fluent English postgraduates don't know how to locate either author or subject in a particular volume by using the letter ranges on the books' spines. Once we explain, they grasp the system quickly. They seem literally thrilled to find so much information in books that, they say, they hadn't known existed.

As we leave the reference room late in the afternoon, some students from the class still work on.

May! Calendulas and poppies brighten the campus. Young women appear in translucent dresses innocent of slips. We don't see any male Chinese heads swiveling, but they can't be indifferent. More couples commune along secluded paths in the park.

A new source of protein turns up in market—garter snakes. Our almost daily trips for food, now that the weather has moderated, never fail to amaze. Peanut sellers have returned to sit companionably side by side on the curbs. They keep open sacks before them. Often a plump, bright-eyed baby, which the row of sellers take turns watching, plays on rough cement blocks behind them.

The old lady with the blind eye clacks her wooden block steadily on her rolling ice cream cart to remind customers she is back on her corner. Today, a man ahead of us in the throng spots something on the pavement. He bends, picks up an eel, a frantically wriggling stray from some other shopper's bicycle bag. Finders keepers. The man laughs at his good fortune.

Our students have just survived a double psychological whammy: Dan's linguistics exam and a First of May holiday that gave everyone a three-day weekend. Now it's back to classroom demands, stepped up as the semester moves toward its scheduled July end.

Morale in class, for both students and teachers, seems to be on a yo-yo. This morning, all but Miss Bin Qilin come unprepared. A week ago, I announced, "Begin reading the first two pages of Plato's 'Myth of the Cave.' Next week, bring to class a drawing of his central image in the dialogue to show your interpretation of it."

When I call for their drawings, they look at me, dumbfounded. "We forgot," several say. "You should have reminded us."

They do the assignment in class. Then we compare sketches. This "show" and discussion lift everyone's mood temporarily. We all like comparing the visual results, the height of shadows leaping on the wall, what length chains shackle the prisoners, where classmates have placed Socrates' fire and sun. When we finish, the whole process, for starters, has literally drawn the class to a clearer understanding of Plato's meaning.

Midweek, prolonged lightning, thunder, and rain during the night apparently silence the entire campus loudspeaker system. No 6:00 A.M. blast anywhere! At 7:30, when we splash into the classroom (the new building has sprung a major leak; an inch of water floods its entrance hall), only three students are present. Ten straggle in during the next twenty minutes. Six remain absent.

Those present settle slowly into in-class writing on individual projects. Miss Lü Shu sits upright, still, her eyes half shut, deep in thought. Miss Bin, having scratched out one paragraph, puts her head down on a pillowing arm. I assume she is also thinking. If not, if she's catching forty winks, let her. She can do the writing later outside. It's her choice.

Morning dawns grey as a water buffalo's flank, sodden with rain.

In class, we hear two longer presentations by Mr. Xue Hai and Mr. Fan Rui, based on their encyclopedia research. Mr. Xue has abandoned his announced report on Robert Burns in favor of "an important figure—Gloria Steinem."

Mr. Fan has found Hemingway fascinating, especially his four wives. Throughout Mr. Fan's report, one student reads a newspaper tucked under her desk.

This afternoon, it helps our morale to pick up and reread two essays from yesterday's independent writing. Mr. Zuo Niannian, responding to the final words in Joan Mondale's speech to Macalester College graduates, makes his title "Choose One's Own Path to Fulfillment—Joan Mondale."

> Recently, I have often been haunted by the dream that I might get rich and have a lot of money to do whatever I like to do, such as eating deli-

cious food, traveling a great deal and buying new clothes for my wife and myself. I have envied those who are rich. I have been very disappointed to find that I must be prudent in spending the money I have.

I know that a businessman can be rich. Could I become one? I have asked myself such a question frequently. The answer, as I see, is that I was not born as a businessman. I don't know how to sell. I wouldn't know how to praise the products. And I would be frightened. As a salesman, you should run from one place to another. In short, it would be a bankruptcy rather than riches for me to be a businessman.

I asked myself too: If I had enough money to spend as I would, what pleasure would it bring me? Would I really like it? For me, the answer is hard to be a positive "yes."

The culture in this country didn't encourage people to be rich until recent years. I was born and raised in this culture. I have lived in it for over three decades. I am familiar with it. I find the simple life is comfortable and suitable for my getting the goals of my life, that is, to understand the nature and to understand the people.

I have done teaching for nearly a dozen years. It is a way for me to get at the fulfillment of my life. During my working for and with the students, I have been understanding the people. I find myself to be useful to some of them, which gets rid of the dullness of my life.

Now, I am continuing to study what I should learn to be an advanced teacher. My life is not rich in material goods, but it promises well in fulfillment. It is this path that I have found and continue to choose to take.

For the same assignment, Mr. Xue Hai has written an account of a memorable experience.

ON MY WAY TO UNIVERSITY

Bikes passed in both directions, their bells ringing. Cars came and went, their horns honking.

I rushed to the bus stop holding several pieces of pancake in one hand and carrying a briefcase in the other. I managed to squeeze on a bus. The door shut, catching the back of my jacket.

"Comrade, my jacket is caught in the door," I said.

"Please buy tickets or show your monthly tickets," the conductress called over the microphone again and again, drowning my voice.

"If you are not getting off, Comrade, let's change places," suggested a young lady.

"Change places? OK." I tried to move forward, but I failed. My jacket held me tightly. I apologized, "I'll get down first at the next stop."

She moved onto the step above me, her white, white neck just opposite my face. Her wide-open collar showed a red woolen sweater. My heart beating very fast at that time, I turned my head to avoid staring at her.

There was a sudden commotion in the bus. One of the women passengers standing in the middle had lost her purse. She cried loudly and tearfully, "Who steals my purse? Hand it over to me quickly! I lost nearly one hundred yuan. What's wrong? My God, my God . . ."

"Hand it over! Whoever took it!" yelled the conductress.

The bus stopped at the side of the highway.

"Give it back quickly! Give it back quickly! We don't want to be late to work!" other passengers in the bus shouted.

At that time, I was in a dilemma. I couldn't advance, nor could I retreat. It was a rush-hour. Passengers were urgent to go to work, so the bus I took was packed.

"What lousy luck!" I murmured. "I never met such a difficult problem before. Probably I'll be late for classes today. How can I explain it to my students?" My heart beat faster than ever. I broke into a sweat all over my body.

"Hand it over at once! Don't waste our time!" the conductress yelled again angrily. "Otherwise we'll drive to the police station."

Pushing forward, a young girl was in a great hurry and trod on an old woman's foot with her high-heeled shoes.

Granny screeched, "Are you blind, young devil!"

The young girl turned a deaf ear to it and pushed her way hard and directly to the driver.

"Comrade driver, I must reach the hospital at 7:30. There is still half an hour to go. I have enough time to change buses. You may open the door and let me get off." The young girl's voice was supplicating.

"No, no, I'm sorry," the driver said politely. "We serve all passengers and are responsible for everyone. We have to go to the police station now."

The driver started the bus and drove passengers along [the] road. The bus was running so fast I could not see clearly the buildings, trees, or pedestrians' appearance passing by.

Within less than ten minutes, the bus reached a police station. The driver jumped off the bus from the door at his left and rushed into the station. Soon the driver came out with several policemen. These police stood around the bus door forming a ring of encirclement.

The door of the bus opened, I nearly fell out. The police waved me to go. As I moved about and gasped for breath, I found that sweat trickled down my neck gently.

At that moment, a voice suddenly came from the bus. "It's all right, I have found the purse," someone called out, stooping to pick up the purse. The others pressed forward.

"Look and see if anything's missing."

That woman passenger examined her purse, and said, "Nothing's missing." She thanked the driver and those policemen again and again.

I got on the bus again and stood behind the driver, urging him to drive quickly.

When I reached the University, I heard the bell for class just ringing. As I neared the classroom, I saw my students were waiting for me in it. Forgetting to put my pancakes into my pocket, I hurried into the class-room like a gust of whirlwind.

45 . So Big a World in a Moment

Despite warnings to narrow and focus their reports, Li Yanping announces she will give us a bird's-eye view of Shakespeare, covering "the man, his career in the theatre, his early poems, sonnets, plays (comedies and tragedies), and his influence"—in twenty minutes. In haste, she omits a crucial *t* when she reads from her report, "Sonnets 18 through 125 promised to bestow immorality on the young man."

Li Jian tackles the Rossetti family, writing his major points on the board. He interrupts his speech part way to hack and make a deposit in the classroom spittoon. We would condemn this habit more if we didn't know for ourselves how blown dust and ever-present coal smoke in this part of China cause everybody, native and foreign alike, constant sinus drainage and phlegm. At the moment, my problems are compounded once again by a painful sore throat.

The next morning, my voice could qualify me as a Russian bass. "You talk today," I croak to Sieg. It's lucky we've scheduled in-class writing after two more presentations.

Miss Zhuang Zi brings us Mark Twain—again. Because Mr. Ku Qiu has already told us much about Twain's works in his report, Miss Zhuang says she will concentrate on the following headings: (1) Early Life, (2) Western Years, (3) Marriage, and (4) Hartford Years. She puts each category on the board in capital letters.

Yesterday, while I could still talk, I asked the students whether their Chinese teachers used this same system of outlining their lectures. The class said yes, adding they felt very comfortable with this custom. "It helps us take notes."

For variety, Mr. Mao Yanyang gives us D. H. Lawrence. He had first started researching Freud, but one day he stopped Sieg in the library, saying, "I can't go before the class with *that* material!" As it is, the mere mention of *Lady Chatterley's Lover* (an editor was fired recently for publishing the controversial novel in China) reaps Mr. Mao knowing leers and sniggers. He coolly faces his audience at that point, and also when they laugh every time he says "hooman" for "human."

Mr. Mao interrupts his prepared talk. "Why do you laugh?"

The class just sits and smirks at him.

Sieg provides the standard pronunciation. Mr. Mao repeats "human" and continues to use it correctly as he finishes his comments on Lawrence's significance in English literature.

Wherever he goes, Mr. Mao will go far.

During the next two hours, while students write, responding to any part they choose from Plato's "Myth of the Cave," I return to our own apartment cave for a warm, welcome, mid-morning, throat-indulgent nap.

In the afternoon, Sieg and I begin reading student papers. Mr. Zuo Niannian starts his essay with a comparison:

> One Chinese parable says that there is a frog living in a dry well. All he can see is the little piece of the sky from the well-mouth. He thinks that the whole sky is just as big as the mouth of the well because he has never left the dry well once. We may see what a false image he has formed from his limited point of view.
>
> When I read the first paragraph of "The Myth of the Cave" by Plato, I couldn't help thinking of our limitated view of our world.

Miss Bin Qilin chooses a later paragraph. She begins by quoting, in part: "he would rather suffer anything than entertain those false notions and live in this miserable manner."

> When people get light, they know what is the truth and where the truth is. They will pursue the truth. During "the Great Cultural Revolution," many people got fooled and mad. They didn't know what was the truth. They did destruction, but thought they were revolutionary. They made our country poorer and poorer, but thought China was developing forward.
>
> However, there were still a few people who saw that China at that time was really a mess. They found that if the situation continued, China would be destroyed. In spite of many, many difficulties, they stood forward to tell and guard the truth. They knew they would die for doing that. They still couldn't believe the false notion. Some of them really died. Now, people can see they are true. "The Great Cultural Revolution" was really a terrible period when some people would "suffer anything" rather than "entertain false notions."

I put down Miss Bin's paper with a prickle of pleasure. Her hard work this semester to improve her writing is paying off. And if only she and her generation can just keep hold of their new perceptions!

Eagerly, I pick up Mr. Li Jian's response. He addresses a later part of Plato's dialogue:

> In our times, Socrates' view that "the happiness was to be in the whole state" is very modern, especially among some high officials in order to show their high spiritual level. But in fact, how many of them keep to their slogan?
>
> Chronologically speaking, those who joined the revolutionary course at the early period of Chinese revolution were devoted to the goal, the liberation of the exploited Chinese people. Most of them built their reputation on the solid foundation of hard work and the spirit of self-sacrifice. However, after China entered the peaceful and developmental period, a few of the former revolutionaries degenerated. Some of the newly nominated officials say one thing but do another.
>
> Let me leave the old generation and come to their juniors. Quite a few climbed to high position by either backbiting the opponents or flattering their superiors.

Let me show you an example. One of my friend's classmates at college holds a considerable post at the college by this means.

I've heard quite a lot of students complaining about having dull and boring political classes. My friend's classmate went to the opposite viewpoint. In order to show he had done a great deal of work and to be promoted, almost every Thursday afternoon he summoned all his classmates to a big room to study the so-called documents of the Central Committee.

What did he do at the time? He just sat at the back of the classroom dozing. The students who brought magazines or newspapers read their own favorites. Others who did not bring anything with them felt on pins and needles because they had nothing to do in the classroom. They couldn't go due to his checking names at the end of two hours in the classroom.

By sacrificing the time of his classmates and by his compliments to his superiors, he stayed at the college and was promoted as a vice-dean of the department.

What's the whole happiness? It's all gone to the sole person!

"I wonder if this is what goes on in the library when it's closed every Wednesday afternoon for political study?" I manage to whisper.

"It's possible." Sieg hands me Mao Yanyang's paper. "You should know, while he was writing this, Mr. Mao knocked himself on the head three times with a closed fist."

"Did it work?"

"Read it and see."

Mr. Mao heads his essay "Ignorance and Knowledge."

Plato stated that the man "dragged up a steep and ragged ascent" would gradually become accustomed to the real world. . . . The man would also begin to have a pity for his past image world, for his past fellowmen who were now still living in the false and dark world in which they had great faith. He would firmly believe in his new situation. . . .

I was brought up in a relatively cultural-closed town. The people had a limited cultural background. They didn't know foreign countries. They didn't know how to understand and act. They had lots of traditional concepts which are today hampering their development. To some extent, they were ignorant.

But before I received any kind of high education, before I came out to see more of the world, I was a member of that environment and never sensed that. I never even thought of another wide world around. I got used to that small world.

So when at first I began to move out of this dark and small "cave," I felt a little "dazzled." I couldn't accept so much fresh knowledge, so big a world in a moment. But gradually I began to change. I learned lots of things, saw enough of the world to become a completely different man in nature from my past, from my fellowmen living still in that poor situation.

As a result, when I came back home, I often felt a sense of loneliness. I couldn't join them as much in their ideas. They couldn't receive my information and way of thinking either. Alienation cropped up, but I was not regretful.

Perhaps in their eyes, I was abominated, but they should understand such a simple truth: ignorance and knowledge can never coexist. A man can never share those two features. What is more, a man is more abominable when he is ignorant without knowing his ignorance.

I glance over Mr. Mao's paper again. "Looks like it did work," I whisper. "What would he have written if he knocked four times?"

46 : May Moods

Monday, on top of spring with roses blooming and ginkgo tree leaves fully out, saps student powers of concentration. They sit up straight and cheer, however, when we postpone a paper due Friday, to lighten this week's assignments. But something else weighs them down, something we haven't yet been able to identify.

We know they held a postgraduate class meeting Saturday, because Monitor Lao Sheng announced it in Chinese last week before class.

This morning Sieg asks, "Was there anything in your meeting we should know about?"

"Someone will talk to you later," Mr. Lao answers.

No "someone," no "later" comes at the break or after class. At 11:15 everybody vanishes for lunch.

Dan drops by after our own customary heap of rice, pork, and greens. He's had a meeting at the office with the interim head of postgraduates, who is filling in during Guo Kun's absence. That gentleman has conveyed the complaint that our mutual students feel they are "working too hard." Facing Dan's regular journal assignments, his demanding content and handouts (without textbook) in linguistics, our once-a-week outside papers and other interrelated assignments, plus twenty hours of classes each week, they feel they have "too much!"

Dan has uncovered two other sources of pressure on them: the students' university allowance, hurt by rising inflation, is not enough to meet their food expenses now. Those who can find work outside are doing extra teaching, or translation, or whatever they can locate.

In addition, their department recently had to score three thousand Hehai student entrance papers. The office put some of the postgraduates to the task, fortunately with pay. But often these students worked six hours a day on the exams, sometimes until 10:30 at night, and *then* began their own classwork preparation.

Yet no one hinted to us about this extra drain on their energies. If we hadn't happened to give a sample projective inventory last week, a way of tapping into students' feelings about their work through statement completions, we wouldn't have sensed their increasing stress. Why in China must so much information come indirectly, often too late? Only our chance joining of facts today with Dan's reveals arguments our students could justifiably have raised for earlier relief.

"They've made another request through channels." Dan grins. "They want to spend the last week before their exam study week reviewing this semester's materials. 'No new work,' they say. That means my final week of new instruction moves back to next week!"

"If the same holds true for us," Sieg says, "this will be a much shorter semester than we planned."

We'll wait for the next interesting shoe to drop.

Today's *China Daily,* delivered to the Guest House days after publication, bears the date May 14. The "Letters to the Editor" column has a cheering blooper. It's impossible to tell whether paper or author created it.

The writer, who signs a Chinese name, rails against Japanese unwillingness to admit they have been repeated "invaders." The letter writer warns his readers, "I think a degree of vigilance is highly necessary. Philosopher George Santayana said it very well: Those who forget their past are condemned to report it."

We ease up slightly on assignments. Sieg and I take turns giving more lecture-type material about authors and subjects scheduled for class discussion. The students are grateful. Their spirits rise.

Mr. Lao Sheng's command to Tuesday's conversation group: "Everybody prepare a joke. If no joke, tell us a happy or sad experience."

"Once there was a Chinese beggar," Miss Feng Yunxia responds. "When fifty years old, he is now rich. He wants to get married, but he is a cripple, with a badly injured leg.

"The matchmaker says, 'Go see your future wife. Ride a horse.'

"The beggar accepts her advice. He goes to see the woman. He finds *her* on a horse. You see," Miss Feng explains, "they are both cripples. Neither one wants to be the first in bed.'

Everybody laughs.

With his question of the morning, Mr. Lüe Shi returns us to sterner stuff. "Please say two or three concise sentences on your summer resolutions." He waits.

"The chairman," Mr. Xue Hai suggests, "should go first."

"The chairman," Mr. Lüe echoes, "should draw conclusions."

Slowly, the circle begins to answer. Many of them say they plan to rest, read, and do housework, but all somewhere include their acute need to earn money.

"My uncle and aunt from Taiwan brought an English book on economic managements," Mr. Ku Qiu says. "I will try to translate it. If book is published, I will be paid. Also, I will find a work place for own teaching. If I can pay ten thousand yuan, I can be released here."

"Wait a minute," Sieg says. "Explain that. Ten thousand yuan?"

The students rush to enlighten us. Having received their government-sponsored training free from Hehai, they are bound to teach English classes in this or in an allied hydraulic engineering institution unless they can buy their way out of their contract. Sometimes a business or a unit outside that really wants their services will pay the huge sum, but it's hard to find one.

"You see," one student says, only half joking, "we are really slaves."

"Perhaps it is not ten thousand yuan. Perhaps only six thousand," someone says hopefully.

No time for more airing of this issue. The next conversation group is at the door.

Over lunch in a downtown restaurant, Sieg asks Dan about this morning's discussion of payment to purchase educated students.

"They told the truth," Dan says. "Hehai trains them, gives them housing and a stipend, so they're obligated."

"Are Hehai's costs as much as they get from an outside 'buyer'?" Sieg asks.

"Probably not, but it varies. The price can drop, especially if Hehai and its sister institution don't need all the teachers it trains. I've heard they're going to use about ten of the nineteen in the present class."

"And another group of postgraduates starts next fall!"

"Which should add to their profits." Dan finishes his bean curd and pushes his plate aside to study the dessert list. "I think I'll have 'Glutinous Rice Dumplings with Red Bean.' "

47 . Livestock and Other Surprises

Friendship Hill has acquired some newly active inhabitants. Within the apartment, a family of huge black cockroaches, fast and determined enough to win the Boston Marathon, keeps trying to invade our sealed-up foods. We escort as many as possible outdoors. Either they or their cousins keep returning to the hunt.

Outside, on window screens at night, tan lizards catch white moths. The lizards run when I tickle their fast-pulsing tummies with a broom straw, but just to the corner of the screen. Beyond them, the season's first tree frogs have turned up their vibrant mating calls. So has a wild, scrawny, black and white tomcat. It lives on rats from the ever-renewed canteen garbage heap, on birds, and on frequent leftovers we set out on plantain leaves behind the Guest House.

Our hilltop has acquired a new form of lawn mower. Those two cheerful peasant ladies who plucked and weeded the grass down on their knees last fall have not reappeared. Instead, a young white goat with small horns works the job. Every morning early, someone from the kitchen tethers the goat to a succession of trees. The goat chomps grass in hungry circles. In going round and round any tree, however, the goat snubs itself ever closer to the trunk until it can't move at all and bleats in protest.

Again and again, Sieg steps over the hedge to unwind the goat or refill its dumped water pan. Is the creature grateful? No way. It tries to butt Sieg's legs every chance it gets.

We're sad to discover the true purpose of the small animal. One morning it disappears. That night it turns up on the banquet table to help Muslim foreign students celebrate the end of Ramadan.

Shi Changmei has been absent from the Waiban office for some days. She's gone north to Beijing, trying to arrange for our tickets home and the final partial conversion of our salaries. It's a long trip, eighteen hours' train ride one way. We hope she's able to enjoy her "vacation," at least in part. She's taken our passports with her. When she returns, her news is unsettling. *Perhaps* we have tickets for July 2. She isn't sure. She might have to go again. The salary matter hasn't yet been cleared up. "There is a difficulty." She doesn't explain. We don't press. It's quite possible Hehai has used up its allotment of hard currency for the year.

Sieg asks for our passports back.

"Oh, they are still in Beijing."

We feel politically naked.

In class, Mr. Fan Rui mentions a traditional Chinese belief that the earth is square but heaven is round. Recalling the round kivas of our own southwestern Indians and the traditional preferences of past and present Native Americans for round groupings of all sorts, I ask the class more about the Chinese belief. They explain the old idea came from the people's sense of horizon: heaven was round and held up by pillars.

In a later class discussion, they question what Westerners mean by "Protestant work ethic."

"If you worked hard and prospered," Sieg explains, "people used to believe you were clearly one of God's elect. Some people still think so." He looks around the class. "All over the world, Chinese people are known for working very hard. Does this pattern have anything to do with religion?"

Not at all, they insist. "It's just to be successful. It's practical."

Today, we check sentences the students have written in response to Orwell's "Politics and the English Language." I've asked them to make up "bad" sentences showing at least one fault Owell criticizes and to revise their examples into English he would have approved.

Their sentences show they understand Orwell's recommendations: wherever possible, cut long or unneeded words, passives, confusing negatives, tired figures of speech, and fancy words when a plain one will do.

Mr. Li Jian revises his "The *crème de la crème* student is said to have committed suicide" to "Some said the top student killed himself."

Mrs. Ching Chao edits her "As far as I am concerned, I am not an unlucky person" to "I am a lucky person."

If this had been a contest, Mr. Xue Hai might have won a prize for his contribution. He changes "Our teacher said that that that that he wrote in his exercise book was wrong" to "Our teacher said the pronoun 'that' he wrote in his exercise book was wrong."

On Friday, a sunny warm morning, the students are as flighty as butterflies. They have a hard time settling down to their in-class independent writing. Several of them buzz, giggle, and chatter about more than exchange of dictionaries.

A few serious students, trying to concentrate, look up, annoyed. By turns, Sieg and I patrol the aisles—a policing action we dislike intensely. Miss Li asks me if I think she could write about a beautiful mountain path she once took. I try to get her to voice what she'd like to say about that path. She can't recall it clearly.

After her second trip to the restroom, she turns around in her seat again. "I once had an experience in middle school working at a beach. How about that?"

She sounds enthusiastic. "Go ahead!" I tell her.

She goes to the restroom again and hasn't come back by the end of class.

Sieg spreads on the table the students' linguistics journals, which Dan has given us to distribute. All the students rise at once as if controlled by a single set of strings. They rush for the table, grab their journals, and read Dan's responses intently.

Class is over for the weekend, except for one final exchange. Mr. Lao Sheng and Mr. Lüe Shi present a new request. The class has end-of-semester travel plans now. There is money in the department budget to provide almost a week's tour for everybody. Of course, everyone wants to go. This means exam week must move back another week. Study for exam week comes before that, with all classes canceled. The formal semester will end in two weeks—just ten more days of regular classes.

Our original understanding was that the semester finished after the first week in July. This semester now ends the third week in June. If we had known this before Shi Changmei traveled to Beijing to buy our tickets, we could have gone home a full week earlier!

Once again, too little knowledge, too late.

I cheer up when I read Mr. Xue Hai's paper. This fine spring morning, he titled it "A Drizzle in the Fall."

> Extremely tired and bored after a long time preparing for my graduate-student examination, I reached for my pack of cigarettes. Ph! It was empty! But I was eager to smoke. Where did my wife hide my recently-bought cigarettes? For the sake of my health, she did not allow me to smoke. Maybe, she put them in the newly-made clothes press.
>
> I walked to it on tip-toe and had a look. Its door was open. It was empty inside. Maybe, she put them under her pillow!
>
> Take them, I thought. I walked to her bed dauntlessly, but gently.
>
> "No." I stopped, hesitating. "She worked a whole day, let her have a sound and sweet sleep."
>
> I looked at my watch. It was ii o'clock. Maybe, I could buy some on the street. I left my reading-room and locked the door into the corridor with a click. Then I came down stairs.
>
> Outside, all was silent. There were a few pedestrians, and some dim street lights shimmering. A chilly breeze made me shiver. I quickly pulled my coat closer.
>
> As I went further, I saw two vague figures under a light, one in red and the other in green. Getting nearer, I found two little girls selling cigarettes, each sitting opposite the other and shaking with the cold.
>
> They saw me coming nearer and turned their eyes toward me.
>
> "What poor girls!" I thought. "Why don't you go home and sleep since it is so late?" I felt for my purse in my pocket. But then I hesitated as I saw both of them gazing at me eagerly, as if to ask, "Are you buying mine?"
>
> Whose should I buy? If I bought from one, I would disappoint the other. Finally, I passed each of them one yuan without buying any. But I felt their thankful looks as I passed.

Now it was drizzling. Some raindrops fell on my face. Their anxious eyes seemed still to flash at me.

I suddenly hit on an idea. Why not buy some packs from each. I turned back and walked quickly toward them.

The two little girls still sat closely together under a beautiful green umbrella.

"I want to buy some Yu Lin cigarettes," I said, as I took out five yuan. Neither of them took my money.

"How many packs have we sold today for Granny Wu?" The girl in red turned to her friend.

This moment, I saw both of them clearly. The girl in red had small eyes, thin eyebrows, and pretty lips. The one in green had two short pigtails, with a big nose under her big eyes.

"Who is Granny Wu?" I asked curiously.

"Granny Wu? She is an old widow living in our village," replied the girl in red. Pointing at her friend, she said, "She has no school on Sundays. So both of us help Granny Wu with her selling."

The girl in green smiled bashfully.

"Yu Lin cigarettes? How many?" asked the girl in red, taking my money.

"Five packs," I said.

I took the cigarettes and walked home. As I walked, I turned back my head at times and saw the two little girls under the dim light in the drizzle, looking like flower buds under a greenish leaf.

"What fine qualities they have!" I couldn't help saying out loud. "I must tell my students about them tomorrow."

So thinking, I reached my home. I opened the door and found my wife still snoring softly and sleeping soundly.

"Aha!" I made a face in the corner and said softly, "I have bought packs of cigarettes again, dear. What will you do with me?"

48 . "What I Believe"

Sunday, during his prebreakfast walk, Sieg meets at the gate an English-speaking guard, Mr. Ren Shi, with whom he has become acquainted.

"Are you going out for breakfast?" Mr. Ren asks.

"I'm going for my walk."

"May I ask how old are you?"

"Sixty-five," Sieg says. "How old are you?"

"Sixty-eight. When were you born?"

"In September. How about you?"

Mr. Ren hesitates. "That's hard to say. By Western calendar, B.C.—" He stops, laughs. "I'd be dead, wouldn't I? A.D., probably in March. Maybe April."

"What difference does it make at our age?" Sieg says.

"That's right. We're just waiting to die." Mr. Ren bursts into a wild cascade of laughter.

Sieg is still amused when he comes up the hill and reports the exchange.

Later, after buying fresh plums at the market, we take our favorite back street to return to campus. It leads past a six-story apartment complex under slow, interrupted construction since last September.

Sunday is a normal workday. Hard-hat laborers at ground level are all women—young, round-cheeked, rosy. While they shovel coarse sand through wire screens to mix cement for the modest high-rise, they talk and joke, showing full sets of white teeth.

Only a few yards beyond them, in the shadow of the modern building, an old hunchbacked woman crouches in front of her brick, earth-floored hovel. Its interior looks dark. It's probably damp. Broken stone steps drop precariously from her shelter perched on a slight rise of earth to the narrow, unpaved lane.

Often, in all weather, we see this woman sitting on a four-inch stool. She holds an ax in one gnarled, arthritic hand. Patiently, stiffly, feebly, but with plodding results, she chops, chops, chops at bits of green wood or pieces of board, reducing them to shorter lengths for her cooking fires. She looks brown and furrowed as the dirt at her feet. Her baggy trousers and worn slippers match, both in color and texture, the bark of the stump she hacks today.

She doesn't look up as we pass. Her bent back forces her face a bare eight inches from the ground. She works intently. Behind us, we hear the weak chop of her ax counterpointed by strong laughter from her working neighbors, the young construction crew.

Sunday evening, shortly after our one Western cultural fix for the week (Mickey Mouse in Chinese on TV), Dan appears carrying a plate of pizza and a bowl of chocolate chip cookies. Somehow he's managed, triumphantly, to bake both in a borrowed oven. He also brings with him a Chinese friend.

Mr. Sun wants to try out some card tricks on us. The first two baffle us, much to his satisfaction. The third bombs. Mr. Sun lays out four cards, a two and a king of spades, a queen of hearts, and a seven of clubs. He hands me a folded piece of paper to open later.

"Now, please, choose two cards in your head, but don't tell," he says.

Silently I choose the two and the seven.

Mr. Sun takes away the two and the king.

"Now choose one of those two," he tells me.

This time I choose the seven.

He removes the seven and points to the paper in my hand, which I open. It reads, "Queen of hearts."

"That is what you choose, yes?"

"No. I chose the seven. You know why?"

The stumped magician says: "Yes. Why?"

"I'm always for the underdog. The unimportant ones. Two and seven are much less than a queen and a king."

"No wonder the trick didn't work on you!" He laughs. "In China, seven is an unlucky number, and Chinese people, who associate red with happiness, would always pick the queen of hearts!"

We agree cross-cultural magic can fool more than the audience. Then Mr. Sun begins teaching us a game that has successfully crossed many borders—mahjong.

Throughout the semester, we've had many discussions centering on what various authors believed. We also remember something an older Chinese friend said to us one day last fall: "Young people in this country no longer believe in anything!"

This sweeping declaration doesn't seem to fit some of the hopes and ambitions we've heard our students express. So we ask them, early in June, to write an essay about "What I Believe" and to share it with the class unless they want to restrict their audience just to us.

Mr. Mao Yanyang ends his

> I believe in myself; in economy [that leads to a decent living]; spiritual life; in solitude sometimes but not selfishness; in consideration for others; in frank friendship.
>
> That is me, a clear "me."
>
> Life is a long path. I'll be walking or running on this path with optimistic self-confidence and rockful endurance, without a stop, even of a moment.

Miss Chun Xu writes on the same subject:

> I am only twenty-two years old, so I have a very bright future before me. In many people's eyes, I am a very joyful girl as if I have no worries.
>
> To some extent, I am. But why is it so?
>
> Because I believe in dreaming. Whatever I cannot get in real life, I will enjoy by my imagination. Dreaming brings me into a lovely world. In

dreaming, I may live in a brilliant castle, I may become a singing bird, I may have a walk on the moon, or I may be on the top of the Eiffel Tower.

Dreaming is a very important part of my life. It helps me to choose my goal in life. When I was in middle school, I often envied those who had a chance for further study in college. Sometimes I could see myself walking in the beautiful campus of a famous university, reading in the big library, listening to a well-known professor's speech, taking part in various recreational activities. . . .

In order to realise this beautiful and fascinating dream, I began to put my effort on study. When I was dull with my study, the dream would appear before me. In this way, I remained the top student of my class. At last, my dream became true.

So believing in dreams doesn't mean indulging in illusions. The most important thing is to make every effort to realise your dream.

A different student takes the subject in an opposite direction.

To tell you the truth, I believe nothing.

From my childhood, I was deeply affected by my teachers around me, the newspaper press, and the radio that the communism is the best kind of social system and Mao is the best man, and everything that he said is absolutely right. When the Cultural Revolution ended in 1976, I was still very young, in primary school, ignorant. But I was deeply impressed that the Cultural Revolution was not so good as it used to be and the communist party also could sometimes make mistakes.

I was influenced by my parents. They didn't have any interest in politics. Neither of them is a communist party member. But I needed the honor of being a little red guard when I was in primary school, and I was glad I was.

When I got into middle school, the Cultural Revolution was over. I became more and more indifferent to politics and finally found that politics was more of a challenge than I wanted. But I didn't tell anybody. I kept silent. At that time, I was really a student. A good student should take part as the League Member. More and more of my classmates joined. Many of my friends and some teachers persuaded me to join them. They said, "You will find it's a help for you to get a job, or go to college after graduation." I thought they were right. But I would have felt awkward if I had done what I wouldn't like to do. Well, at last, I was not a league Member, up till now, let alone a [party] member.

I don't regret that I'm neither a league nor a member, although I've lost many things because of it. I never win any fame about politics. I'm glad I'm faithful to my mind. I don't pretend.

Now I'm interested in some credoes of some religious beliefs. For instance, I believe human beings need fraternity and charity. . . .

Mrs. Ching Chao starts, "I believe in reading, especially good, thoughtful books." Her final paragraph, after four marshaled points, concludes,

I always feel very excited and rich in mind after reading a good book. I learn so many things from my books. Now I start to observe the world with a new and curious eye. And I indeed find that beauty exists everywhere around me. In the past I found life was dull. Everyday was the same for me. Now, because I am able to find a lot of beauty and appreciate it, I think life is beautiful, which makes me feel happy!

Mr. Xue Hai's response in part reminds me of the old woman we saw chopping wood in the lane. He begins:

Peasants often asked me what I really believe in while I was staying in the countryside to receive the reeducation from them. Such as, "Do you believe in God?" "Do you believe your destiny?" "Do you believe the important social relations?"

"No," I said, "I only believe in my persistent efforts in my life. Persistency is the best policy."

So peasants thought I was ignorant, but I thought I was clever because I could master my own destiny in my hands.

When I was in my primary school, my mother often told me a story about the early learning of Li Bai (a famous Tang Dynasty poet) in order to urge me to study hard.

Li Bai was a naughty boy. He all played and no work all day long. One day, he left school for home. On his way, he saw an old women with grey hair sitting on a stone beside a small stream and grinding a small stick.

Li Bai was curious about this. He went up and asked, "Granny, what will you do with this stick?"

Granny answered him with a smile. "I want to make a pin."

Her words astonished Li Bai, and he asked her further, "Granny, how many years do you need?"

Granny said, "There is no difficult thing in the world as long as one sticks to it. Persistent efforts are very important."

Li Bai was enlightened. After that, he studied very hard from morning till night. He even read books by means of lightning bugs in the deep night. As a result of his hard studies, he became a well-known poet in the Tang Dynasty, standing at the top of all poets at that time.

Since then, my mother's story urged me a lot in my studies. I always kept it in my mind. Whenever I was tired and neglected my studies, it would come into my mind at once.

In 1976, during the years I was staying in the countryside, I took my spare time in my English studies by myself even though I met many difficulties because I never studied English in my middle school. But I persisted in it whenever possible. I even studied English in the break time of working in the field.

As a result of my persistence, hard studies, I passed the entrance examination in 1977 successfully and became a university student. Really, I had succeeded in my career by my persistent efforts.

The year 1987 was the turning point of my life. By my hard studies and persistent efforts, I also became a graduate student. So I believe one's personal persistent effort because "Persistence is the Best policy." It can make an ambitious young man succeed even though he has no important social relations around him.

49 . Continuing Glimpses

In some ways, these ten months in China have accustomed us to typical off-campus scenes. In other ways, as we near the time for our return home, we look with sharpened interest at how China goes about its daily business.

June has turned fiercely hot. Air streaming through wide open bus windows, on our way to the Xinjiekou, carries heat waves we would have welcomed last winter.

The rattling bus halts momentarily near a happening attended by police and a dense crowd in the middle of the street. The policeman moves. The crowd moves with him. An angry Chinese man harangues the entire group. Blame must be placed on the one who is at fault, and the victim must be exonerated. People are so packed around the central participants that even from the vantage point of our bus, looking down, we can't make out who the main characters are and what the situation is. Two little girls run toward the crowd in their haste to see too.

We have lunch at the Jinling, pick up a few items in the hotel supermarket, and start home on foot by back alleys and lanes. We pass a Nanjing form of ambulance. An old man, ill, his eyes closed, his age-spotted skin pale, lies curled with his head propped on a pillow in the open bed of a tricycle truck.

It's much too hot for a cover over him. The young man and woman accompanying him have paused for a moment in the skeletal shade of an electric pole and a small dusty plane tree. Concern knots their foreheads. The patient's face twitches with discomfort. He licks his lips, as if thirsty.

Whether they are waiting for someone or have simply stopped to ease the cart's painful jolting for their rider on that rough road to the hospital, I don't know.

They will get him to doctors and nurses in a little while. Perhaps, they fear from the look of him, too late.

It's so steaming in the classroom this morning that students have set both ceiling fans circling and droning at 7:30 A.M. Some of the women carry black fans to flutter when perspiration starts to roll.

We work first on vocabulary and their original sentences using the new words. Five student examples are distinctly Chinese:

draconian: "Taking a home made airplane," that is, blowing someone up, was a draconian way, invented during the Cultural Revolution, to treat a captured rival.

Malthusian theory: Chinese economists used to believe that the Malthusian theory provided a reasonable excuse for war.

malleable: In China, people need to be more malleable than in the West because of the many changes.

nepotism: Nepotism is very important in China, as the saying shows: "When one man gets on the top, all his friends and relatives go up with him."

nepotism: The nepotism in China is like the twisted roots of a banyan tree.

I like one student's subtle complaint in an altered slang phrase: "*on the go:* My heavy homework always keeps me on the gone."

Friday, the students click their tongues in disapproval when we hand out a new reading. They cheer up when they see how short the Prodigal Son story is. We have a double reason for wanting to introduce this. One is up front.

Sieg begins, "This is perhaps the most famous parable in Western literature. You'll run across countless references to it." As usual with short pieces, he has the class follow through with him, reading it aloud for sound as well as meaning. Their voices rise in a jagged chorus of bass, tenor, soprano, alto. "Once there was a man who had two sons. . . ." Miss Feng reads aloud faster than the others.

Our second reason for introducing the parable is teacher anticipation. Next Monday, when we read to them Lord Kenneth Clark's moving statement of his personal credo, stated at the end of his series "Civilization," they will hear, among his other beliefs, that "forgiveness is better than vendetta."

Clark's words were published in 1969. We want these current students to have the chance to grasp possible links between Clark's humane position, Luke's timeless model, and perhaps some present or future crucial events in their own lives.

In the discussion that follows, Mrs. Ching Chao objects to the father's treatment of his elder son.

"Why doesn't he recognize the good deeds of his first son?" she asks and immediately answers her own concern. "Perhaps, after this, he will."

50 · Smiles and Frowns

Things are definitely winding toward an end.

Saturday morning, obeying Monitor Lao Sheng's command, we gather on the plaza for the formal class picture. Two students who weren't in class Friday are here, like the others, dressed in their best for this important event. Two others are missing. One has been called home by her father ("but not for serious reasons," her friends say). The other has felt an urgent need to see his girlfriend.

Lining up with us are Dan Younkin and two Foreign Languages Department officials—the acting head in Mr. Guo's absence and, naturally, the unit's Communist Party secretary, a kindly, diffident man.

Men in back, women in front. The group poses looking straight into a glaring sun. Will we all, in this record for remembrance, show smiling mouths and scowling foreheads?

The class wants a different shot. "Boys and girls separate," they dictate, "with teachers."

244

Sieg looks at the milling bunch, all in their twenties and thirties, almost a year older than when we first met them. "When do you stop being 'boys' and 'girls'?" he asks.

"Perhaps when we are married," they say.

Mr. Zuo Niannian and Mr. Lao Sheng, both husbands and fathers, confirm they are no longer "boys"—"except in the eyes of our elders."

Once the picture taking is over, the group disperses.

Sunday, on our walk through the market, we see a watermelon squad in action. Two women stand in the bed of a truck parked outside a store. They hand watermelons, one at a time, to a man on the sidewalk. He throws a forward pass to his receiver, a second man standing well within the store's open front. This man catches each watermelon, turns, and tosses it to a third man in the rear, who stacks the ripe fruit ready for eager customers. The store owner stands watching, smiling but anxious. Nobody drops a pass.

Monday is a hodge-podge day. We start with our request for no individual parting gifts from the students—to save their money and our backpacking space. (They're already preparing a small class gift for us by designing and getting our name carved in Chinese characters on the bottom of a stone lion chop.)

"Besides," Sieg says, still trying to ward off their generous impulses, "all year long, each one of you has given us priceless gifts in sharing your writing and thinking. That fits neatly into our heads and needn't pass customs."

We convey to them a request from Mr. Guo Kun in Texas. He has asked us to rename the courses taught this semester. He wants course titles that will transfer more easily to U.S. transcripts, on the chance his postgraduates some day link their studies with a sister institution abroad.

We've thought over his request. Does it matter if what we've called "vocabulary" and "speech" combine into three hours of "Lexicology, Conversation, and Speaking?" Or "reading" becomes two hours of "Selected Readings in Modern Literature: Short Stories; Poetry" plus three hours of "Analysis and Application of Reading Selected Prose?" It's easy to turn "writing" into a grander but still accurate description—"Creative Writing: Essays, Short Stories, Poetry, and Letters."

The class copies down these official changes with wry smiles. Reading George Orwell's "Politics and the English Language" has taught them to recognize how handily words can serve purposes.

A wild windstorm during the night brings branches crashing down. Pro-longed slashes of rain ground mosquito squadrons and diminish, but don't eliminate, the usual parade of singing cyclists along the street below. The road streams with sheets of water as we slosh downhill to class.

It's final reading exam day. Everyone is there at 7:30 prompt. The students work silently, intensely. Only a few take the allotted ten-minute break.

This open-book exam asks them to apply their varied reading experiences this semester to analyze, make connections, and link authors' ideas with their own observations. They would feel much more secure with a spew-back-what's-taught demand or a multiple-choice exam.

Mr. Zuo Niannian, untypically absent for headaches the last two days, puts his head down on his deak about 9:10. He is the first to hand in his paper and leave. Mr. Xue Hai, who dislikes margins because they limit his room for ruminations, and Miss Lü Shu, who loves extended examples, are the last and most reluctant. It takes our stand-up cajolery to pry them loose from their papers.

Apparently, students rush out of exams and immediately begin comparing what they answered to specific questions. We aren't five minutes up the hill and settled into reading at the coffee table when Miss Bin Qilin, all agitated in her frilly red blouse and black and white checked skirt, rushes in.

She feels she has blown the first question and wants to correct it, if possi-ble, or at least to find out whether her interpretation or her classmates' is "right."

In a blend of fairness to other students and our own self-defense, we insist we can't discuss her answer yet. Dissatisfied, still torturing herself, she leaves.

In the evening, Mr. Xue Hai, rattled for the same reason but over a differ-ent question, comes to talk over the exam. Same answer to Mr. Xue. He is so unwilling to give up that we have to reach further to reassure him or he'll never sleep.

"Remember," Sieg says, "even if you did have trouble with that question, you may have done better on other parts, so your total score may be good."

Mr. Xue shakes his head. His sense of error concentrates on that one answer, which he feels doesn't agree with those of the other students he's talked to. In anguish, he sits on the edge of the overstuffed chair. His eyes blink anxiously.

I remind him again of what we've told all the class. "Don't forget—your grade in this part of the course doesn't rest on one exam. You've had a mid-term. You've written five other reading papers. All those grades will be averaged for your final grade."

His traditional Chinese set, regarding one exam as crucial to his life, overrides his ability to reason or to accept our wider basis for evaluation.

We finally ask him to spread the word among other students that we cannot discuss individual answers now, that we're still in the process of looking at them. At last, he leaves.

The next morning, at 8:30, Mrs. Ching Chao knocks on our door. She is also agitated about her answers. She too wants to find out what was "right."

What do these wretchedly up-tight, genuinely suffering students really expect? Surely not that they can change their answers? Do their Chinese teachers allow postexam elaboration? Or do they feel that we, as Westerners, are more open to compromise? Or we don't know Chinese exam customs and are therefore more vulnerable to questioning?

We still have so much to learn!

Meanwhile, we also have their final reading projects to consider. One story they could choose to write about is Björnstjerne Björnson's "The Father," a tale of a boy who literally drowns because of his total dependence on a loving but dominating father. Three student responses to this story reveal contemporary parent-child relations in China.

Miss Bin Qilin heads her essay "Let Child Be Independent."

I once saw a pair of cartoons. In the first, a boy, very young, was sitting on a small chair before his father who is feeding him. In the second, the boy, now an adult with long hair, suit in western style and pair of pointed leather shoes, is still sitting before his father, now old and white-haired. The father is still feeding the son with a spoon.

At the first sight, I only felt it funny. Now I understand its deep meaning after reading "The Father" by Björnstjerne Björnson. If a father cares too much about his son, the son can never get independent and is of no ability after growing up. . . .

Such a tragedy may often happen in our society. The young man in the cartoon I have described can't even feed himself as an adult. In China, many parents spoil their children and don't let them do anything except study at home so that when they become university students, the children still have to have their parents come to them to wash clothes and make up bed. Some university students have no ideas of themselves, have no ability of self-living. Only then do they complain that their parents have never let them be independent. And the parents also regret that they should have given their children no chance to practice and to grow up themselves.

Traditional Chinese parents always think that they should be responsible for their children, taking them to school, finding them a good job, and marrying them, etc. Many of them are doing so. Therefore, I should say to these parents here, "Don't do so. You are destroying your children."

Mr. Ku Qiu's essay, "Father's Devotion for Son," confirms Miss Bin's. He writes:

We can see that Thord loves his son from the bottom of his heart and devotes himself to his son.

In real society, such a thing widely exists.

Take Mr. Yu, one of my acquaintances, for example. He has a son whom he considers his center of life. He saved money for his son's education. He himself ate rough food and wore the cheapest clothes, but he tried to let his son dress well. Mr. Yu cooked the best dishes for his son when his son was at home. When his son went to the university, he bought a tape recorder for him by selling wood in the market. Even when his son got an ideal job after graduation, Mr. Yu occasionally sent money to his son to let him live better. Now that his son has married and has a child, Mr. Yu takes care of his grandson so that his son has more time to work and rest.

No doubt our fathers love us and are devoted to us. Can we devote ourselves for our next generation?

Responding to the same story, Mr. Mao Yanyang calls his essay "Dominance Means Destruction." He concludes:

In China now, the birth-control policy makes it impossible for parents to have more than one baby. So the one baby has become their asset. There is nothing which they don't do for him, even when the child is growing older.

Lots of people are complaining that the young people of the present generation is a "generation in arms." They have no independence. You can often see the scene if you are in a university that nearly every freshman student is accompanied by their elders. On the first day of enrollment, the parents make the bed, buy meal tickets, buy other living necessities for him. The child does nothing and seems to have little shame as if all these are natural enough.

Is this the kind of people we need for the country? Absolutely not. No matter how high his marks might be, he would be handicapped in his future work and future life unless he became concerned with his independence and began to say, "Let me have a try myself."

Miss Lü Shu responds to a different story. August Strindberg's "An Attempt at Marriage Reform," in which a married couple strive to retain their individuality, moves Miss Lü to develop "My View on Marriage Reform."

In most Chinese minds, men usually go out to do heavy work or work in offices, and they'd better get much money. Women just take some professions like nurses, teachers, or shop assistants. If vice versa, they would be laughed at. And men would not like this kind of womens: women might not enjoy this type of men.

But I'm not the case. If a man is a good one and his character suits me, why don't I like him and make friends with him, even love him? If my job is physical labor and if there is a brave man loving me, I will really appreciate his eyesight [glance] and immediately decide to accept his feeling since he recognizes a good suitable woman. I want to choose the person I love, and not care too much about his job or profession.

In China, most men hope their girl friends or wives will be inferior to them on points like record of formal schooling, ability in dealing with problems, and height. If these women are better than they are at some subjects, men will feel uneasy and cannot bear it. The result is that they have to say good-bye. . . .

We Chinese always think that wife must follow husband. Wives cannot do different things or say different words with their husbands. This is indeed the traditional relation between husband and wife. . . .

But I won't be the same case. I'll do some job similar to him. I'll also have the right to differ with him on condition that we respect each other. I want to be independent both in economy and in thought. To Chinese women, it's no problem to have economic independence. The main problem is thought independence, thinking by ourselves, not always being influenced by men. We want to think whatever we like, to do what's right.

Strindberg's story on marriage reform sends Mr. Xue Hai in a different direction. His title is " 'An Attempt at Reform' Makes Me Think More."

Nothing can stop the seven human emotions, namely, joy, anger, sorrow, fear, love, hate and desire. . . .

In reading "An Attempt at Reform," I am reminded of the years of the Great Leap Forward—a great social reform in China in 1958.

In 1958, our authorities said conditions for entering into communism were favourable. So they put up a slogan, "Run into the communist society!" They took some radical measures at once in some aspects of our country. People were asked to go to public dining-halls to eat three times a day, or to fetch [food from there] back home to eat. Those owner peasants were organized into members of 'People's Communes' without regard to peasants' willingnesses.

Anything made of iron, even cookers and teapots, was thrown into steel making furnaces. The high tide of making iron and steel was really on a large scale. Peasants were asked to give up farm work and make iron and steel.

There was an unexpected natural disaster in our agriculture in 1959. We failed to bring in a single grain, whereas we had a bumper harvest in making iron and steel. But they could not be turned into grains to help people get over their difficulties.

During the years of the Great Leap Forward, people suffered a lot. If we had adhered to the combination between ideals and realities more closely, we would not have been frustrated and punished by the natural law. . . .

In reading the story "An Attempt at Reform," I think a lot. I worry about the social and political reform going on in China today.

"Will this reform be successful?" I ask myself thoughtfully.

"Maybe it will," I assure myself with a lightsome smile on my face.

51 . Final Days

We reach the classroom early Wednesday for the final writing exam. Students have asked to start as soon as possible because, incredibly, some of them face a four-hour French exam immediately after this one.

Yesterday, when we discovered this bad timing, we asked the students why they didn't protest the schedule.

"In China," they explained again, "you don't question the authorities."

"Yet your government is calling in the newspapers for more ideas from below, for everyone to help things change for the better!"

"We don't wish to make trouble," they said.

Most of them begin writing quickly. Miss Chen Hong has forgotten to bring the text she needs for the open-book exam. Fortunately, I brought my copy against just such a lack.

Miss Feng Yunxia's pen quits. Sieg lends her his.

Mr. Fan Rui has a different problem that makes him disturb his neighbors. He feels the desk surface is too hard under Hehai's thin exam paper. He wants a book to slip under his sheets of paper.

Miss Chun Xu, across the aisle, provides one.

At last, all three can begin to work. Dictionaries travel from neighbor to neighbor, but that's usual, nondisruptive exchange.

The single exam question directs them to reread a brief paragraph that mentions arts and habits William Cory felt students acquire through a good liberal education. We ask them to comment on any part or parts of the passage that seem especially useful to them in their educational development.

Many students finish early. Those who aren't off for their French exam are anxious to start studying for their last dreaded linguistics exam Friday morning.

Mr. Lao Sheng pauses to give us a message. "At three o'clock, Friday afternoon, please be here in this classroom for our final meeting."

"We'll be here," Sieg promises.

For several days, Nanjing has been soaking under a grey, cool, rainy spell, unwelcome opposite to everything assumed pleasant about June. Still, it's good weather to read exam papers by. Miss Zhuang Zi, the one who last September told us she liked most to "sing and cook," writes with an assurance we've enjoyed seeing her develop during these months:

THE ART OF EXPRESSION

According to William Cory in "Arts and Habits," "You go to school not for knowledge so much as . . . for the art of expression."

I agree with his point of view, since I have a personal experience.

How I am surprised to find that I can calmly deliver a speech in front of a crowd of people. Seeing that I am talking on and on in a flow of eloquence, people can hardly believe that I spoke with a slight stutter when I was a child.

I was brought up by my grandmother, my mother's mother. She was a housewife and lived in the countryside. There were no books, no TV set at her home. She could not teach me anything because she never received any education from school.

Everyday before she went out to work in the fields, she told me again and again not to go out to play, or she frightened me if I did. She told me somebody would kidnap me. Therefore, I stayed at home honestly, looking at the outside world through the gate.

When I was seven years old, I was sent back to my parents and went to a primary school. At that time, I was very timid so I just kept silent either in class or outside class. I was a lonely girl then.

Being afraid of answering the teacher's questions in class, I always bent my head. My teacher, however, often picked on me to answer questions. I stood up trembling. My face streamed with sweat because of fright. By and by I began to speak with a stutter. My classmates laughed at me, so I felt more embarrassed. Just then, my teacher said to me, "You speak very well. Keep on please." I looked at my teacher gratefully and I went on.

Since then, I often answered my teacher's questions in class. Although I still spoke with a slight stutter, my classmates never laughed at me any more. I became more brave and self-confident.

But I still kept silent after class. In order to let me speak more and be active, my teacher suggested my taking part in some recreational activities. I was asked to give performances in front of a crowd of people. For example, to sing songs, to dance, or to play a part in a play.

At first, just like when I was asked to speak in class, I felt very nervous. My voice was trembling; my hands and legs were shivering. The worst thing was I often forgot my lines. My teacher encouraged me instead of blaming me. Gradually I acted better and better. . . .

With the help of my teacher, I not only corrected my stammer, but also I could give a fluent speech in front of people. When I was studying in Nanjing Normal University, I once won a prize in a speech competition.

Therefore I should say I went to school not for knowledge so much as for the art of expression.

I put down Miss Zhuang's paper, which Sieg has already seen. "Good for that teacher—or series of teachers!"

"What was it Miss An wrote—'Students need more laud than criticism'? Apparently it worked for Miss Zhuang."

One week from today, we head for Shanghai and home, always assuming "the authorities," those unseen persons in charge of arrangements, can get train tickets at this crowded travel time. We asked Shi Changmei about air connections. She clicked her tongue.

"*Impossible* to get tickets!"

Between that date and now, we must assign final grades, write summary reports, see what will pack and what we can pitch, manage farewell visits with students and friends, and confront our own feelings—the usual mix of sad and glad whenever we head home.

Already, it's Friday. Time for the class farewell party.

We enter the familiar classroom at 3:00 P.M. Our whole bunch is here, tired from exams, excited about the class trip they begin tomorrow, painfully aware, like us, that these are our final moments all together.

They ask us to sit down in the front row. They have brought refreshments —wrapped candies, sweet peanuts, a fried dough ball in sesame seed. Its grease obliterates deep scratches on the desk top. They also distribute to each person a cylindrical cardboard tube filled with ice cream that somehow, miraculously, doesn't melt. Everyone gets a generous portion of every treat.

Behind the lectern, Mr. Lao Sheng announces this afternoon's agenda. There will be a welcome by Mr. Sun, Guo Kun's assistant, who is soon to go to the United States himself; two speeches by us (surprise!); a presentation of class gifts by Mr. Fan Rui; and a speech by each of the students in farewell.

Mr. Lao turns the podium over to Mr. Sun.

All speeches are mercifully short, including ours. Sieg and I try to tell the class how much their sharing with us over these months has meant and will continue to mean, no matter how many miles and how much time separate us. The students touch on highlights of the year. From their remarks, we gather the most memorable by far was the Thanksgiving feast we provided in a local restaurant. They do acknowledge, however, considerable food for thought as well.

Mr. Fan presents the class gift to us, a blessedly small chop with our Chinese name carved on its base. Mr. Xue shows us how to hold the chop by the lion's mouth when we stamp it on an ink pad so we don't, in ignorance, get our names upside down.

They have one last, unexpected "very beautiful priceless gift"—a large, thick photograph album. On the cover is a fuzzy white and yellow cat with green glass eyes, pink nose, red mouth, and red bow, the whole under a round plastic bubble.

"Be sure to pack a cloth over the bubble to protect it," Mr. Xue advises. "You probably cannot get it repaired in the United States."

"Look inside," Miss Chun Xu urges.

We open the album. Each student has slipped in a favorite, individual color picture of himself or herself.

"So you will remember us," Miss Zhuang Zi says.

In the pictures, Mr. Lao Sheng and Mr. Zou Niannian stand proudly, each with his lovely young wife and child.

Mr. Ku Qiu stands, arms behind his back, chin lifted slightly, in front of a flowering white crab apple tree.

Miss Bin Qilin and six of her classmates pose separately in front of the now completed, newly landscaped science building on campus. Miss Bin, Mr. Xue Hai, and Mr. Mao Yanyang each stand on the steps. Mr. Mao holds his arms crossed, hands hidden beneath elbows. There's a typical wait-and-see quirk to one eyebrow.

Miss Feng Yunxia sits smiling on the low abutment, her skirt pulled decorously low over her knees.

Mr. Lü Shi stands solidly at the foot of the same steps. He has his sleeves rolled up, hands on hips, legs spread wide.

Mr. Li Jian sprawls, looking uncomfortable, on the grass below.

Miss An Ran, leaning slightly in a grove of spring bamboo, smiles as she grips one slender bamboo stalk in both hands.

Mr. Fan Rui sits relaxed on a rock in front of a park lake. Mrs. Ching Chao, upright against a similar rock, parallels a pagoda in her background.

Miss Li Yanping, an alluring red scarf draped around her throat, lays one delicate hand, free of chilblains, on a dragon's head in another park.

Miss Xi Yang stands beside a white car in front of an unnamed hotel.

Miss Liu Jie has left off her tinted glasses. She smirks as she wraps both arms loosely around a brick pillar.

Shy, soft-voiced Miss Chen Hong reclines enticingly in deep grass at the foot of the president's administration building hill. One pink-sweatered arm props her chin.

Miss Chun Xu sits demurely on the ground in front of a row of palm trees. Her long ponytail hangs over her shoulder, its blackness against her rose sweater matching the blackness of her slacks.

Miss Zhuang Zi's eyes almost disappear beneath her long bangs. She thrusts one white stockinged leg and high heel forward, somehow curving it against a background of lake, mountain, and traditional buildings.

Behind Miss Lü Shu are a crowded beach and a brilliant sunset. Miss Lü has raised one hand high, palm up, as if to say, "How beautiful the evening is!"

"We will treasure these—" I can't go on.

Quickly, we shake hands with each student, once a stranger, now so richly known.

It's time to go. They are eager to discuss arrangements for their class trip, which begins tomorrow.

We walk out, not looking back, not now, leaving them as teachers must to their own important days and years ahead.

About the Authors

Lois Muehl, author of children's books, popular and professional articles, and light verse, received a B.A. degree in English from Oberlin College and an M.A. in English education from the University of Iowa. She directed the college-level Developmental Reading Lab at the University of Iowa and also taught rhetoric.

Siegmar Muehl holds an M.A. in philosophy from the University of Chicago and a Ph.D. in educational psychology from the University of Iowa. He taught educational psychology and headed the Children's Reading Clinic at the University of Iowa. His published articles span the fields of reading research, language usage, and nineteenth-century German-American history.

Together they have traveled extensively, teaching educationally disadvantaged African American students at a predominantly black college, Hmong and Khmer refugees in Thailand and in California, university students in Korea, and postgraduates in China.

Between trips they visit with their four children and five grandchildren and pursue many and varied interests.

 Production Notes

Composition and paging were done on the Quadex Composing System and typesetting on the Compugraphic 8400 by the design and production staff of University of Hawaii Press.

The text and display typeface is Galliard.

Offset presswork and binding were done by Malloy Lithographing, Inc. Text paper is Glatfelter Offset Vellum, basis 50.